THE
ENVIRONMENTAL
BUSINESS
HANDBOOK

THE
ENVIRONMENTAL
BUSINESS
HANDBOOK

Euromonitor Publications Limited, 87-88 Trunmill Street,
London ECIM 5QU

THE ENVIRONMENTAL BUSINESS HANDBOOK
First Edition 1989

Published by

EUROMONITOR
87-88 Turnmill Street
London EC1M 5QU

Tel: 01-251 8024
Telex: 21120
Fax: 01-608 3149

British Library Cataloguing in Publication Data
Jenner, Paul
        The environmental business handbook.
        1 Environment. Conservation
        I Title II. Smith, Christine
333. 7'2

ISBN: 0 86338 317 3

Printed in Great Britain on 100% recycled paper by Redwood Burn Ltd,
Trowbridge, Wiltshire

CONTENTS

Continued...

Continued...

LIST OF TABLES

Continued...

Continued...

LIST OF FIGURES

LIST OF ABBREVIATIONS

ACE	Association for the Conservation of Energy
ASH	Action on Smoking and Health
BiC	Business in the Community
CARICOM	Caribbean Community
CBI	Confederation of British Industry
CEED	UK Centre for Economic and Environmental Development
CEGB	Central Electricity Generating Board
CEP	Corporate Environmental Policy
CFC(s)	Chlorofluorocarbons(s)
CHP	Combined Heat and Power
CIA	Chemical Industries Association
CITES	Convention on International Trade in Endangered Species
CO2	Carbon dioxide
DoE	Department of the Environment
E102	Tartrazine
EC	European Community
ECU	European Currency Unit
EEC	European Economic Community
EEZ	Exclusive Economic Zone
EIRIS	Ethical Investment Research Service
EMEP	Co-operative Programme for Monitoring and Evaluation of the Long-range Transmission of Air Pollutants in Europe
EYE	European Year of the Environment (1987-8)
FAO	Food and Agriculture Organisation (UN)
FoE	Friends of the Earth
GDP	Gross domestic product
GEC	Gross energy consumption
GNP	Gross national product
HEP	Hydroelectric power
ICNAF	International Commission for the Northwest Atlantic Fisheries
IFOAM	International Federation of Organic Agriculture Movements
IIED	International Institute for Environment and Development
ILO	International Labour Organisation
INCPEN	Industry Council for Packaging and the Environment
IUCN	International Union for the Conservation of Nature and Natural Resources
IWC	International Whaling Commission
LRTAP	Long-range transport of air pollution
MAC	Maximum admissible concentration
MDB	Multilateral Development Bank

Continued...

MIT	Massachusetts Institute of Technology
MORI	Market and Opinion Research International
MSC	Manpower Services Commission
mtce	Million tonnes coal equivalent
mtoe	Million tonnes oil equivalent
NAFO	North Atlantic Fisheries Organisation
NCC	Nature Conservancy Council
NEF	New Economics Foundation
ODP	Ozone-depleting potential
OECD	Organisation for Economic Co-operation and Development
PAN	Pesticides Action Network
PIRC	Pensions and Investments Resource Centre
PPP	"Polluter pays" principle
RDF	Refuse-derived fuel
SEAN	Scientific Event Alert Network (Smithsonian Institution)
SO2	Sulphur dioxide
TFAP	Tropical Forestry Action Plan
TGWU	Transport and General Workers Union
TOES	The Other Economic Summit
TUC	Trade Union Congress
UN	United Nations
UNEP	United Nations Environment Programme
UNESCO	United Nations Educational, Scientific and Cultural Organisation
UV	Ultraviolet
WCED	World Commission on Environment and Development
WEC	World Energy Conference
WHO	World Health Organisation
WTO	World Tourism Organisation
WWF	World Wide Fund for Nature (previously World Wildlife Fund)

PART ONE
INTRODUCTION

1.1 THE SCOPE OF THE HANDBOOK

The Environmental Business Handbook sets out to analyse the constraints on and opportunities for business, due to the growing environmental consciousness. Its intention is neither to vindicate nor attack environmentalists, governments or industry, rather to present objectively information which businessmen need to take into account if profitability is to be maintained.

Furthermore, although the book provides briefings for business on the current environmental issues and assesses their significance (Part Two), it is much less a function of the book to pronounce on the rightness or wrongness of the environmentalist case. It starts instead with a simple proposition: the environment movement *exists*. Given that it exists, what are the implications for business and how should they respond?

This proposition occupies Part Four, the largest part of the book. We conclude that the implications are profound for almost every aspect of business activity. For example, there is evidence of a greening of capital; the ethical investment movement is growing and environmentalism is an important component of it. More important than that, unenvironmental businesses face a growing threat to profits and even the least ethically concerned of investors must take account of that. There are also implications for employment, not merely in terms of the quantity or nature of employment but with regard to the pressure an environmentally conscious staff can bring to bear on the direction of a company.

These two subtle forces, money and people (both sometimes not so subtle) are at work, as it were, within the company itself. There are also external and more overt pressures. The book shows the green consumer to have become a real force in the marketplace. Every aspect of a product's marketing can be affected, from research (a reaction against animal testing, for example) through to packaging and public relations. Industry is increasingly the subject of environment legislation, and leading-edge companies are actively encouraging that legislation, fearful of the additional costs of their own environmentalist posture and therefore anxious to see uniform standards imposed. (The book notes instances of environmentalism *reducing* costs.)

What is quite clear is that the environment is itself acting quite directly on business. In many cases businessmen who blame environmentalists or legislators for the problems they face are effectively blaming the messenger for the message. Part Three of the book describes how resources are being depleted - to the detriment of business. In the shorter term businesses are damaging one another through pollution, a situation about which the victims are increasingly vociferous; in the longer term those same businesses are damaging themselves.

Finally, the book demonstrates the very positive side to environmentalism: incorporated into production processes, conservation ideas actually reduce costs. Using more raw material than is necessary, discarding materials that can be of value, creating wastes that have to be disposed of, consuming energy that could be saved, none of these are good business practice. This is one aspect of the environmentalist message. Objectively, it is true to say that conservationists have often been ahead of businessmen at the businessmen's own game. This positive side to environmentalism (looked at from the business viewpoint) is creating markets for new products and, in some cases, revitalising otherwise stagnant consumer industries. From catalytic converters for cars to scrubbers for power stations there are big new markets for pollution abatement equipment, for example. Low-energy versions of widely owned products have reintroduced growth in place of saturation. That there will be many more instances of this is clear.

1.2 THE GROWTH OF ENVIRONMENTALISM AND ITS IMPLICATIONS FOR BUSINESS: AN OVERVIEW

Short-term structural problems for industry should not be minimised by environmentalists, but business opposition to environmentalism often concerns the question of image as well as that of pragmatism at work. There is a widespread misconception that the green movement comprises "beardie-weirdies", dangerous radicals, anarchists, trouble-makers, hippies - at best romantics who have no understanding of the real world. The evidence shows, of course, that numbers of these do support environmental ideas, but they are far from being the majority in terms of either numbers or influence. On the contrary, the most influential part of the environment movement is headed by ex-civil servants, ex-government scientists, ex-bankers - all very much part of "the Establishment".

The International Union for Conservation of Nature and Natural Resources (IUCN), for example, appointed Dr Martin Holdgate as its Director-General from April 1988. Holdgate had been Chief Environment Scientist and Deputy Secretary (Environment Protection) of the UK Department of the Environment. Although he had, for example, argued for UK membership of the 30% Club (to reduce airborne pollution) he was also willing to defend UK intransigence on the issue at the 1984 Multilateral Conference on the Environment, in Munich. His reason was that action had to be based on "a proper understanding of the factors that change and damage the environment": hardly the words of a dangerous radical.

The World Wide Fund for Nature (formerly the World Wildlife Fund), founded in 1961, has as its president HRH the Prince Philip, Duke of Edinburgh, a man who is not only a member of "the Establishment" but who enjoys hunting. Indeed, the WWF is *not* opposed to hunting, provided the species is not threatened; it is even prepared to support hunting in order to give a commercial value to wildlife and therefore to its conservation. HRH Prince Sadruddin Aga Khan is a vice-president of WWF. Members of the trustees of the WWF International Council include David Ogilvy, founder and director of the Ogilvy Group, and Ralph P Davidson, chairman of the board of Time Inc. Members of the Council include Sir Kenneth Kleinwort, director of Kleinwort, Benson, Lonsdale; John H Loudon, the former chairman of Royal Dutch Shell; and Senator the Hon. Alan A Macnaughton, chairman of Olivetti Canada.

None of these could be accused of favouring world economic collapse. Some, like Loudon, have even been associated with projects other environmentalists have attacked. (Shell is the sole manufacturer worldwide of the organochlorine pesticide aldrin, banned as a plant protection in all EEC states except the UK. It also manufactures dieldrin, used against tsetse fly but classified by the WWF as "extremely hazardous" and estimated by environmentalists to have caused the death of 10,000 people. Hence the Friends of the Earth campaign: Tell Shell To Go To Hell.)

And what of Friends of the Earth? Again, FoE members are well-educated *consumers*, with more or less the same trappings of Western lifestyles as everyone else. The FoE movement began in the USA and was established in Britain in 1970. One of its first actions was to dump Schweppes' new non-return bottles on the steps of the company's head office. But the high-profile publicity stunts masked a less than revolutionary approach, and the more militant moved towards Greenpeace following a staff strike in 1982.

One of the FoE campaigns has been about acid rain. In July 1988 the Nature Conservancy Council (NCC), the government's own advisory body, reported: "It is almost impossible to put a price on the damage that has occurred and is still occurring as a result of acid deposition. It has been estimated that the effects of acid deposition on buildings and drinking water cost the whole of Europe thousands of millions of pounds a year." The message may be unwelcome to industries contributing to the acid rain problem, but it is *not unbusinesslike*. On the contrary, the FoE position is justifiable in business terms. Companies involved in forestry, fishery, civil engineering, tourism and water supply know that acid rain can and is damaging *their* profits.

Another campaign has concerned depletion of the ozone layer which protects the earth from ultraviolet radiation. In the 1970s chlorofluorocarbons (CFCs), which are responsible for the problem, caused sufficient concern in the USA that they were banned there for aerosol use in 1978. Their continued use in aerosols elsewhere illustrates one of the new business dictums: companies which fail to take environmental problems into account when devising business scenarios can expect to run into problems in the future. The combination of legislation and public opinion has now caught up with CFC manufacture. But the ozone problem does not end, even with the complete cessation of CFC use (which has not yet been achieved). CFCs in the atmosphere can last up to 100 years, releasing chlorine; one molecule of chlorine can destroy 100,000 molecules of ozone. The *business* problems of that could be formidable. In fact, environmental issues are invariably business issues; threats to the environment *are* threats to business.

There has been a clear shift in emphasis by the environmental movement, towards co-operation with business. At the highest institutional level this is reflected in the 1985 opening statement to the UNEP Governing Council by executive director Mostafa Kamal Tolba: "We have been directing too much attention to governments, when 75% of the world's development is financed by the private sector."

At the previous year's World Industry Conference on Environmental Management, held at Versailles, France, Tolba used the opportunity to point out that:

> A mainstay of sound environmental management is that anticipation and prevention of environmental difficulties are far preferable to reaction and cure. This is cost-benefit analysis of a sort that businesses consider every day in the course of their operations. To remain viable and profitable, industry must foresee change, not react to it. Here, we in the environment movement have a massive contribution to make by providing industry with early warnings on environmental trends - for example, on rates and likely consequences of marine pollution, carbon dioxide build-up, desertification and tropical forest destruction.

Not all environmentalists, of course, aim for Tolba's restrained dialogue. Although it would be wrong to talk of a split in the green movement, it is certainly true to say that there is the view (classified "social ecology" by some, or "realo") that economic activity and growth (as understood by the businessman) should continue but on the basis of sustainability; and there is the view (classified "deep ecology" or "fundy") that the problems lie with over-consumption. In this philosophy the crisis is one of energy supply, not energy consumption; accordingly economic growth is itself wrong.

Those who feel threatened by environmentalism and who look for comfort to the potential destructiveness of this apparent rift will not find it, however. A handful of the more politicised greens may indeed occupy either extreme, but the vast majority are pragmatists. For example, energy conservation through improved product and building design, better insulation and so on would be approved by the bulk of consumers and businessmen. Yet conservation of energy is also the deep ecology, the apparently *extreme*, view.

There are other issues on which the majority of environmentalists and the majority of businessmen can also agree: sustainability is one. The term perhaps needs some explanation. In a speech to the International Institute in 1984, Tolba set out *his* view of the concept:

1. Help for the very poor because they are left with no option other than to destroy the evironment.

2. The idea of self-reliant development, within natural resource constraints.

3. The idea of cost-effective development using different economic criteria to the traditional approach ... that is to say, development should not degrade environmental quality, nor should it reduce productivity in the long run.

4. The great issues of health control, appropriate technologies, food self-reliance, clean water and shelter for all.

5. The notion that people-centred initiatives are needed; human beings, in other words, are the resources in the concept.

But sustainability is not a word exclusive to the environmental movement. It has formed part of the philosophy of leading companies for more than a decade, although the word itself probably first appeared in this context in the World Conservation Strategy published in 1980. In 1985 the UK Centre for Economic and Environmental Development held a conference entitled "Sustainable Development in an Industrial Economy".

Sustainability is no less significant a business concept than profit.

PART TWO
ENVIRONMENTAL ISSUES:
BRIEFINGS FOR BUSINESS

ISSUE: ACID RAIN

Relevance Power station operation and design; pollution abatement industry; car manufacturers; tourism; forestry; ancient monuments; freshwater fishery; water supply.

New industry created: manufacture of catalytic converters.

Impact Worldwide, but primarily in developed countries.

In brief Acid rain is a generic term covering various chemicals and chemical interactions. The complex chemistry has hidden the acid rain issue for many years, the link between sulphur dioxide emissions and rain acidity having been discovered by the Manchester chemist Robert Angus Smith and published in his "Air and Rain: the Beginnings of a Chemical Climatology" in 1872. The mechanism involves not only sulphur dioxide but also nitrogen oxides, hydrocarbons and ozone, acting either alone or together. Source of the pollution is the burning of fossil fuels, primarily in coal-fired power stations and motor cars although there are also natural sources, especially for sulphur dioxide.

The effects of acid rain include forest dieback, now severe in many areas, acidification of lakes leading to loss of fish stocks, erosion of stone buildings, corrosion, crop losses, pollution of groundwater through the release of metals in soil and an increase in human respiratory complaints.

The Swedes were the first to be seriously concerned, leading Sverker Astrom, Swedish ambassador to the UN, to propose an international conference, materialising in Stockholm in 1972 as the UN Conference on the Human Environment. Since then have come the Co-operative Technical Programme to Measure the Long-Range Transport of Air Pollution 1973-1977 (LRTAP) by the OECD; the Convention on Long-Range Transboundary Air Pollution, signed in 1979 and ratified in 1983; and the 1982 Conference on the Acidification of the Environment in Stockholm, which led to the proposal for the 30% Club, rejected by the Executive Body. In 1984 the 30% Club was formed by the ten countries which had supported the proposal, and by 1985 membership had increased to 21 - notable exceptions being Britain and the USA. Members of the 30% Club are committed to reducing their sulphur dioxide (SO_2) emissions by 1993, by 30% of the 1980 figure. EC proposals now go beyond this. Environment groups are calling for an 80% reduction in SO_2 emissions by 1993, a 75% reduction in nitrogen oxide by 1995 and a 75% reduction in ozone formation as soon as possible (in all cases taking 1980 as the baseline). It should be noted that ground level ozone is a hazard but is vital in the stratosphere (see *Issue: Ozone/CFCs*).

Energy saving is the most effective way of controlling emissions. In addition, flue gas desulphurisation equipment and catalytic reduction equipment will need to be fitted to power stations, and catalytic converters to cars. Such a converter fitted to a vehicle's exhaust can cut carbon monoxide, nitrogen oxides and hydrocarbon emissions by up to 90%. Tighter vehicle-pollution controls in the EC and elsewhere will accelerate the spread of catalytic converters, a market Johnson Matthey looks set to dominate in Europe, having constructed a plant in Belgium. Catalytic converters do, however, depend on use of lead-free petrol since they are sensitive to lead. Lean-burn engines can meet the pollution requirements for smaller cars.

Meanwhile, badly hit countries are trying to tackle the symptoms of acid rain. Sweden, for example, had limed 4,000 lakes by 1988 and plans to continue rescue operations at a rate of 200 lakes a year, spending £10 million annually on grants for acid rain clean-up. However, liming is only a stop-gap measure, lasting three to five years in the case of a lake in Sweden, considerably less in Norway.

Conclusion A switch to low-sulphur oil and coal wherever possible. A big market for pollution abatement technology ... but high cost will encourage energy saving. Acid rain has hastened the "polluter pays" principle and international co-operation in tackling environment problems.

ISSUE: ADDITIVES

Relevance Food and chemical industries.

Impact Developed countries worldwide, also developing producer nations; concern is growing.

In brief The additives issue was one of the first wider environmental problems to be taken up by consumers, largely as a result of preoccupation with diet and the possible link with health problems. There are about 3,000 additives in food - some are intentional, others, like pesticide residues, unintentional. The average Briton is said to consume over 5lb of additives a year. Around 40 additives used in the UK are alleged by some environmentalists to be carcinogenic; hyperactivity has been linked with tartrazine (E102) and there are other possible problems with allergies. The long-term effects of additives are simply not known - no one has been taking them long enough in current quantities.

12

Conclusion Despite public unease the market for additives (worth £200 million in Britain) is set to expand, but there is also an expanding demand for additive-free foods.

ISSUE: AGROCHEMICALS

Relevance Chemical manufacturers; governments; farmers; agricultural workers; food importers; wholesalers; retailers; consumers.

Impact Worldwide. Even areas *not* using agrochemicals can be affected through importing chemically tainted products. Land and water pollution are a growing problem.

In brief Increasing demand for food and the perceived greater sophistication of consumers have led to a boom in the use of agrochemicals in the worldwide production of food. The problem is gravest in developed countries with intensive farming industries, but is rapidly mounting in developing areas. Ironically, the problem is associated both with excessive food production, as in the north, and the severe food shortages experienced in the south. Agrochemicals are used widely for pesticides, herbicides, and fertilisers and their history is one of widespread destruction of wildlife, serious pollution and long-term imbalance in agricultural practice. Although greater attention is paid to immediate toxicity, a number of substances being banned, there is also serious concern about the continued usage of many products. Apart from pollution and poisoning, agrochemicals have been proved to cause considerable havoc to the natural process, with consequent problems for farmers caught in a vicious circle of pest resistance/increased chemical application. Nitrates are contaminating groundwater and causing health concern. Even chemicals banned in certain countries are being discovered on foodstuffs, often having been manufactured for Third World use and then reimported on products.

Conclusion Consumer awareness is leading to increased vigilance about food content, and inevitably this will result in concern about chemical treatments and a suspicion of certain blacklist products, especially imports. Organic growing methods are gaining greater credibility and a number of no-chemical guarantee schemes are in operation. Excessive use of chemicals also leads to soil degradation and perhaps even desertification (see *Issue: Desertification*), with a long-term reduction in worldwide agricultural land. There are also fears of the long-term health problems associated with the widespread manufacture and use of agrochemicals, problems which affect agrochemical factory personnel, agricultural workers and even those living in rural areas who come into contact with spray drift and the like.

ISSUE: ALUMINIUM

Relevance All individuals; water authorities; medical profession; food processing and packaging; kitchenware manufacture.

Impact Mainly developed countries; there is slight but growing concern.

In brief Researchers have linked aluminium with Alzheimer's disease, the condition once described simply as "senility". The evidence is inconclusive but compelling. In 1907 the German neurologist Alois Alzheimer examined the brain of a woman aged 55 who had died demented, and found tangled and twisted patches within the nerve cells. Chemical analysis of such patches taken from seniles who have died has revealed abnormally high concentrations of aluminium. A major source of aluminium is water. It occurs naturally in water where soil is acid but it is also added, in the form of alum, to cause dirt particles in reservoirs to sink. Statistics suggest a link between high-aluminium water supplies and the increased incidence of senility. Other sources in the diet include aluminium cookware, certain food additives, medicines such as antacids, and canned food and drink. The incidence of dementia is increasing; in Britain in 1987 the Medical Research Council puts the figure at 570,000.

Conclusion The apparent link between aluminium and Alzheimer's disease is neither well known nor widely accepted by governments or water authorities. However, the evidence is strong and the disease's cost to health services, society and families cannot be ignored. Companies using aluminium in ways which could result in human ingestion should review their operations.

ISSUE: THE ATMOSPHERE

Relevance All companies emitting pollutants into the air; logging; aerosol manufacturers; tourism; agriculture; all individuals.

Impact Pollution of the atmosphere is generally getting worse; it could become critical early in the 21st century if no action is taken.

In brief Air is one of the world's most vital renewable resources. It is also one of the "commons", which makes its protection difficult. Its pollution could become the source of major global political conflicts, even of a shift in the world power structure. Damage to the ozone layer and the build-up of greenhouse gases are contributing to a global warming which could drown coastal cities and radically change the geographical spread of agriculture. Ultimately human life on the planet could be threatened.

Conclusion Artificial atmosphere management will be the only solution if natural systems are not maintained.

ISSUE: BIOTECHNOLOGY

Relevance Technology companies; waste disposal and recovery; legislators; an increasing number of companies of all kinds.

Impact Biotechnology has the potential to become a major industry – and major environment issue – in the 21st century.

In brief The 1980 Spiks Report defined biotechnology as "the application of biological organisms, systems or processes to manufacturing and service industries". On that broad definition, biotechnology has long been in use. The leading-edge biotechnology companies, however, are concerned with something more than that: the genetic engineering of organisms creating new "superbugs". A fungal enzyme, naturally existing in the wild, has been used by ICI in a process to detoxify cyanide, a common industrial chemical. Such biotechnology does not arouse environmentalist concern. Projects such as the creation of sheep one-third larger than normal through genetic engineering of growth hormones have caused widespread concern, however. Few countries have yet legislated or even know where to begin legislation. The Danish government has banned the release of organisms engineered by the addition, subtraction or rearrangement of genes (recombinant) except where prior clearance has been given. Many are talking of a moratorium to allow further research to take place.

Conclusion Public and environmentalist response to biotechnology depends very much on the applications to which it is put and the safety record achieved in its early days. Talk of giant sheep will undoubtedly set the industry back; other applications, such as waste processing, are likely to meet wide acceptance. Environmental groups are watching the situation very closely but generally reserving their positions.

ISSUE: BRUNDTLAND REPORT

Relevance Politics, business, individuals.

Impact Worldwide but slow and partial.

In brief The World Commission on Environment and Development (WCED), headed by Gro Harlem Brundtland, Prime Minister of Norway, was set up by the UN as an independent body in 1983. Its 1987 report, *Our Common Future*, is the latest of a number of global perspectives, which have included Brandt's Programme for Survival and Common Crisis, Palme's Common Security and the World Conservation Strategy. The legal principles proposed by the WCED have been summarised into 22 points (see Section 4.9), including:

1. All human beings have the fundamental right to an environment adequate for their health and well-being.

2. States shall conserve and use the environment and natural resources for the benefit of present and future generations.

3. States shall maintain ecosystems and ecological processes essential for the functioning of the biosphere, shall preserve biological diversity, and shall observe the principle of optimum sustainable yield in the use of living natural resources and ecosystems.

10. States shall prevent or abate any transboundary environmental interference which could cause or causes significant harm . . .

11. States shall take all reasonable precautionary measures to limit the risk when carrying out or permitting certain dangerous but beneficial activities and shall ensure that compensation is provided should substantial transboundary harm occur even when the activities were not known to be harmful at the time they were undertaken.

21. States shall cease activities which breach an international obligation regarding the environment and provide compensation for the harm caused.

Conclusion Unlikely to bring about much change but forms part of a wider lobby for which some tangible gains can now be seen - for example, the growing acceptance of the "polluter pays" principle.

ISSUE: CARBON DIOXIDE

Relevance All individuals; all industries burning fossil fuels; all organisations associated with deforestation; cement manufacturers; transport users.

16

Impact Worldwide. Increasing problem.

In brief Emission of carbon dioxide (CO_2) into the atmosphere is primarily through the combustion of fossil fuels. There is also biological release of CO_2 through the destruction of forests (see *Issue: Deforestation*), mainly by burning and decay, which is almost as substantial as fossil fuel sources, in the range of 5 billion tonnes of CO_2 each year. Over the next hundred years the CO_2 content of the atmosphere is likely to double from its pre-industrial level of about 260 parts per million. Like other trace gases in the atmosphere, CO_2 (one of the "greenhouse" gases), is transparent to incoming solar radiation which heats the earth. However, it is also relatively opaque to the longer-wavelength radiation reflected from the earth's surface, and this trapping of radiation means that the earth is heated - and is likely to become warmer as heat continues to be trapped.

Conclusion The projected rise in global temperature predicted to result from this "greenhouse" effect (see *Issue: "Greenhouse" Effect*) will substantially affect climatic conditions in many parts of the world, according to scientists. An average temperature rise of 2-3°C is forecast, which may change rain patterns and could lead to a rise in sea levels, perhaps by as much as one metre through thermal expansion alone. If ice-melting at the poles takes place the sea would rise more rapidly, perhaps by 30 metres or more, causing widespread flooding. Many major cities such as London or New York, as well as entire low-lying countries, could be submerged - with almost unimaginable social disruption following.

ISSUE: COMBINED HEAT AND POWER (CHP)

Relevance Most companies; energy industry; many individuals.

Impact CHP technology is in use in many of the world's major cities, including Berlin, Munich, Paris, Rotterdam, Stockholm, Vienna, Moscow and New York, is well established in Scandinavia and is now being introduced in the UK.

In brief CHP sounds so obvious from every point of view that it is hard to understand that it *is* an issue. In conventional power stations, less than 40% of the energy released by burning fuel is converted into electricity, the remainder being lost in the cooling water and flue gases. The concept of CHP is that the heat generated is not wasted but used for space- and water-heating. CHP stations are less efficient at electricity generation but the heat recovery increases overall efficiency to as much as 80%: typically, from an input of 100 units a CHP station could produce 20 electricity and 60 heat units. The same input into electricity generation would produce an output of only 40 units.

There are drawbacks to CHP, however, mainly that it is not very flexible and is therefore best suited to industry where the ratio between heat and electricity usage is stable. (For factories and offices there are small installations known as minichips.) CHP stations must also be local to the heat users.

Conclusion CHP stations will make an increasingly significant contribution to energy needs in developed countries, and in much of the developing world.

ISSUE: CONSUMER ATTITUDE

Relevance All companies, especially those in the front line of consumer demand patterns: also importers; public organisations; national and local government; public relations firms; financial organisations.

Impact Worldwide, but particularly in democratic countries where consumer freedom of choice can substantially affect demand. Status: increasingly sophisticated.

In brief There are up to 3 million members of environmentalist organisations in the UK alone. All over the world these consumers are being increasingly called upon as high street troops in environmental campaigns. They are readily inclined to flex "green" muscles, both spontaneously and at the beck of organised action, and are increasingly well informed and prepared to take action (eg protest, boycott etc) in political and indirect consumer issues such as acid rain, nuclear power and species endangerment. Consumer attitude to environmental concern is beginning to feature strongly on business agendas and planning.

Conclusion The green movement has found its way into homes, schools and businesses and is here to stay and flourish. Consumer environmentalism is as important for business to acknowledge and act upon as any other consumer trend - but it will prove more enduring.

ISSUE: CONVENTION ON INTERNATIONAL TRADE IN ENDANGERED SPECIES (CITES)

Relevance Wildlife trade.

Impact Worldwide and increasingly effective, but many infringements continue.

In brief Wildlife exploitation is actively promoted by many environmentalists as a means of giving economic value and therefore an argument for management as a sustainable resource. However, all environmentalists oppose trade in endangered species. CITES is now supported by nearly 100 countries and lists over 700 species that should not be traded in. Trade Record Analysis of Flora and Fauna in Commerce (TRAFFIC) offices around the world investigate wildlife trade to help ensure enforcement.

Conclusion Time running out for companies trading in species covered by the convention, no matter what happens - either CITES will bite or the species will become extinct. (See also *Issue: Genetic Diversity*)

ISSUE: DEEP ECOLOGY

Relevance All organisations and individuals.

Impact: Influencing committed environmentalists and strategies but unlikely to make significant change in consumer behaviour for at least a decade.

In brief The term "deep ecology" (also known as ecosophy) was coined by the Norwegian ecologist Arne Naess. In an interview in the magazine *Resurgence* he explained:

> The essence of deep ecology is to ask deeper questions . . . For example, we need to ask questions like, why do we think that economic growth and high levels of consumption are so important? It is a shift from being dominated by means, instruments, gadgets, all the many things we think will give us pleasure or make us happy or perfect. The shift comes about when we seriously ask ourselves: in what situation do I experience the maximum satisfaction of my whole being? For instance, we can see that instead of an energy crisis we have a crisis of consumption . . .

Conclusion Long-term change in consumer attitudes possible.

ISSUE: DEFORESTATION

Relevance All manufacturers utilising timber and forest products; wholesalers and retailers of wood and wood products; agriculturalists; pharmacists; exotic food industries; all individuals. (See also *Issue: Tropical Rain Forest.*)

Impact Direct and short-term devastation of lifestyle, livelihood and production capacity of many tropical countries, especially Africa, America and Asia. Long-term reduction and possible total depletion of certain tropical woods and many natural medicines, shortages and possible depletion of natural foodstuffs and potential extinction of many living species. Soil erosion, flooding, possible climatic change.

In brief Two major areas of concern: tropical forests and northern temperate forests. The former concerns the unmanaged harvesting of tropical woods, the localised gathering of wood for fuel on an increasing scale and the desperate but destructive lifestyle of shifting agriculture. About 200,000 square kilometres of primary rain forest are destroyed every year, and secondary forest is considered substantially less rich in product or species. Experts state that at current rates all primary rain forest, with its wide diversity of animal and plant life, will have disappeared within 50 years. Because of its contribution to weather patterns (tropical rain forest both uses and *recycles* rainfall) it is thought possible that massive destruction of these forest systems will radically alter rainfall patterns and contribute to desertification.

Tree damage in northern temperate forests is generally attributed to the effects of air pollution; there are records of conifer plantations in the British Pennines being abandoned in the 1930s due to high levels of sulphur dioxide air pollution killing the trees. Germany and Sweden are particularly badly affected, and fears for Britain's tree health are increasing. Deforestation is also caused by development: some mountain holiday resort developments in European mountains are though to have led to a higher incidence of avalanches and mud-slides.

Conclusion Conservationists are working at both national and international levels to try to alleviate all pressures brought to bear on the world's forests, mounting a Europe-wide campaign to reduce consumer – and therefore manufacturer – demand for non-sustainable tropical hardwoods. Consumer attitudes towards companies continuing to use and trade in endangered species will harden. Both UK and European industry must expect a continuing tightening of anti-pollution legislation. New plant and process development should take this into account.

ISSUE: DESERTIFICATION

Relevance Agriculturalists; importers; international businesses; retailers; consumers.

Impact Worldwide. Anywhere employing either intensive methods of agriculture or responding to continuing demand for product from the land by exploiting marginal and therefore easily degradable soils.

In brief As demand for increased agricultural production grows, farmland is being more intensively cultivated and marginal land brought into production. This can lead to soil degradation and, without remedial steps, desertification within a relatively short time. Estimates state that 6 million hectares of previously productive land are converted into new desert each year, with a further 21 million hectares rendered economically useless. The problem is particularly prevalent in arid or semi-arid regions where production is already constrained by lack of moisture. This leads to the shortening of fallow periods and use of unsuitable land, which in turn lead to increased use of chemical fertilisers (see *Issue: Agrochemicals*) and soil exhaustion. Overgrazing also leads to soil erosion, which can in its turn silt vital rivers and irrigation channels. Drought and the salinisation of poorly managed irrigation schemes exacerbate the problem. Africa is severely affected; the intensely farmed regions of the US Mid-West are causing grave concern and the USSR is known to be experiencing problems.

Conclusion Unchecked desertification will ravage, possibly irrecoverably, traditionally important food production areas (such as the USA) with devastating effect, not just for the country in question, but for importers of its products, retailers and consumers. World prices will become unstable and vulnerable to manipulation. One-third of the world's agricultural land could be desertified by the end of the century. To reverse the march of the deserts, greater funding of research and relief programmes is needed as well as a rethink of both consumer and political demands on agriculture. Greater husbanding of soil resources, less reliance on chemicals and subsidy-led quotas, and more use of organic and non-destructive methods of food production are essential.

ISSUE: ENERGY

Relevance Government, individual and corporate – especially civil engineering, components, property.

Impact Environmentalists causing worldwide and urgent reassessment of energy policies, although practical impact so far limited.

In brief Environmentalists have no uniform voice on energy, except for a clear commitment to avoid whatever is unsustainable or environmentally damaging. Nuclear power is their most common target but all forms of energy production have their environmental problems. Only energy conservation is virtually problem-free, but determined steps to reduce petrol consumption by vehicles, to insulate houses and to develop low-energy appliances are still awaited.

Certainly energy demand has not grown as fast as was anticipated in the early 1970s, but environmentalists believe that much more could be done: Earth Resources Research, for example, believes that UK energy demands could be cut from 369 million tonnes of coal equivalent (mtce) in 1979-80 to 259 mtce by 2000, the electricity component reducing by half without any fall in standards.

The majority of environmentalists are opposed to nuclear power because of the appalling consequences of major accidents, the problems of waste disposal, the feared consequences of increased low-level radiation and the links with nuclear weapons. Many also dislike the political and social implications of highly centralised energy production. The environmentalist viewpoint therefore tends to be in favour of various small-scale energy sources, including coal and oil (with suitable cleansing techniques); hydroelectricity (but not major dam-building which involves flooding and the spread of water-borne diseases such as malaria and bilharzia); biogas; refuse-burning combined heat and power (CHP) plants; solar, wind and wave energy; and energy crops.

Conclusion Taking a global perspective, Chernobyl has been a major setback for nuclear power. There is a shift towards the environmentalist perspective, which industry should take account of.

ISSUE: ENERGY CONSERVATION

Relevance All individuals, organisations and governments; energy industry; building industry; transport.

Impact Small, but growth of interest is accelerating.

In brief Energy conservation is the least glamorous area of energy technology. Energy consumption has always been seen as related to living standards: high consumption is synonymous with the good life. Some environmentalists believe that governments fear reduced reliance on centralised energy generation as a development that could equally reduce their political power. As long ago as 1979, the International Institute for Environment and Development (IIED) published *A Low Energy Strategy for the UK*, showing that GDP could treble by 2025 - with energy consumption remaining at its 1975 level of 330 (mtce). The view from the UK Department of Energy was that such a rise in living standards necessarily required 270 mtce by 2025. In industry, better building design and insulation, heat recovery from industrial plant and increased efficiency in transport could all make a significant contribution to energy conservation and at the same time increase profits - *saving* energy is much cheaper than generating energy.

Conclusion Impetus for energy conservation coming from drive for profits in commerce, rather than from governments. In time, governments are likely to follow.

ISSUE: THE ENVIRONMENT AS A PUBLIC RELATIONS TOOL

Relevance All companies.

Impact Environmental policy and profile are increasingly becoming an aspect of successful marketing.

In brief Public relations has been under-utilised in connection with environmental aspects of business. There is evidence this is changing, with some pioneering companies notching up substantial benefits not only from the adoption of environmentally sound business practice but also from being *seen* to be green-minded. Award schemes, participation in local projects and publication of corporate environmental policies are becoming legitimate business tools.

Conclusion Environmental pressure groups such as Friends of the Earth report that it has become "fashionable" for companies to be *seen* consulting with the greens. Consumer and legislative pressure will continue to grow and companies without an environmental policy (and practice) may find themselves at a disadvantage. Both within the company and outside, PR identifies the environment-friendly organisations.

ISSUE: THE ENVIRONMENTAL EMPLOYEE

Relevance All companies.

Impact Currently confined to sensitive industries in specific countries (eg National Union of Seamen in the UK) but ultimately far-reaching.

In brief Trade unions are becoming active on environment issues, especially those connected with their work. In 1983 the National Union of Seamen banned the dumping of nuclear waste at sea, even though the ban posed a threat to jobs. Subsequently the union has also opposed dumping toxic waste in the North Sea. Unenvironmental companies will possibly meet recruitment resistance. Exchange Resources is a recruitment agency specialising in candidates having a strong ethical position.

Conclusion Environmental pressures building from inside companies. Corporate environment strategies should be devised and announced through internal PR.

ISSUE: ENVIRONMENTAL IMPACT ASSESSMENT

Relevance Planners; all businesses.

Impact Rapidly gaining worldwide acceptance.

In brief The US National Environmental Policy Act 1969 was the first to formalise environmental impact assessments (EIAs); the European Community and over twenty other nations are now following suit. According to UNEP, the purpose is "to promote a better appreciation of the environmental implications of industrial projects". UNEP accepts, however, that "often, but by no means always, environmental protection adds to the direct costs of goods and services . . . decision makers need to be assured that such additional costs are justified by the benefits of environmental protection". The procedure "hinges upon the exercise of development control by appropriate public authority" and a full study requires a team with specialists in ecology, natural resources, socio-economics and process engineering. However, aside from such major projects, a growing number of smaller companies are authorising EIAs in order to minimise later contingent liabilities, particularly public liability, and to maintain a good public relations profile.

Conclusion EIAs to become a standard management tool.

ISSUE: ENVIRONMENTAL RISK MANAGEMENT

Relevance All individuals and companies.

Impact Worldwide.

In brief Risk managers and underwriters have become increasingly concerned at the huge contingent liabilities faced by the corporate sector in respect of the pollution of ground and surface water, air and foodstuffs. Disasters like Chernobyl and Bhopal are causing a reassessment of acceptable risk and of insurance premiums. There is even growing acceptance of a link between the incidence and severity of many "natural" disasters and human activities; landslides are associated with tree felling in many cases, drought could be linked to the "greenhouse" effect, and a connection has even been established between the severity of hurricanes and the amount of carbon dioxide in the atmosphere caused by industrial and agricultural activity.

Conclusion Risk managers are increasingly conducting environmental audits and taking steps to limit exposure to financial risk.

ISSUE: ENVIRONMENTALISM AND EFFICIENCY

Relevance All companies.

Impact Worldwide.

In brief Environmentalism has often appeared to be the enemy of efficiency and profit, seen in conventional business terms. In fact, many aspects of environmentalist thinking have been adopted by industry – energy conservation is a clear example. Other less immediately tangible aspects of green thinking are also now beginning to work their way into the industrial consciousness: What will happen to agricultural efficiency if the predicted "greenhouse" effect becomes reality? What will happen to the efficiency of forestry if trees are damaged by acid rain? A "new economics" is emerging that sees the earth's resources as assets of "The World plc", such that withdrawals of or damage to those assets must be taken into account in the world balance sheet, just as stock withdrawal or damage would in any commercial balance sheet.

Conclusion There is growing recognition of the link between environmental and business efficiency, but it will take a generation at least before the "new economics" takes a grip.

ISSUE: ETHICAL INVESTMENT

Relevance Large corporations and public companies but, increasingly, smaller companies via environmentalist pressure on banks; civil engineering financed by multilateral development banks (MDBs); privatisation of industry.

Impact Significant in the USA; growing in the UK and elsewhere. Ultimately muscular.

In brief Value of "socially screened" US securities estimated at over $350 billion. UK ethical unit trusts were worth £100 million by January 1988, other ethically constrained investment funds many times more. Environmentally screened investment is a small but growing part of this. Banks affected; Ethical Investment Fund says "no" to banks as it is "unable to obtain sufficient information on the companies, organisations or institutions to which banks lend money". World Bank aims to curb non-environmental projects; admits "ecology is good economics". Privatisation impeded; in the UK potential privatised energy companies fight shy of nuclear power over decommissioning costs and contingent liability.

Conclusion Non-environmental companies face strangulation of funds.

ISSUE: FISHERIES

Relevance Fishing fleets; food processing and packaging; agricultures; retailing.

Impact At least a quarter of the world's fisheries seriously depleted.

In brief The annual growth of fish catches has fallen to 1% a year after running at 6-7% between 1950 and 1969.

Conclusion Fishery cannot keep pace with human population growth.

ISSUE: GAIA HYPOTHESIS

Relevance All companies and individuals.

Impact Potential to induce subtle philosophical changes.

In brief The essence of the Gaia Hypothesis, developed by atmospheric scientist James Lovelock, is that the conditions suitable for human life on earth did not pre-exist but were created by the gradual development and interaction of other life forms. The carbon dioxide that formerly made up 30% of the earth's atmosphere, for example, has been deposited over millions of years in the form of limestone cliffs and coral reefs, to leave a concentration - suitable for human life - of only 0.03% today. The implication is that severe disruption of other life forms on the planet could make earth uninhabitable for humans, once again.

Conclusion In the longer term, a possible re-evaluation of the economic value of wild places and of animal and plant species.

ISSUE: GENETIC DIVERSITY

Relevance Agriculture; pharmaceuticals; cosmetics; chemicals; fashion and leisure industries.

Impact Worldwide but the effort to preserve biological diversity is minute in relation to the scale of the problem.

In brief Humanity has investigated only a tiny fraction of the earth's fauna and flora for possible benefit. There are believed to be 75,000 edible plant species, for example, but only 3,000 are actually used and only 150 of them are widely traded. In the fight against AIDS, the US National Cancer Institute in Bethesda, Maryland, is checking some 10,000 substances a year, including algae, fungi and other plants. In all there are believed to be 30 million species on earth, of which some 2 million have been studied. Only a few thousand are not at risk - it is forecast that the next fifty years will see the elimination of at least a third of species; extinctions are believed to be currently running at between 1,000 and 10,000 a year, and accelerating.

Conclusion Although various schemes exist to establish "gene banks", such as the plant conservation by botanic gardens, a high rate of extinction will continue; conservation measures may inhibit some business activity but not as much as the losses themselves.

ISSUE: "GREENHOUSE" EFFECT

Relevance All organisations and individuals.

Impact Unknown - but could lead to new patterns of energy production and consumption and to atmospheric management.

In brief At the beginning of life the earth's atmosphere is believed to have contained 30% carbon dioxide, a level intolerable to humans: today the proportion is around 0.03% (due, according to the Gaia Hypothesis, to the action of developing life forms). However, the proportion is now increasing, particularly due to the burning of fossil fuels and the world's forests. This in turn will create a "greenhouse" effect, leading to an increase in global mean temperature. Carbon dioxide is not the only gas involved; methane, nitrous oxide, other oxides of nitrogen and chlorofluorocarbons are also believed to add to the effect. The present-day level is around 350 parts per million and the annual rate of increase seems to be 1.5 parts per million. No one knows what the impact of this will be but a widely accepted forecast is that the global annual mean temperature will be around 2°C higher in 2030 than it was in 1980.

This in turn could lead to thermal expansion of the oceans, the disappearance of the Arctic ice cap, the breaking away of the Antarctic ice sheet, the inundation of coastal cities, regional climatic change, the redistribution of productive land and new patterns of drought and desertification. Some scientists believe the impact is already detectable; it has been postulated that increased carbon dioxide has already caused an increase in hurricane intensity and there appear to be anatomical differences in the leaves of several tree species when compared with herbarium specimens collected during the past two centuries (notably a decline in the number of pores).

Conclusion If models are confirmed by future experience the pressure to develop non-fossil-based energy and to conserve remaining forests will become overwhelming. An atmosphere-management industry could be born . . or a reaction against further industrialisation could develop.

ISSUE: INDOOR AIR POLLUTION

Relevance All individuals; employers of office workers; architects; manufacturers of ventilation systems; health industry.

Impact Small but growing concern in developed world.

28

In brief As many as 90% of office buildings may be "sick", causing low productivity and absenteeism among people working in them. Among the suspect pollutants are asbestos, carbon monoxide, carbon dioxide, formaldehyde, nitric oxide, nitrogen dioxide, ozone, various organic irritants and radon (see *Issue: Radon*). The sources include modern insulation materials, furnishings, building materials and office equipment. The problems can be exacerbated by air-conditioning systems.

Conclusions There is growing recognition that "sick" buildings pose a genuine threat to human health and productivity. As this awareness increases so it will create pressure for new approaches to building design and for solutions for existing buildings.

ISSUE: INNER CITIES

Relevance Planners; businesses moving or expanding; politicians; transport companies; employees; local residents; legislators.

Impact Urban areas, especially in developed and developing countries.

In brief The sorry plight of many of the world's urban areas is often blamed on industry, the debris of industrial demise being left as a stern reminder of the "evils" committed by business and businessmen. Not just the past has received criticism - plans for future development (eg the office blocks in the St Paul's area of London) have been deplored by such headline-catching names as Prince Charles. It is considered necessary first to reverse the trend of both residents and industry deserting inner-city areas for ever-expanding suburbs, then to recreate liveable, workable and, above all, successful cities. Projects include pedestrianisation (with access problems for industry), urban greening and social architecture. Britain is considered to lag behind European city projects. In its Cities for People campaign, Friends of the Earth points out that successful European city projects have improved Copenhagen, Vienna, Hanover, Lyons and Bologna. Pressure to ban or severly restrict all traffic from city centres is growing.

Conclusion There must be more liaison between urban planners and the people using cities. Pedestrian and traffic-restricted zones will severely affect some businesses, interrupting transport schedules for both goods and the workforce. Better public transport systems are essential and industry can lend its strength to this lobby effectively. Building design will be more significant, with stricter environmental requirements regarding not just appearance but noise, smell, dust and discharge. Local communities and organisations will increasingly expect business to play an active role in local affairs, both financially and socially. Organisations such as the Groundwork Trusts already act as liaison for an increasing number of such relationships.

ISSUE: LAND

Relevance Agriculture; all individuals.

Impact One-third of agricultural land is threatened by desertification; 60-80% of irrigated land is threatened by salinity; other land is threatened by acidity.

In brief A combination of human and climatic factors is costing six million hectares of productive land a year through desertification. Additionally, the land is losing its productivity due to pollution by acid deposition, the salinity that is the inevitable result of improper irrigation schemes, and road-building and construction.

Conclusion Agricultural land losing productivity; the world's ability to feed itself is facing decline.

ISSUE: LANDFILL

Relevance All individuals; waste management; companies producing hazardous waste; manufacturers of products with heavy metal and other dangerous chemicals; water authorities.

Impact Worldwide.

In brief Landfill is the standard method of waste disposal almost everywhere in the world: 90% of UK waste is disposed of in this way. Environmentalists have three major concerns: first, that ready acceptance of landfill ignores resources that could be recycled or reused; second, that the majority of landfills do not even recover energy (methane gas); third, that landfills are dangerous, allowing groundwater pollution by toxic chemicals. Even where landfill is operated to the highest available standard leakage does occur. The US Environmental Protection Agency now says landfill regulation must work "on the assumption that migration of hazardous wastes and their constituents and by-products . . . will inevitably occur".

Conclusion Increased impetus to look at recycling and reuse of resources as well as gas supply from landfills; more waste incineration with heat recovery. Tighter control and landfill.

ISSUE: LEAD IN PETROL

Relevance Oil companies, garages, motor manufacturers; manufacturers of catalytic converters.

Impact Worldwide move against lead in petrol.

In brief Lead is toxic to humans, and is already banned in petrol in many countries, notably the USA and Japan. In West Germany more than 50% of cars use unleaded petrol. In the EC generally, unleaded petrol is to be widely available from 1989 and, subject to ratification by the European Parliament, all new cars are to run on it by October 1990. Cars converted to unleaded can run on leaded petrol when necessary. Use of unleaded petrol also permits fitting of catalytic converters to reduce other exhaust emissions. In the UK it was calculated that 78% of new cars registered in 1987 could run on unleaded petrol, 23% without adjustment and 55% after adjustment, with the result that about 14 million cars could run on lead-free. By early 1989 only between 500,000 and one million had changed over. At this time about 3.5% of petrol sold was lead-free with about one in six stations offering it.

Conclusion Unleaded petrol consumption to expand.

ISSUE: "NEW ECONOMICS"

Relevance Politics; business; individuals.

Impact Slow but worldwide and potentially profound in the long term.

In brief There is no precise definition, but "new economists" generally believe that "traditional economics" fails to take account of the quality of life. In conventional economics a person can be described as "rich" despite having no source of unpolluted food, water or air, no access to natural surroundings, and while dying of a pollution-induced disease; in "new economics" the quality of life is taken into account, possibly by ascribing a monetary value to things conventional economics has ignored. In Britain the New Economics Foundation was founded in 1986 and is closely connected with The Other Economic Summit (TOES). "New economists" value the environment, self-reliance but also mutual aid, personal growth and human rights, and tend to favour the report by the WCED. They propose a guaranteed basic income, a shift of taxes from work towards pollution and energy and resource use, recycling and conservation strategies.

Conclusion New economic ideas gradually moving into the mainstream.

ISSUE: NITRATES

Relevance Agrochemical manufacturers and distributors; farmers; water authorities; fish farmers; suppliers of mineral water; possibly developers, estate agents etc if water quality influences property decisions; control equipment manufacturers.

Impact UK especially, Denmark, Holland, West Germany, parts of India and Australia, areas where nitrogenous fertilisers are used in quantity.

In brief The World Health Organisation's *Guidelines for Drinking Water Quality* state that "nitrate is toxic when present in excessive amounts in drinking water". In August 1985 the EC passed a directive which set a maximum admissible concentration (MAC) of 50 mg of nitrate per litre of water. In 1988 about a million people in Britain were receiving drinking water which regularly exceeded that limited; several million others occasionally do.

Nitrate poses a health hazard in two respects. First, bacteria in the mouth and stomach convert nitrate to nitrite, which combines with haemoglobin in the blood. Babies under three months are at greatest risk from the reduced oxygen uptake of the lungs, which can lead to "blue baby" syndrome.

Second, nitrite also reacts with amines in food to produce N-nitrosamines, shown to cause cancer in primates and believed by some specialists to cause stomach cancer in humans. High risk areas in Britain are mainly in the Severn-Trent and Anglian Water Authority regions.

Denmark developed an action plan in January 1987, adopted in May 1987 with amendments by the Danish Parliament's Environment and Planning Committee. Measures include restriction on timing and quantity of manure application and a reduction in nitrogen discharges from sewage plants and from industry. The target is a 50% reduction in nitrogen discharge (and an 80% reduction in phosphorus discharge). Capital costs of the scheme are estimated at Dkr 4.5 billion in agriculture, Dkr 6 billion for sewage plants and Dkr 1.5 billion for industry.

Conclusion Public disquiet will be met by government reassurance due to the high cost and difficulty of implementing nitrate-reduction programmes. In general, a piecemeal response is predicted involving controls on the application of fertiliser taxes and increased expenditure on water purification. Independent sources estimate the cost of bringing much of UK water up to EC directive standards at about £6 billion in 1989 - which in turn may mean a doubling of an average household water bill and increasing pressure on privatisation plans.

ISSUE: NUCLEAR POWER

Relevance All companies and individuals; governments; energy authorities.

Impact Worldwide and growing unease.

In brief Nuclear power is the *bête noire* for most but not all environmentalists. Its environmentalist supporters claim it solves the pollution problems most other energy sources would create. Its opponents, the great majority of environmentalists, point to the problem of low-level radiation, radioactive waste and to the consequences of a Chernobyl-type accident. A paper presented to the 13th Congress of the World Energy Conference in 1986 stated:

> One of the most eye-catching results of risk perception is the low correlation which is found between statistics of average yearly fatality rates and subjective judgements of seriousness of risk . . . A number of studies reveal that catastrophic potential of risky activities is an important characteristic.

What is the catastrophic potential of a nuclear power station? The breeder reactor design *does* have the potential for a nuclear explosion. The other designs do *not* but they still have the potential for a melt-down should there be a complete failure of coolant supply. Either would cause a massive release of radioactivity.

There is no significant disagreement about the effect of exposure to high levels of radiation: it was seen at Hiroshima. Chernobyl occurred after only 4,000 reactor years worldwide. Three Mile Island, Pennsylvania, released relatively small doses of radiation by comparison but was nearly and overwhelming disaster. There have been a small number of other significant accidents, and hundreds of lesser ones. While it may be possible to improve operational safety, therefore, the possibility of catastrophe sometime before the end of the century remains a fear in the public mind - and a reality.

Conclusion Austria, Sweden, Denmark, Greece, Italy, Norway, Portugal, Luxembourg, the Philippines, Australia and New Zealand are among the determinedly non-nuclear nations while the USA has commissioned no new nuclear reactors (and cancelled many) since Three Mile Island. The World Bank will not finance nuclear energy. In Britain nuclear power is suffering from electricity privatisation proposals because it has failed the economic tests. Nuclear energy *could* be phased out worldwide; on the other hand, concern about the "greenhouse effect" of burning fossil fuels could impose nuclear prospects.

ISSUE: OPPORTUNITIES

Relevance All companies.

Impact Worldwide and growing.

In brief Environmentalism is presenting business with many new opportunities in terms of goods and services in both the consumer and industrial fields. In the high street, green consumers present a market segment to be catered for, and profited from, just like any other. Not only is there a market for new products but stagnant, saturated markets can in some cases be revitalised by the introduction of energy-saving and environmental models. In industry there are huge markets for pollution abatement and energy saving. In the services sector, too, there are new opportunities, especially for environment consultancy.

Conclusion The environment movement is imposing costs on industry but there are opportunities, too, for dynamic companies with the responsiveness to embrace them.

ISSUE: ORGANIC FARMING

Relevance Food production and retailing; chemical companies.

Impact Significant expansion in Europe in the past ten years.

In brief Organic farming eliminates all liquid nitrate fertilisers and the majority of pesticides. Practices varied with the beliefs of individual farmers, but uniformity has arrived with the standards specified by the International Federation of Organic Agriculture Movements (IFOAM) and with the similar standards of the UK Soil Association. Organically grown produce comes from land that has been certified free from non-approved products for a minimum of two years, and where a system of food husbandry involves crop rotations and natural manures instead. Permitted pesticides include derris dust and natural pyrethrum.

Conclusion The introduction of organic produce by supermarket groups such as Safeway has brought the subject from the fringe to the mainstream and, by implication, given credence to the environmentalist argument that pesticides are dangerous to human health.

ISSUE: OZONE/CHLOROFLUOROCARBONS

Relevance Chlorofluorocarbon (CFC) manufacturers; aerosol applications; manufacturers of rigid-foam insulation/packaging and polystyrene food trays; manufacturers of air-conditioning and refrigeration; manufacturers of frozen foods; manufacturers of fire extinguishers; electronics industry. Associated retailers. Fisheries and farming.

Impact Worldwide. In 1980 UNEP asked governments to reduce manufacture of CFCs. In 1985 the Vienna Convention for the Protection of the Ozone Layer was adopted by 21 states and the EC, and subsequently by a number of other countries. The Montreal meeting of the Vienna Convention in 1987 agreed a protocol requiring signatories to freeze consumption at 1986 levels by 1990, reduce by 20% by 1994 and by a further 30% by 1999; decrease to 90% of 1986 production levels by 1994 and to 65% by 1999 (but allowing a production increase to 110% of 1986 levels up to 1990).

In brief CFCs are widely used chemical compounds, which have been shown to damage the earth's ozone layer. Ozone depletion will lead to more ultra violet (UV) light reaching earth, causing climatic change and unquantifiable damage to ecosystems including loss of crop productivity, and a predicted increase in human skin cancers and cataracts.

Ozone in the atmosphere acts as a shield against solar ultraviolet radiation. 90% of atmospheric ozone is in the stratosphere (above 12 km from Earth), and at its highest concentration between 20 and 30 km from Earth. CFCs break apart in the stratosphere to release chlorine, one molecule of which can destroy 100,000 ozone molecules. CFC 11 and CFC 12 are believed to account for 70% of ozone depletion and CFC 113 for 12%; Halon 1301, although produced in smaller quantities, has an ozone-depleting potential (ODP) eight times higher than CFC 11.

Because 1986 CFC production levels were six times higher than the environment is believed able to cope with, the Montreal protocol will not halt or reverse ozone depletion. It is estimated that an 85% reduction in emissions would be required merely to stabilise concentrations.

Major CFC producers are ICI, Du Pont, Hoechst AG and Atochem. Major CFC uses are as propellants in aerosol sprays, refrigerants, blowing agents for plastic foams and solvents.

There are alternatives to ozone-damaging CFCs, including less or non-damaging CFC compounds containing hydrogen, though generally more expensive to manufacture. Hydrocarbons can often substitute for CFCs and there are also other possible propellants. There is the potential for foam production without auxiliary blowing agents. Many CFC uses are non-essential (eg aerosols can be substituted by roll-ons or pump-action sprays).

Conclusion By the end of 1988 UK companies such as McDonalds, Kentucky, Wimpy and Spud-U-Like had pledged to stop using CFCs as blowing agents for fast-food cartons. Supermarkets were also phasing out egg boxes and meat trays with CFCs. Pressure is likely to increase for change of agent in insulation foam plastics, solvents for metal cleaning, and refrigerants.

Scientists and environmentalists will press for further reductions in CFC production and consumption and are set to achieve a near ban on ozone-damaging CFCs by the mid-1990s.

ISSUE: PACKAGING

Relevance Manufacturing and distributive trades; retailers; waste disposal.

Impact Developed world. Economic and environmental pressures combining to make packaging consume less material.

In brief Environmentalists have long been critical of packaging as wasteful and polluting. Minimal or no packaging has not, however, proved popular with the majority of consumers. In the UK the packaging industry has formed a pressure and advisory body, the Industry Council for Packaging and the Environment (INCPEN). As much as a third of UK household waste consists of packaging. However, INCPEN is able to point to positive as well as polluting consequences - a longer life for foodstuffs, less ill-health since packaging protects foodstuffs from germs, less wastage through damage to goods in transit, and the potential to provide detailed product information. In the developed world, packaging waste *is* likely to diminish since most products that can be are already packaged; that packaging, however, uses less and less material as manufacturers compete by reduced costs. The anti-packaging pressure is also being blunted by recycling, in certain instances, and by the interest in energy recovery from waste. These developments bring their own criteria, notably the use of a single material - if two or more materials are combined in packaging the subsequent cost of separation could make recovery uneconomic.

The economic pressure to use less material - known in the industry as light-weighting - is illustrated by the fact that in the past 20 years tin cans have been reduced by 30% in body plate thickness. This light-weighting in turn brings transport savings; it is estimated that the switch from glass to plastic for in-flight drinks sales saves some £10,000 a year in fuel for long-haul aircraft.

Conclusion Companies that fail to light-weight will suffer a competitive disadvantage, less through a bad PR image as through unnecessary costs. Recyclable containers could, in some cases, be an alternative strategy. (See also *Issue: Recycling*.)

ISSUE: PESTICIDES

Relevance Farmers; chemical manufacturers; legislators; food importers, wholesalers and retailers; companies and individuals living or working in rural areas; consumers.

Impact Agricultural regions worldwide, traditionally developed countries practising intensive methods of farming, but recently also developing countries facing increasing pressures from home and export markets.

In brief Each year over one billion gallons of pesticides (including insecticides, herbicides and fungicides) are sprayed on to crops and soil in the UK. At least 38 different types of pesticides are cleared for use in the UK, although banned or restricted on health grounds in other countries. Usage has boomed over the past 30 years with vast acreages worldwide now on the "pesticide treadmill" - a vicious circle of chemical-resistant pests requiring constantly increased applications.

Environmentalists complain that British testing procedure is inadequate to isolate and identify all toxic agrochemicals. They also challenge the government stand that "no evidence" of long-term health damage automatically equals safe. Europe-wide pesticide campaigns have included the Pesticides Action Network's (PAN) "Dirty Dozen".

Another major issue, especially in Europe, is the "pesticides" boomerang", in which toxic agrochemicals (often those actually banned in the country of manufacture) are manufactured for export to developing countries, only to reappear later on imported foodstuffs. Accidental pollution continues, especially in rural areas where aerial spraying is used, but also from ground-level spraying, where spray or vapour drifts affect local residents, plant and pet life. There are also concerns about the levels of complaints from consumers, agricultural workers and agrochemical production employees.

Conclusion The UK government has pledged to seek additional safety evidence from chemical manufacturers applying for relicensing of pesticides. It also stresses the increasing sophistication of safety test technology, but environmentalists argue that testing is neither adequate nor sufficiently comprehensive. Public concern about and resistance to agrochemicals is already demonstrated by the growth in demand for organic methods. A number of organic produce standards stamps have been introduced. The government can expect increasing pressure to ban suspect chemicals, both at home and from the EC and elsewhere. Agrochemicals users producers must be aware of differing (and constantly changing) overseas regulations involving sudden bans. Interest in the fields of biochemicals and plant genetics to replace chemicals is growing.

ISSUE: POLITICS AND LEGISLATION

Relevance All companies.

Impact "Greening" of political manifestos; increase in environment legislation taking place in most countries.

In brief The creation of pan-national policymaking institutions, somewhat divorced from commercial pressure and lobbying, has facilitated the introduction of legislation taking a world perspective of environmental problems. The UNEP is one of these key organisations. The European Commission has also been issuing directives at a faster rate than some member states would themselves have willingly legislated. This body of research, pronouncement and control from international organisations is itself shaping public opinion in countries. At the same time, national pressure groups on the environment have become sufficiently well organised in many developed countries to oblige legislators to take their views into account. Even in the UK, for example, where in 1987 the Thatcher enterprise culture was well established, the Conservatives felt it necessary to incorporate more green ideas into their manifesto than ever before.

Conclusion Industry needs to adopt a more constructive dialogue on environment legislation or face exclusion from the argument.

ISSUE: "POLLUTER PAYS" PRINCIPLE

Relevance All companies.

Impact Small so far, but set to become of more tangible significance in the 1990s.

In brief In 1972 the member countries of the OECD agreed to base their environmental policies on the "polluter pays" principle (PPP). This was as much a trade as an environmental measure, designed to discourage subsidies, since companies which could ignore environmental damage and pollution abatement costs were at a competitive advantage over others. PPP means that environmental costs are reflected in the price of products and services. Environmentalists would like to see the principle given a rather wider application so that it could be used as the basis of legal action by the public. As a concept it suffers from the frequent inability to identify the polluter responsible for an oil slick, a cloud of gas or the result of illegal dumping at a landfill.

Conclusion PPP to continue as a guiding principle.

ISSUE: RADON

Relevance Individuals; architects; office workers; energy industry.

Impact Little-known issue as yet but potentially a major one.

In brief Radon is a naturally occurring radioactive gas that can concentrate in buildings, especially those with a high degree of insulation. In the USA the Environmental Protection Agency has said that eight million homes could require work to reduce radon. In the UK, where a maximum level of 20 milliSieverts per year has been set, 20,000 houses are said to exceed it. That dose is four times the average dose of a nuclear worker. Some 900 deaths a year in Britain are attributed to radon gas, which is a carcinogen. In the USA it has been estimated that construction costs of new homes would need to be increased by 10% to make them radon-safe, while modification of existing homes has been put at anything up to 100% of their value. The cheapest method of tackling the problem could be an electrostatic precipitator. (See also *Issue: Indoor Air Pollution.*)

Conclusion As higher insulation standards are applied in homes and commerical premises so the radon problem is likely to increase, creating a market for radon treatment.

ISSUE: RAMSAR CONVENTION

Relevance Governments; industry using wetland products; tourism developers; fisheries.

Impact Any country with areas of wetland, especially where developing industry could substantially alter natural environments.

In brief Wetlands are the only ecosystem to have their own international convention: the Ramsar Convention of 1971 under which signatories undertake to conserve areas of wetland and, wherever possible, underwrite their future by giving them some form of economic value. Wetland areas have had a low profile, even among conservationists; the normal response is drainage. Consequently, there have been massive reclamation schemes. The Ramsar Convention aims to halt the decline of wetland habitats and lists some important wetlands. This list is kept by the International Union for the Conservation of Nature and Natural Resources (IUCN) and at December 1985 showed 323 sites covering more than 20 million hectares. At the same date there were 38 signatories; 27 developed countries and 13 developing. Lack of money remains a grave problem, hindering both effective conservation effort and expansion.

Conclusion Wetlands are rich ecosystems which, if conserved, protected and carefully managed, can be successfully exploited both for product and environmental benefit. The short-term drain-and-reclaim stand has been seen to be wasteful in the longer term, with some wetland "industry" projects including aquaculture/agriculture combinations producing additional benefits such as local employment, foreign exchange and natural habitat. The convention urgently needs more active and generous signatories.

ISSUE: RECYCLING

Relevance All organisations and individuals, but especially the packaging and waste disposal industries.

Impact Substantial and fundamental.

In brief Increasing raw material costs, scarcity, and the problems and costs of waste disposal have given impetus to ways of reusing many substances and products, especially paper, glass, cans, plastics, metals, textiles and dangerous heavy metals in batteries. In the developed world, the average household produces about one tonne of waste a year - much of it without any environmentally benign method of disposal. According to the Swiss Federal Office for Environmental Protection, for example, about 4% of the cadmium and 80% of the mercury found in municipal wastes comes from batteries: new regulations in 1986 should have increased the collection rate for spent mercury cells to around 90%. Concentration is mainly focused, however, on paper, glass (6 billion glass bottles and jars are used in Britain each year), metals (over 11 billion food and drink cans are produced in Britain each year), plastics, oil and textiles.

Conclusion Companies will increasingly consider recycled material in their manufactures and, equally, the ability of their manufactures either to be recycled or to be disposed of safely. The growing recycling mentality also has implications for the previous acceptance of built-in obsolescence. (See also (*Issue: Waste Disposal* and *Issue: Waste Management*.))

ISSUE: RENEWABLE ENERGY

Relevance All individuals and organisations; governments; energy industry; building industry; high technology.

Impact Worldwide.

In brief Renewable sources are those that are unaffected by man's use: the sun, the wind, the waves and the tides. Generally, however, the term is also applied to geothermal heat from the earth's core, to running water and to biomass, that is, the sun's energy stored in trees and plants. In fact, the wind, waves and running water are also forms of solar energy, connected with the sun's evaporation of moisture and with the heating of the earth's surface. It has been calculated that the incoming solar energy absorbed by the earth in one year is equivalent to 15 to 20 times the energy stored in all the world's recoverable fossil fuel reserves. Put another way, the solar radiation falling on the world's 20 million square kilometres of desert in one year is 400 times the world's present annual energy consumption. Renewables are not without environmental as well as practical problems but their use can undeniably reduce chemical, radioactive and thermal pollution and provide the solution to energy needs when fossil fuels have run out.

Conclusion Development of renewables is inevitable.

ISSUE: SMOKING

Relevance Farming; tobacco industry and retailing; health industry.

Impact Powerful in developed countries.

In brief Opponents of smoking have begun to carry the campaign into the environment field. David Simpson, director of Action on Smoking and Health, has described it as "among the most important environmental issues of our time", due to the deforestation for tobacco curing, the use of land which "could grow desperately needed food crops," the generation of litter, tar and carbon monoxide, the role of discarded cigarettes in starting fires and, most of all, because smoking "is an ecological disaster for the human body". Having gained some tangible results in developed countries and the anti-smoking campaigners are now turning their attention to the issue worldwide: "As smoking declines in the West, the problem is being exported to the developing countries."

Conclusion The linking of anti-smoking with environmentalism will strengthen the lobby against the tobacco industry.

ISSUE: STOCKHOLM DECLARATION

Relevance All companies, governments and individuals.

Impact The declaration has been incorporated into the constitutions of several countries but tangible benefits have been insufficient from the environmentalist viewpoint.

In brief Sverker Astrom, then Swedish ambassador to the UN, suggested convening an international conference to discuss environment problems, especially acid pollution, which remains a major worry for his country. This became the UN Conference on the Human Environment held in Stockholm in 1972. Principle 1 of the resulting Stockholm Declaration is: "Man has the fundamental right to freedom, equality and adequate conditions of life, in an environment of a quality that permits a life of dignity and well-being." The Swedish scientist Svante Oden presented a paper on the transport of air pollutants over long distance which, although received with scepticism at the time, resulted in Principle 21 of the Declaration, that activities carried out in one country should not pollute other countries.

Conclusion The Stockholm Declaration continues to influence national and international law.

ISSUE: SUSTAINABILITY

Relevance All businesses.

Impact Worldwide, long-term evolution in business philosophy.

In brief "Sustainability" is one of the buzzwords of pragmatic environmentalists. UNEP executive director Mostafa Kamal Tolba set out the wider context in a 1984 address to the International Institute:

1. help for the very poor because they are left with no option other than to destroy the environment;
2. the idea of self-reliant development, within natural resource constraints;
3. the idea of cost-effective development using different economic criteria to the traditional approach - that is to say, development should not degrade environmental quality, nor should it reduce productivity in the long run;
4. the great issues of health control, appropriate technologies, food self-reliance, clean water and shelter for all;
5. the notion that people-centred initiatives are needed; human beings, in other words, are the resources in the concept.

In 1980 the World Conservation Strategy coined the phrase "sustainable development" for the optimum management of renewable resources. But as long ago as 1971 IBM laid down an environmental management policy, revised in 1973, without using the term "sustainable" but with sustainability implicit in it:

IBM will reduce to a minimum the ecological impact of all of its activities. Management in IBM is expected to be continuously on guard against adversely affecting the environment and to seek ways to conserve natural resources.

Although IBM is not in business which creates severe pollution problems, IBM is committed to:

1. Meet or exceed all applicable government regulations in any location.

2. Establish stringent standards of its own where government regulations do not exist.
3. Attempt to utilise nonpolluting technologies and to minimise energy consumption in the design of products and processes.
4. Work toward a 1979 goal to minimise dependence on terminal waste treatment through development of techniques to recover and reuse air, water and materials.
5. Assist government and other industries in developing solutions to environmental problems when appropriate opportunities present themselves and IBM's experience and knowledge may be helpful.

Conclusion Sustainability will increasingly be adopted by business as a standard management objective.

ISSUE: TROPICAL RAIN FOREST

Relevance Timber trade; pharmaceuticals companies and medicine; farming; tourism; fast-food outlets.

Impact Worldwide. Environmentalists seek consumer support for boycott of tropical hardwood products unless from sustainably managed forests. Multilateral development banks (MDBs) are under pressure to stop funding deforestation projects. Consumer reaction against secondary targets such as hamburgers and other beef products is being orchestrated.

In brief True rain forests cover some 4.5 million square kilometres of the earth, while tropical rain and monsoon forests together account for half the world's forests, covering some 11 million square kilometres. The annual rate of destruction is estimated to be 45,000 square kilometres to commercial logging, 25,000 to cattle ranching, 25,000 to gathering wood for fuel and 160,000 square kilometres of all primary forest to slash-and-burn. This amounts to some 2% of existing tropical rain forest a year, meaning absolute destruction within 50 years.

The loss of the world's tropical rain forests will have significant impact on the future of business, disrupting the $18 billion drugs industry, which derives many of its raw materials from them; denying agriculture new genetic material; and bringing to an end the source of supply for hardwoods and woodchip for paper-making and packaging. If the destruction takes place it will necessitate increased investment in river-defence and erosion-prevention systems - and possibly in a completely new atmosphere-management technology. For the campaign to save the rain forests to succeed implies a reduction in the consumption of tropical hardwood plus increased investment in "appropriate" and "alternative" technology.

The main hardwood-importing countries are Japan (over $2 billion), the USA (over $0.6 billion) and the UK (over $0.4 billion). These are the target countries for environmentalists but campaigning is taking place in more than 30. What are the environmentalists concerned about? First, the loss of plant and animal species. While the UK, for example, has some 1,443 different plants, Costa Rica, only one-fifth the size, has 8,000. It is estimated that 4 square miles of rain forest could contain 1,500 species of flowering plants, 750 species of tree, 400 of birds, 150 of butterflies, 125 of mammals, 100 of reptiles and 50 of amphibians. The rain forests are equally home to tribal peoples.

Environmentalists also point to the number of products that originated in the rain forest (from rubber to resins, from pharmaceuticals to corn flakes) and the unknown future industries that would be lost. Finally, it has been calculated that 50% of the oxygen added to the atmosphere each year comes from the tropical rain forest of the Amazon Basin.

The International Tropical Timber Organisation has now been formed, representing both producer and consumer countries, with the aim of achieving sustainable use of tropical forests. Meanwhile environment groups like Friends of the Earth continue their campaigns to mobilise consumer action. FoE has specifically targeted companies in oil and gas exploration, mining, construction, cash crop export agricultures, tobacco, logging and commercial bank funding for investigation. The timber industry in Britain has now agreed to a surcharge on imports of tropical hardwoods.

Conclusion A major long-term issue which could prove instrumental in revising conventional economic thinking. Probable move towards manufacture of wood products in supplier countries, with restrictions on export of logs.

ISSUE: VEGETARIANISM

Relevance Farmers, food industry, clothing industry.

Impact Worldwide and growing but with particular relevance for developed countries.

In brief Vegetarians (who object to the killing of animals) and vegans (who object to the exploitation of animals, even if they are not killed) exist for many reasons; the environmental argument is that domestic animals consume -

and therefore actually reduce - protein otherwise available to humans. Beef cattle, for example, consume on average ten times more protein than they supply. According to the WCED (Brundtland Report), the present per capita global average consumption of plant energy for food, seed and animal feed amounts to about 6,000 calories daily, with a range among countries of 3,000 up to 15,000 calories, depending on the level of meat consumption. Less meat consumption, environmentalists believe, would mean more food available to people, with less pressure on the land and less need to practise highly intensive agriculture with its alleged dangerous use of artificial fertilisers and pesticides/herbicides.

Conclusion A trend towards reduced meat consumption in developed countries can only gain in impetus. In the USA the average consumption is some 110 kg per person per year, in the UK 75 kg, in the USSR 51 kg and in Brazil 32 kg. Developing countries and less developed countries, however, are likely to increase meat consumption; in China it stands at 21 kg, in Nigeria 6 kg and in India 1.1 kg. Vegans and strict vegetarians also avoid leather goods, and possibly also silk and wool.

ISSUE: VEHICLE EMISSIONS

Relevance Motor industry; industries using vehicles; legislators; town planners; petrol companies; pollution control equipment manufacturers; all individuals.

Impact All countries with transport systems, involving the use of combustion engines. Particularly the developed world.

In brief Motor vehicles are the main source of nitrogen oxides and hydrocarbons, harmful atmospheric pollutants (see *Issue: Acid Rain*). In the USA, Japan and Australia three-way catalytic converters are already used to control emissions, and regulations are up to four times stricter than those proposed, though not yet fully implemented, within the EC.

Carbon monoxide In a normal city centre, traffic accounts for practically the whole emission of CO. The gas is rapidly absorbed in the lungs and taken into the bloodstream where it inhibits the oxygen transport. Classic symptoms of CO poisoning are headaches and giddiness.

Nitrogen oxides and hydrocarbons There is increasingly strong evidence that these substances are damaging air pollutants both individually and in combination. They are believed to exacerbate health problems such as asthma and have been linked to lung cancer. More than 40% of all NOx in the atmosphere comes from vehicle exhausts.

Catalytic converter A catalyst-covered ceramic honeycomb, cased in steel and fitted to vehicle exhaust systems, it converts harmful exhaust pollutants into less harmful water, carbon dioxide and nitrogen. Used compulsorily in the USA since the early 1970s, they are most effectively used in conjunction with unleaded petrol (see *Issue: Lead in Petrol*).

Lean-burn engines These are a much-debated alternative to catalytic converters, supported by the British motor industry, for one, for use with engines up to 2 litres. Increasingly sophisticated engine design including modification of cylinder heads and hi-tech electronics can create conditions where fuel is burned much more leanly, with an air:fuel ratio of up to 24:1. Apart from reducing carbon monoxide and nitrogen oxide emissions, lean-burn engines can be 10-15% more fuel-efficient. However, there are suggestions that medium-size vehicles using lean-burn systems may increase damaging emissions at higher speeds and will need also to use catalytic converters.

Conclusion Legislation will force cleaner technology on to the indisputably polluted roads of Europe sooner rather than later. It is also clear that pressure will continue for ever tighter controls: not just the lean-burn engines and catalytic converters now proposed, but also reduced speed limits and tax penalties *against* cars will be considered. New transport technology is a virtual certainty and, in the long-term, promises industrial growth. Companies and individuals should be aware of the legislative mood and be able to respond both retrospectively and, for competitive gain, in advance.

ISSUE: WASTE DISPOSAL

Relevance All companies.

Impact Considerable, worldwide.

In brief Current methods of waste disposal are coming under increasing criticism in respect of a number of substances. Landfill poses a potential threat to water supply, so that unlined sites have been banned in many countries. But sites lined either with clay or synthetics are also known to leak. Dumping toxic wastes and sewage sludge at sea has received much adverse publicity, especially at the time of the 1987 North Sea Conference in London. Incineration, especially refuse-fired CHP stations, look potentially the best solution but many existing incinerators are emitting toxic gases, especially dioxin.

Conclusion Companies under increasing pressure to design products with minimum waste, that can be recycled or disposed of safely. New markets emerging for advanced waste disposal technology, including biotechnology. Increase in industrial costs to take account of safer waste treatment and disposal. (See also *Issue: Waste management.*)

ISSUE: WASTE MANAGEMENT

Relevance All companies.

Impact Worldwide and growing.

In brief What was once regarded as waste is increasingly seen as a resource. In Britain, for example, in 1984 the House of Commons Trade and Industry Committee found that £1,800 million of materials were being reclaimed each year but that Britain could benefit by at least a further £750 million by more widespread and better techniques. The 3M company is the most frequently quoted, having in 1975 introduced worldwide the 3P Programme: "Pollution Prevention Pays". 3M figures show that it has since saved nearly $300 million, reduced air pollutants by over 100,000 tonnes, water pollutants by more than 15,000 tonnes, waste water by around 2 billion gallons and sludge/solid waste by some 200,000 tonnes.

An example of the philosophy in action: the Minnesota plant producing magnetic oxides installed a $0.5 million evaporator to a waste stream to produce ammonium sulphate worth $150,000 a year; the alternative non-productive, conventional pollution control equipment would have cost $1 million.

Conclusion Waste management is a vital part of competitiveness for many industries. (See also *Issue: Recycling.*)

ISSUE: WATER

Relevance All companies and individuals.

Impact Worldwide problem of water pollution; growing problem of inadequate supply.

In brief The UN's goal of clean water for all by 1990 has been abandoned. A target of the year 2000 also looks impossible. A combination of population and industrial growth is making demands that neither natural nor artificial systems can meet. Even in countries like the UK that have taken drinking water and bathing water quality for granted there are problems of pollution by nitrates, aluminium, landfill leakages, sewage and various toxins.

Conclusion Commercial and even domestic consumers will have to be metered in many parts of the world. Industry will have to look to water recycling if it is to meet its needs and contain costs.

ISSUE: WHALING

Relevance Whaling industry; food manufacturers; pharmaceuticals; tourism.

Impact The 1982 IWC moratorium (see Section 3.2) is now significant mainly for Iceland, Japan and Norway; touristic whale watching particularly significant for California.

In brief Whale catches rapidly declining through over-hunting even before the International Whaling Commission quotas and subsequent moratorium.

Conclusion Whales one resource that has been over-exploited such that most commercial whaling is unlikely to prove economic for many years. That which is or becomes economic will face strong political barriers to exploitation.

ISSUE: WILDLIFE EXPLOITATION

Relevance Fur, meat, fish, cosmetics and pharmaceutical industries; tourism; pets; hunting.

Impact Worldwide and profound, especially for targeted species.

In brief Environmentalists are divided on the exploitation issue. On one side are those who argue that wildlife can be preserved only if it gives an economic return, on the other those opposed to management, culling etc. The former lobby is in the ascendant. Bodies like the World Wide Fund for Nature (formerly the World Wildlife Fund) generally accept that wildlife can be "harvested" where species are not threatened, for food, sport, hunting, souvenirs etc. The Convention on International Trade in Endangered Species (CITES) was drawn up in 1973 and is gradually growing in strength as more and more countries enforce it; however, there is still a considerable trade in wildlife and wildlife products, despite CITES protection.

Conclusion The management of wildlife and the harvesting of non-endangered species, together with the protection of endangered species, is a growing trend.

PART THREE
WORLDWIDE RESOURCES

3.1 INTRODUCTION

Industrial production has grown more than 50-fold in the past century; four-fifths of that growth has taken place in the last 40 years. If the world's population grows in accordance with official predictions, by the time it stabilises in the 21st century, industrial output will need to increase by a further five to ten times. But can it?

Past predictions of "limits to growth" have proved premature: new reserves have been discovered, yet other resources have *already* proven finite. Today the whaling industry is virtually ended; open-sea fish stocks will never again keep pace with human demand; and within the next 50 years tropical rain forests may exist no more. These are all examples of so-called renewable resources which, unlike coal, oil and minerals, should never run out. Yet some already have and others are following to extinction. Part Three examines the resource crisis for whaling, fishing, tropical rain forests, the atmosphere, the land and water.

3.2 WHALING

Introduction

Whaling has been a worldwide industry for almost ten centuries, but careless husbanding of the raw material has resulted in the long-term suspension and possible permanent cessation of harvesting and an enforced switch to other livelihoods for whalers and alternative products for users.

Most of the traditional industrial uses for whale products (see Table 3.1) are now met by alternative natural and man-made products. Japan is virtually alone, however, in claiming whales are an irreplacable domestic commodity. This will be discussed in detail later.

Table 3.1   USE OF WHALES 1980

Category	Source	Product
Whale meat	Baleen	Prime meat (steak); salted meat (baked or boiled); frozen meat and Sashimi; sausage and pressed meat, cold cuts; hamburger; canned and dried whale meat; feed for livestock, pet food; flavouring, extracts.
	Sperm	Solubles (used in processing animal feed).
Whale oil	Finback	Margarine, lard, shortening; cosmetics; crayons, candles; used in manufacture of explosives, cigarettes; soap for laundry and industrial use; rubber fillers and special greases.
	Sperm	Coatings (paints and varnishes) and printer's ink; sulfated oil, precision machine oil; pharmaceuticals; cosmetics candles, crayons and ointments; detergents; lubricants.
Skin	Sperm/Baleen	Boiled skin for use in stews; slab and sliced bacon; gelatin (puddings and confection); salted and dried skin; handbags, belts and drums.
Internal organs	All	Seasonings (for noodles and other fast foods); pharmaceuticals (liver oil, vitamins and hormones), insulin, cortisone, pepsin and flavourings.
Other	All	Meal (livestock feed); squid hooks, letter openers; seals, pipes and ornaments.

Source: Tokyo University of Fisheries

Since whales were first used by modern man, stocks have been over-exploited. Despite increasing scientific understanding, the pattern has been one of stock depletion leading in turn to a shift in target species and hunting ground. First the right whales of the Bay of Biscay, then the sperm whales and humpbacks were exhaustively hunted wherever they could be found. With the introduction of mechanised hunting apparatus, the whales' defences were weakened and the hunting grounds expanded.

The giant blues first felt the might of the explosive harpoons. Comprehensive harvesting then followed in direct relationship to the size of the prey: first the fin whales, then the sei and, in recent years, most attention has focused upon the relatively small minke whale.

At the turn of the century the US whaling fleets brought the bowhead whale close to extinction in the Bering Sea and Arctic, and in the 1930s the US and European fleets hunted tens of thousands of blue whales in the Antarctic, severely depleting stocks.

The IWC and its Moratorium

The International Whaling Commission (IWC), the main internationally recognised body regulating the industry, has taken a series of conservation measures which, by the 1970s, ensured that most seriously depleted stocks were protected from commercial whaling. But stocks of blue, bowhead, grey, humpback and right had already been exploited to critically low levels before being protected. Now scientists fear for the survival of the North-West Pacific humpback and the blue and right whales of the North-West Atlantic.

Decreasing catches (see Table 3.2) - consistently lower even than IWC quotas - and increasing conservationist pressure eventually resulted in the 1982 IWC moratorium on all commercial whale hunting. This temporary ban came into force in 1985 and is regularly reviewed so that it may be lifted when stocks once again become viable.

Whether commercial whaling will ever again become viable in conservationist terms must be in question. The reproduction rate of the great whale is such that populations are unlikely to grow by more than 2% per annum. The rate can rise for smaller whales but, given the additional pressures of over-fishing of food sources and marine pollution, the probable growth rate is only 1% per annum.

Table 3.2   GLOBAL CATCH OF SELECTED WHALE SPECIES 1973-1983

number of whales caught

	Sperm	Species Sei	Fin	Minke
1973/74	21,421	6,239	2,142	10,446
1974/75	21,228	5,001	1,552	11,662
1975/76	17,422	1,870	741	11,273
1976/77	12,329	2,021	310	10,199
1977/78	11,064	695	711	12,447
1978/79	8,655	163	730	9,078
1979/80	2,211	102	472	9,948
1980/81	1,595	100	410	11,828
1981/82	621	71	356	10,406
1982/83	414	100	277	11,660

Source: UNEP

Whaling must therefore be seen as an unattractive investment. Given that long-term predictions cast serious doubt on the creation of substantial whale populations until the second half of the 21st century, it is a safe assumption that existing whaling organisations will by then have allocated manpower, plant and investment to other activities. Table 3.3 shows the pre-moratorium state of investment in plant, and employment and production data for leading whaling nations. Whaling activities had already been substantially curtailed by increasingly restrictive quotas and diminishing stocks. Nations were complaining of social problems associated with unemployment and displacement of the workforce, and pressures on other industries attempting to absorb redundant plant.

Not every IWC member nation has agreed to the moratorium. By 1987 world whaling was restricted to scientific catches by Iceland and the Republic of Korea and to a small catch - 200 minke whales, again for scientific purposes - by Norway. Japan and the USSR continued to operate whaling although both had agreed to end commercial activities after a given period. More than 11,000 whales have been killed since the moratorium, many in the name of scientific research - and IWC-approved reason for whaling, seen by many as a loophole for determined nations.

Table 3.3   PLANT, EMPLOYMENT AND PRODUCTION OF LEADING WHALING NATIONS

| | | Plant and Employment | | | | Production | | |
| | | | Store station/plant | Employment | | Oil (tonnes) | Meat and other (tonnes) | Value ($000) |
	Year	Vessels		Direct	Indirect			
Australia[1]	1978	3	1	96	200	3,931	2,706	2,600
Brazil	1978	1	1	290	nk	808[2]	2,817[2]	3,614[2]
Canada[1]	1972	6	3		372	68[3]		3,000
Chile	1977/9	3	1	208	–		173[3]	–
Iceland								
Pelagic[1]	1979	4	1	220[4]	nk	1,194	6,127	8,364
Coastal[2]	1979	11		105[4]	nk	200[5]		
Japan								
Pelagic	1979	23	10	2,330	50,000[6]	2,400	15,600	36,693
Coastal	1979	15	13	629	–	5,100	8,500	12,912
Korea	1979	21[7]	–	280	3,000[8]	–	2,000	5,000
Norway	1979	92	38	516	1,960[8]	–	4,000	5,357
Peru	1979	3	1	250	500	nk	nk	nk
South Africa[1]	1975	5	1	468		7,000	8,150	4,700
Spain	1980	3[9]	2[10]	493		nk	nk	nk
USA	1971	3[11]	1	55	nk	53[3]		nk
USSR	1980	12[11]	0	1,013	nk	3,600	16,000	nk

Source: IWC

Note: nk = not known

1 whaling terminated; 2 30% export; 3 number of whales; 4 seasonal; 5 minke whales; 6 1975 figure; 7 subsidy for capital plant 1980; 8 220 seasonal; 9 plus 2 out of service; 10 plus 2 dependent cold stores; 11 includes 2 factory vessels

Japan

Japan refuses to approve the ban. Its continuing demand for whale products keeps the world's small, but tenacious whaling industry alive. In early 1987 it announced its intention to catch 825 minke and sperm whales in Antarctica for research purposes. Conservationist outcry and a US government threat to halve Japan's quota in the US 200-mile economic zone (an action it is empowered to take under the Magnuson-Packwood Act, a domestic law designed to curtail the fishery catch of nations that ignore IWC recommendations) forced Japan to review its position. Ultimately it agreed to restrict its scientific catch to 300 minke, no sperm whales.

Japan is unique in that it has cultural, historical and dietary as well as industrial claims to whaling (see Table 3.4). Whaling has traditionally been big business for Japan: in the 1960s it used to catch over 20,000 a year valued at around 30 billion yen ($200 million). In 1980 the Japanese delegation to the IWC stated in a submission about the effects of a whaling ban: "The whale and whaling are deeply embedded in Japanese dietary, economic, social and cultural life." It predicted that the imposition of a total ban would mean: "The Japanese will be totally deprived of the opportunity to eat whale meat to which they have been accustomed since prehistoric age. This is equivalent to the negation of a national culture by foreign nations."

Table 3.4   SOCIAL ATTITUDES TO CONSUMPTION OF WHALE MEAT IN JAPAN 1980

%

1. *Do you remember eating whale meat as a child?*
    Ate it frequently   53
    Ate it occasionally   36
    Did not eat it very often   11

2. *How often does your family eat whale meat in one month?*
    1-5 times   62
    Hardly ever   27
    6-10 times   9
    More than 10 times   2

Continued...

Table 3.4 cont'd

3. *Where do you usually buy whale meat?*
    Fish store   41
    Supermarket   38
    Whale speciality store   21
    Direct from whalers   0

4. *Who is especially fond of whale meat in your family?*
    Whole family   48
    Father   24
    Mother   19
    Children   5
    Grandparents   4

5. *Would you and your family like to be able to eat more whale meat?*
    Yes   62
    No   38

6. *(Asked only of those responding "yes" to 5.) Why are you*
    unable to eat more whale meat although you want to?
    Too expensive   65
    Not as much whale meat available   17
    Unable to get type of whale meat wanted   14
    Don't know   4

Source: Tokyo University of Fisheries

It was predicted that 3,000 whalers would lose their jobs and, with no suitable alternatives available locally for their unskilled labour, local community economic and social life would collapse. In addition, Japan foresaw that all companies involved in whaling or with its products would go bankrupt; that existing plant would be wasted and that the whole nation would regard a ban as "a challenge to its own cultural and traditional inheritance".

Today the Japanese whaling industry is subsidised to the extent of 350 million yen ($2.6 million). Were this level of subsidy to become politically less favoured, it is likely that enthusiasm for the activity would similarly wane.

Other Reactions to the Moratorium

Other nations have also reported to the IWC on the effects of, first, severe reduction and then the proposed ban.

USSR

The USSR reported that between 1970 and 1980 it had "made inoperative and destroyed" 35 whaling boats valued at 56 million roubles. Retraining redundant whalers had cost 10-11 million roubles; by 1980 the total economic loss as a result of quota reduction was about 250 million roubles, lighting, food and medical industries being hardest hit.

Brazil

Brazil reported unemployment, suspension of the food supply, negative effects on balance of payments and reduction of government revenue.

Norway

Norway's report stated that in 1980 it had a fleet of 92 catching vessels employing about 500 crew. About 1,070 people were employed in cold storage plants and another 890 in oil refineries.

Australia

In 1987 Australia presented the IWC with a report, *The Socio-Economic Implications of the Termination of Australia's Whaling Operations.* Australian whaling operations had ceased in 1978 with the closure of the Cheynes Beach Whaling Station in Albany, Western Australia. The main reason was said to be economic, although the industry conceded that it was aware of "mounting public concern and antipathy towards whaling". Among other things, the report stated that, of the 100 employees forced to obtain alternative employment, nearly 75% had found jobs within three months, most of the remaining unemployed then being over 45 or under 25. Those who did find employment had to accept an average salary level 25% below their previous salary at Cheynes Beach; one-third accepted positions of lower skill status. Approximately 75% had chosen to remain in Albany.

3.3 FISHERIES

Introduction

The amount of fish caught in the world's seas has been increasing since the Second World War, the global catch rising at a steady 6-7% annually, from 20 million tonnes in 1950 to 65 million tonnes in 1969. After a peak around 1970, the average annual growth rate dropped to about 1% as more and more stocks were depleted.

Table 3.5 shows the growth patterns by region for 1975-1985. Growth was maintained in some cases, such as the Northern Pacific (up 7.1 million tonnes, or 36.5%, over the decade), but decreased in others, for example North Atlantic (fell by 2.1 million tonnes, or 13.1%). Table 3.6 gives 1985 data for selected species.

Table 3.5   CATCHES OF FISH BY REGION 1975-1985

'000 tonnes		Atlantic		Indian		Pacific	
	North	Central	South	Ocean	Northern	Central	Southern
1975	15,783.6	6,203.4	3,394.8	3,151.3	19,530.0	5,969.4	4,645.8
1976	16,562.5	6,370.4	3,570.1	3,140.0	19,991.0	6,401.2	6,122.7
1977	15,556.4	6,268.1	3,969.6	3,469.9	19,970.4	7,184.4	4,470.5
1978	14,464.5	6,332.4	4,830.2	3,659.5	20,316.4	7,527.9	5,930.3
1979	14,667.6	6,039.4	4,419.8	3,546.4	20,301.8	7,545.0	7,278.0
1980	14,675.0	6,847.6	3,895.7	3,690.2	20,725.1	7,916.9	6,717.2
1981	14,489.0	6,858.3	4,028.8	3,734.8	21,906.7	8,322.6	7,340.2
1982	13,602.3	7,251.5	4,342.2	3,879.3	22,592.7	8,181.4	8,437.2
1983	13,900.0	7,311.9	4,312.4	4,015.2	23,668.0	8,026.9	6,856.1
1984	14,081.6	7,214.0	3,915.2	4,341.8	26,426.1	8,475.4	9,151.1
1985	13,723.3	6,941.7	3,991.9	4,490.6	26,663.1	8,859.2	10,211.0

Source: FAO

At least 25% of the world's fisheries are seriously depleted. There is particular concern for specific species in some regions and these are monitored by the UN Food and Agriculture Organisation (FAO). Table 3.7 shows nine listed as

Table 3.6   REGIONAL FISH CATCHES 1985

000 tonnes

	North	Atlantic Central	South	Indian Ocean	Northern	Pacific Central	Southern	World* total
Flounder/halibut/sole	577.4	49.3	11.7	24.9	653.9	28.6	5.0	1,350.7
Cod/hake/haddock	4,378.5	104.7	1,041.5	1.4	6,706.8	–	175.2	12,408.1
Redfish/bass/ conger	1,253.9	564.9	408.3	706.6	1,427.9	661.1	241.6	5,264.3
Jack/mullet/ saury	2,480.6	666.1	619.0	342.6	865.3	765.2	2,227.9	7,966.9
Herring/sardine/ anchovy	2,229.4	2,800.4	942.3	621.5	5,510.8	2,227.3	6,845.4	21,177.0
Tuna/bonito/ billfish	61.2	458.6	84.9	495.3	451.5	1,556.9	45.1	3,153.6
Mackerel/snoek/ cutlass	548.0	254.4	154.5	204.2	1,860.4	577.3	115.4	3,714.1
Shark/ray/chimera	112.7	80.9	48.4	130.3	102.5	97.7	34.5	606.9
Miscellaneous marine fish	150.8	751.1	82.2	1,330.2	4,344.6	1,679.3	106.1	8,444.4

Source: FAO

Note: * not including diadromous fish, crustaceans, or molluscs

"severely depleted", all except the capelin showing a marked drop over the 1965-1983 period. The drop in cod and haddock catches cannot be compensated by increased catches of capelin and mackerel.

Table 3.7   DEPLETION OF SELECTED FISH CATCHES 1965-1983

'000 tonnes

| | N.W. Atlantic | | | |
	A	B	C	D
1965	1,462	249	7	3,735
1970	1,199	48	7	1,471
1975	639	29	367	1,078
1976	530	26	361	855
1977	469	40	229	708
1978	483	61	93	644
1979	574	54	33	633
1980	598	80	27	677
1981	617	83	39	737
1982	704	67	42	803
1983	697	56	42	976

| | S.E. Atlantic | N.E. Pacific | | S.E. Pacific | |
	E	F	G	H	I
1965	985	39	445	62	7,681
1970	607	34	121	36	13,060
1975	665	17	69	44	3,319
1976	640	16	65	48	4,297
1977	326	13	38	45	811
1978	149	113	20	59	1,416
1979	96	13	13	70	1,413
1980	62	13	31	84	823
1981	99	15	29	40	1,550

Continued...

Table 3.7 cont'd

| | S.E. Atlantic | N.E. Pacific | | S.E. Pacific | |
	E	F	G	H	I
1982	89	17	23	17	1,826
1983	100	24	26	12	126

Source: UNEP
Notes: A = cod, B = haddock, C = capelin, D = herring, E = South African
pilchard, F = halibut, G = ocean perch, H = king crab, I = Peruvian
anchovy

The FAO warns that care should be taken when interpreting statistics as data supplied are not always reliable due to the existence of production quotas as a means of managing stocks and a subsequent tendency to under-report catches. In some cases, however, the internationally agreed catch quotas are higher than actual catches. The present global catch of about 80 million tonnes will probably rise to about 100 million tonnes before levelling out. It is clear that with conventional management, the growth era of the industrial fisheries is over, even if full productivity is restored in now-depleted stocks, enabling full quotas to be met.

The predicted 100 million tonnes of fish per year will fall far short of anticipated demand. The world catch has failed to match population growth and indications are that 95% of the world's fish stocks (marine and fresh water) are in the unhealthy position of being either fully or over-exploited. Indeed, current catches are 20-24% below what they could have been without such high levels of over-fishing. This must have a serious impact on human protein sources. Three-quarters of the world's fish catch is used directly for human consumption, the rest processed into fish meal, oil and fertiliser.

The greater part (76.8 million tonnes in 1983) of the world fish supply comes from marine fisheries, with inland waters providing significant amounts, especially in areas far removed from the seas. As Table 3.8 shows, the growth in inland areas is modest but steady: a 45% increase between 1975 and 1985, from 7.0 to 10.1 million tonnes.

Table 3.8   TOTAL FISH CATCHES IN INLAND WATERS 1975-1985

000 tonnes

Year	000 tonnes
1975	6,974.0
1976	6,938.9
1977	7,165.3
1978	7,096.1
1979	7,257.3
1980	7,661.8
1981	8,180.6
1982	8,510.1
1983	9,225.9
1984	9,493.4
1985	10,121.4

Source: FAO

Pollution and Degradation

As with marine fisheries, inland waters are hit by consistent over-fishing, but habitat and water quality degradation are also serious problems. In coastal waters and semi-enclosed areas, pollution and the impact of land development can be severe. An increase in the settlement of coastlines, industrial and recreational exploitation and the increasing incidence of agricultural pollution take their toll. Even the open oceans are beginning to suffer from pollution. Millions of tonnes of pollutants are pumped into the seas each year (Table 3.9 gives some examples), and sediments brought to the oceans by huge rivers such as the Amazon can be traced up to 2,000km out to sea. Heavy metals and other contaminants can reach the open oceans via the atmosphere. As much as 1.5 million tonnes of oil is spilled annually from tankers. No wonder there are increasing fears about the long-term effects of such substantial pollution.

Inland waters are vulnerable to industry, agriculture - especially where intensive farming methods are employed - and habitat degradation. For instance, the building of dams can restrict the free movement of spawning and migrating fish. Even variations in water temperature, as caused by power stations, can seriously damage fish health.

Wetlands draining is a serious threat to some fish stocks. The Wadden Sea, Europe's largest wetland (held as one of the world's most important wetland areas), for instance, supports almost 60% of the North Sea's brown shrimp, more than 50% of its sole, 80% of plaice and almost all herring during some period of the life-cycle. The dockside value of these species was $100 million in 1983 and yet this major resource base is severely threatened from several quarters, including development, pollution and over-exploitation. There are schemes to protect and perhaps preserve the area as a valuable ecosystem.

Waste

Waste is another major cause of the world's much weakened fish resources. Accidental catch continues to be a serious problem in fish harvesting: for every tonne of shrimp landed, at least 3 tonnes of fish are discarded, dead (often because the catching of immatures and, of course, protected species is illegal). With well over 2 million tonnes of shrimp caught annually, over 6 million tonnes of fish are wasted. Countries such as India are probably losing up to 1 million tonnes of fish a year, Thailand 548,000, Mexico and Indonesia both about 360,000: an unnecessary waste of valuable, and not easily replaceable, protein.

Waste can be reduced. Poor recovery of stocks of Pacific halibut, severely depleted during during the 1960s, was partly blamed on high levels of accidental catching of immatures by trawling vessels. Restrictions were imposed on fishing in the Bering Sea and Gulf of Alaska, with positive results. Herring, haddock, whiting and other cod-like fish are still harvested wastefully in the North Sea and North-East Atlantic despite restrictions on net size.

Fishing is Big Business

The world annual export values of the herring and cod families alone exceed $700 million each. Nineteen countries earn more than $100 million annually - Norway, Canada and Denmark each earn more than $600 million annually. Table 3.10 shows the fishing catches of selected OECD countries as a percentage of the world total. Japan is dramatically ahead in marine terms, taking 15%, almost 40% of the OECD's 39.3% share of the world total marine catch. The USA comes next with 6.3% followed by Norway (2.8%), Denmark (2.7%) and Iceland (2.2%). Japan also leads in inland water catch, with 2.03% of the world total. In all, the OECD takes only 6.13% of the world total inland catch.

Table 3.9   POLLUTANTS DUMPED AT SEA BY SELECTED COUNTRIES 1977-1983

000 tonnes	1977	1978	1979	1980	1981	1982	1983
Australia	432*	425*					
Belgium	288	299*	702*	534*	671	588	648
Canada		3.6*	7.2*	8.5	140	na	na
Denmark	6	6	12	9	5	4	1
France	1,978	2,557	3,076	3,257	2,855	2,571	1,596
	811	854	704	751	370	530	727
Ireland	114	124	94	97	132	83	139
Netherlands	1,256*	1,501*	1,671	16	14	11	7
Spain	525*	525	453	304	518	513	549
UK	2,386	2,469	2,886	2,500	2,495	2,249	2,506
	7,791**	8,254**	8,469**	8,907**	8,485**	8,144	7,297
USA	1,844**	2,548**	2,577*	3,154*	2,049**	na	na
	5,134	5,535	5,932	7,546*	6,094	na	na
West Germany	759	728	740	1,676	1,757	1,339	1,265
	272	272	236	217	215	17	5

Source: UNEP
Notes: * Data refer to industrial wastes; for France, UK, USA and West Germany, the second figure refers to sewage sludge
  * Amount licensed for disposal
  ** Data expressed in tons

Table 3.10   FISH CATCHES OF SELECTED OECD COUNTRIES 1985

% of world total

	Marine areas	Inland waters
Japan	15.0	2.03
USA	6.3	0.73
Norway	2.8	0.00
Denmark	2.7	0.24
Iceland	2.2	0.00
Canada	1.8	0.43
Spain	1.8	0.26
UK	1.2	0.13
France	1.1	0.29
Turkey	0.7	0.43
Netherlands	0.7	0.04
Italy	0.6	0.41
TOTAL	39.3	6.13

Source: FAO

Developing countries, on the other hand, take proportionately huge amounts of inland water fish - much traditionally for home use although export earnings are increasing. In the five years from 1975, for instance, Asia averaged 4.25 million tonnes of freshwater fish catch - well over the total catch of almost 3 million tonnes for the rest of the world's inland waters during the same period. The second largest annual freshwater catch, that of Africa, is just under 1.5 million tonnes, as great as Europe and all America combined. Inland fishing is vital for many developing countries. Freshwater species supply 10% or more of per capita protein intake in 16 countries and 20% or more in 13 countries in Asia and Africa.

In the early 1980s both freshwater and marine fishing were beginning to make a serious impact on developing countries' foreign revenue earnings. Table 3.11 shows that during 1974-78 seven countries had annual fishery exports over $100 million. For three of them, Peru, Panama and Senegal, these exports provided over 10% of total export income.

Table 3.11   DEVELOPING COUNTRIES WITH ANNUAL FISHERY
COMMODITY EXPORTS AVERAGING OVER $10 MILLION
1974-1978

	Average annual exports 1974-1978 ($'000)	% of total exports
Korea	443,537	5.5
Peru	231,838	16.4
India	176,811	3.3
Mexico	171,314	4.6
Thailand	150,869	4.9
Indonesia	119,261	1.3
Hong Kong	104,523	1.2
Chile	98,280	4.5
Malaysia	85,270	1.6
Morocco	76,773	5.2
Argentina	64,137	1.4
Brazil	60,097	0.6
Ecuador	56,840	4.7
Senegal	55,446	10.7
Panama	34,543	14.3
Philippines	33,992	1.2
Pakistan	33,921	3.0
Nicaragua	22,849	4.4
Papua New Guinea	20,518	3.3
Ivory Coast	17,488	1.0
Venezuela	17,430	0.2
Colombia	17,353	0.9
Turkey	15,614	0.9
Madagascar	15,074	4.9
Tunisia	12,875	1.4

Source FAO

Despite this relative importance, developing countries have also suffered severe stock depletion. Stocks have been maintained in areas where harvesting is carried out by traditional methods, but it is different where modern fishing vessels and fish location technology are used. It seems that, rather than exploiting new offshore areas, motorised fishing vessels with modern

69

equipment have tended to fish the inshore areas to which traditional fishermen are confined.

Aquaculture

Developing countries have shown more interest in aquaculture (here considered to be the cultivation of aquatic organisms through their entire life-cycle, rather than giving stocks assistance at certain stages). China alone accounts for more than 1 million tonnes of Asian inland catch, much of which comes from aquaculture.

Yields from aquaculture have doubled during the past decade and now represent about 10% of world production in fishery products. A five- to ten-fold increase is projected by the year 2000. Aquaculture has the advantage that it can be undertaken in waste or otherwise under-utilised areas such as paddyfields, abandoned mining excavations and small ponds. Carp, crayfish, shrimp and oysters are particularly suited to being farmed. Table 3.12 shows the aquaculture activities of selected OECD countries. Japan again leads in production terms, but the significant proportion of aquaculture in Italy (19.9%), France (16.5%) and Greece (13.5%) is worth noting.

Table 3.12   AQUACULTURE PRODUCTION IN SELECTED OECD COUNTRIES 1983-1984

'000 tonnes

	Aquaculture production		1983 as % of total marine catch	Main species
	1983	1984		
Japan	1,154.0	1,206.0	9.7	Seaweed; oysters; yellowtail
USA	308.0	na	7.4	Crayfish
France	129.0	110.0	16.5	Oysters; mussels
Italy	95.0	95.0	19.9	Molluscs; trout
Denmark	23.0	26.0	1.2	Trout
Norway	22.7	25.9	0.8	Salmon
West Germany	na	24.0		Trout; carp
UK	14.0	16.3	1.7	Trout; salmon
Greece	13.5	14.0	13.5	Trout

Continued...

Table 3.12 cont'd

	Aquaculture production		1983 as % of total marine catch	Main species
	1983	1984		
Ireland	8.5	na	4.2	Mussels; oysters
Finland	7.5	9.3	4.8	Trout
Canada	5.0	na	0.4	Oysters; catfish
Sweden	1.8	na	0.7	Trout
Iceland	0.1 [1]	0.1	–	Trout

Source: UNEP
Note: [1] *Iceland's 1983 production actually 50,000 tonnes*

The luxury crayfish is the speciality of American aquaculture and a system of multiple cropping has been tried with successful yields reported. In artificial ponds in Louisiana, yields can exceed 1.8 tonnes/hectare and have been combined with cypress plantations for extra efficiency. Another good combination crop is rice, the flooding and draining of paddyfields presenting suitable breeding and feeding grounds for the crayfish. In other areas fowl and fish are reared in close proximity, the droppings of the one providing good nutrient for the other.

Developing nations are increasingly interested in developing aquaculture in a substantial way, not just to meet local protein demand but to earn valuable foreign currency. Indonesia exported 26,000 tonnes of shrimp in 1983 to earn $190 million. The country predicts a rapid growth to 44,700 tonnes annually, worth $530 million. In the early 1980s Thailand was producing 24, 90 and 180 tonnes a year of cockles, oysters and mussels respectively. Increased conversion of wetlands and water bodies continues to increase production.

Malaysia suggests that fish farming will not only become a major revenue earner in the next decade, but will also bring back some "wasted" land into useful production. Projects proposed include 2,000 acres of coastal mudflats for the expansion of cockle culture - adding up to 84,000 tonnes annually to production; brackish pond development in mangrove forests along the coast, bringing some 570,000 hectares into production and yielding some 220,000 tonnes of shrimp. Surveys have also identified about 6,000 hectares of abandoned mining pools for the culture of freshwater fish and prawns, for production of up to 28,000 tonnes.

A note of caution must, however, be sounded over the wholesale conversion of natural mangrove lands into fish farms. Not only are rich ecosystems being threatened, but the eventual "farmed" product is not always as valuable a commodity as the natural product.

In developed countries, farming "luxury" fish and crustacean products is economically viable only when favourable price conditions prevail. However, as a means of producing fish protein, aquaculture can move some way towards filling the shortfall left by the world's man-emptied oceans.

Table 3.13 shows the steadily increasing catch from inland fisheries.

Table 3.13   WORLD FISHING CATCH FROM INLAND FISHERIES
             1979-1984

'000 tonnes

1979	1980	1981	1982	1983	1984
7,240	7,603	8,138	8,455	9,131	9,716

Source: FAO

The 1987 NAFO Review

The Northwest Atlantic Fisheries Organisation (NAFO) was founded in 1979 as a successor to the International Commission for the Northwest Atlantic Fisheries (ICNAF). NAFO aims to "investigate, protect and conserve fishery resources in order to provide the optimum utilisation and rational management of these resources". Its 1987 review reported on a number of species, and the principal details are given below.

Capelin

Opening of offshore fishery in 1972 led to a rapid increase of catch to more than 360,000 tonnes in 1975 and 1976. The decline to 30,000 tonnes in 1980 was due mainly to quota restrictions and low stock size. Yield increased to 50-60,000 tonnes in 1984-85.

Cod

Fishery peaked at 1.9 million tonnes in 1968 due to increases at Greenland, Labrador and East Newfoundland, then suffered a steady decline to a low of 468,000 tonnes in 1977. It ultimately stabilised, under management regulations, at about 600,000 tonnes in mid-1980s. West Greenland and Flemish Cap stocks remain quite low.

Flounders

Combined catch of species (mainly American plaice, witch flounder, yellowtail flounder and greenland halibut) peaked in 1969 at 315,000 tonnes. About 200,000 tonnes annually was fished during the 1970s, declining to an average 150,000 tonnes in the mid-1980s.

Haddock

Fishery peaked in 1965 at 250,000 tonnes due to heavy exploitation of incoming year-classes in the southern part of the Conservation Area, then declined to about 25,000 tonnes in the early 1970s due to poor recruitment. For several years from 1974 there were zero catch quotas. Catches increased to about 80,000 tonnes in 1980/81, then stabilised at 50,000 tonnes in the mid-1980s.

Herrings

Fisheries increased rapidly to more than 950,000 tonnes in 1968 and 1969 but dropped back to less than 200,000 tonnes in 1982-85. Much of the decline was due to the collapse of the Georges Bank stock in the mid-1970s - no sign of significant recovery to date.

Mackerel

Catch peaked in 1973 at 420,000 tonnes after opening of inshore fishery in 1965. Despite quota restrictions the catch declined rapidly to about 30,000 tonnes in 1978, stabilising until 1983. It then increased to about 60,000 tonnes.

Redfish

Intense fishing by USSR in the late 1950s resulted in a peak catch of 390,000 tonnes in 1958. It was then stable at 230,000 tonnes annually until 1975, then declined to about 130,000 tonnes in the mid-1980s.

Silver Hake

Mainly fished by USSR, it peaked at 394,000 tonnes in 1965, declined to 100,000 tonnes in 1968 and peaked again to 435,000 tonnes in 1973. A decline to 60,000 tonnes in the early 1980s (partly due to quota restrictions) was followed by an increase to about 100,000 tonnes in the mid-1980s.

Overall

Total catch of all fish and invertebrates exceeded 4 million tonnes annually 1966-74 (peak at 4.6 million tonnes 1968), declined rapidly to about 3 million tonnes in 1977 and remained slightly below that level 1980-85.

3.4 TROPICAL FORESTS

Introduction

It is possible to claim tropical forests are *not* a renewable resource in the strict sense of the definition. Scientists state that it is not possible to exploit primary forest for its many goods and services and still end up with the same product. Virtually any cropping ultimately alters the size, type and mix of species in these delicate ecosystems. However, it is also true that with good silvicultural and other management practices it should be possible to give the resource a sustainable role, providing goods and services while maintaining vital genetic diversity. Appropriate management is, however, practised only sparingly throughout the world's tropical forests.

To businesses in the developed world, tropical rain forests (mainly closed-formation broadleaved types) mean timber first and foremost. Less generally recognised is the contribution to medicine, the food industry and other raw materials such as petrol alternatives. In addition they affect climate and protect genetic diversity.

Deforestation and Degradation

Every year 20 million hectares (an area about the size of England, Scotland and Wales) of primary tropical forest is destroyed or seriously degraded, at least a quarter of this by commercial logging.

Table 3.14 gives the FAO/UNEP 1985 forestry survey estimates of the areas of closed broadleaved tropical forests, together with the average annual deforestation rates in 1981-1985, based on its test area of 76 countries, representing 97% of the regions popularly called "the tropics". It should be noted that deforestation figures in the FAO/UNEP survey almost always appear substantially lower than other reports. This is due to its strict definition of "deforestation" as "the complete clearing of a forest and its replacement by another form of land use (usually agricultural and grazing)". Thus Table 3.14 shows just over 11.3 million hectares of tropical forest *completely* deforested annually. Another major survey - Norman Myers for the US Academy of Science 1980 - shows an annual deforestation rate of 18-20 million hectares a year and refers to the destruction of *pure* tropical forest, as being modified from the original state. Unlike FAO/UNEP, this measurement reflects biological value.

Forest clearance in Brazil to create grazing land for beef production for exports has been increasing in the last few years (although even up to 1980 72% of rain forests clearance in Brazil was for cattle ranching).

While it is quite clear that commercial logging is not a leading cause of world deforestation - shifting agriculture and fuel wood harvesting are far more significant - the international timber business does cause substantial degradation of the resource. The consequences of this example of poor husbanding are already being felt in Western world markets. Once-common species such as the true mahoganies from Cuba and Africa have become commercially extinct and others, such as ramin and keruing, are increasingly scarce in the wild.

Industrial Logging and its Effects

The other major threat to Western tropical timber importers is the exporters' twofold change of attitude. There is a growing concern for a specific trade deficit which, in 1985, saw developing countries *importing* $8,964 million of wood products while exporting only $6,052 million (Table 3.15). Already there is a growing move towards greater self-sufficiency in wood, which must, inevitably, lead to a contraction of exports. Coupled with this is the

Table 3.14   CLOSED BROADLEAVED FORESTS: TOTAL AREAS 1985 AND ANNUAL DEFORESTATION/ PLANTATION RATES 1981–1985

'000 hectares

	Productive forest			Total	Unpro-ductive	Annual deforestation			Annual plantation	Plantation deforest-ation ratio
	Unmanaged		Managed			Closed	Open	All		
	Undisturbed	Logged								
Tropical America	437,196	54,650	14	491,860	142,033	4,339	1,272	5,611	535	1:10.5
Tropical Africa	113,889	39,914	1,672	155,475	52,330	1,331	2,345	3,676	126	1:29.2
Tropical Asia	85,139	59,017	36,450	180,606	102,342	1,826	190	2,016	438	1:4.6
TOTAL	636,224	153,581	38,136	827,941	296,705	7,496	3,807	11,303	1,099	1:10.3

Source: FAO/UNEP

Note: the 76 countries comprising the FAO/UNEP test area, from which these data are drawn, are:

Continued...

Table 3.14 cont'd

Tropical America (23 countries)
Central America and Mexico: Costa Rica, El Salvador, Guatemala, Honduras, Mexico, Nicaragua, Panama.
CARICON: Belize, Guyana, Jamaica, Trinidad and Tobago.
Other Caribbean: Cuba, Dominican Republic, French Guiana, Haiti, Surinam.
Tropical South Latin America: Bolivia, Brazil, Colombia, Ecuador, Paraguay, Peru, Venezuela.

Tropical Africa (37 countries)
Northern Savanna Regions: Burkima Faso, Chad, The Gambia, Mali, Niger, Senegal.
West Africa: Benin, Ghana, Guinea, Guinea–Bissau, Ivory Coast, Liberia, Nigeria, Sierre Leone, Togo.
Central Africa: Angola, Cameroon, Central African Republic, Congo, Equatorial Guinea, Gabon, Zaire.
East Africa and Madagascar: Burundi, Ethiopia, Kenya, Madagascar, Malawi, Mozambique, Rwanda, Somalia, Sudan, Tanzania, Uganda, Zambia, Zimbabwe.
Tropical South Africa: Botswana, Namibia.

Tropical Asia (16 countries)
South Asia: Bangladesh, Bhutan, India, Nepal, Pakistan, Sri Lanka.
Continental South East Asia: Burma, Thailand.
Insular South East Asia: Brunei, Indonesia, Malaysia, the Philippines.
Centrally Planted Tropical Asia: Kampuchea, Laos, Vietnam.
Oceania: Papua New Guinea.

acknowledgement of the economic and ecological flaws in wood resource depletion with the result that some countries - such as the Philippines and Indonesia - have banned exports of some tropical logs. Other restrictions will follow.

Table 3.15   WORLD TRADE IN MAIN FORESTRY PRODUCTS 1985

$ million

	Developed countries		Developing countries	
	Imports	Exports	Imports	Exports
Wood-based panels	3,587.3	2,653.8	1,063.2	1,832.1
Industrial roundwood	5,595.9	3,583.2	1,885.0	1,856.2
Sawnwood and sleepers	9,319.8	8,504.2	1,898.9	1,572.5
Paper and board	18,970.5	20,739.9	4,116.5	790.9
TOTAL	37,473.5	35,481.1	8,963.6	6,051.7

Source: FAO/UNEP

Such has been the intensification of industrial logging that there are serious fears for even short-term substainability if management and replanting are not substantially increased. As Table 3.16 shows, timber production has been rising (except for softwoods from natural forests) steadily over the past decade (from 126.1 million cubic metres of hardwood taken from natural forests annually to an estimated 146.3 million cubic metres). It is doubtful that this trend will continue and of the 33 developing countries which are net exporters of tropical timber today, only ten are expected to be in business by the end of the century.

Table 3.16   AVERAGE ANNUAL PRODUCTION OF WOOD FOR
              INDUSTRY 1978-1987

Unit: millions cubic metres

1978-82

	Hardwood			Softwoods		
	Natural forest	Planted	Total	Natural forest	Planted	Total
Tropical America	22.0	12.9	34.9	15.5	10.7	26.2
Tropical Africa	15.8	1.6	17.4	0.2	2.8	3.0
Tropical Asia	88.3	3.4	91.7	3.2	-	3.2
TOTAL	126.1	17.9	144.0	18.9	13.5	32.4

1983-87

	Hardwood			Softwoods		
	Natural forest	Planted	Total	Natural forest	Planted	Total
Tropical America	27.6	18.8	46.4	12.1	22.2	34.3
Tropical Africa	16.7	2.6	19.3	0.2	4.6	4.8
Tropical Asia	102.0	4.6	106.6	3.4	0.1	3.5
TOTAL	146.3	26.0	172.3	15.7	26.9	42.6

Source: FAO/UNEP
Note: 1983-87 figures are approximate

The World Bank has identified ten African, nine Asian and 11 Latin
American timber-exporting countries whose forest estates have reached critical
condition as a result of destructive logging policies: "rough estimates show that
economic costs of unsustainable forest depletion in major tropical hardwood
exporting countries range from 4-6% of GNP, offsetting any economic growth
which might otherwise have been achieved".

Some of the famous forest estates of the past - much used by British
importers - are seriously threatened. Malaysia, the Ivory Coast and the
Philippines are expected to run out of export timber within the next decade

(if logging practices and planting are not improved). Other major forest resources are likewise vunerable (Table 3.17).

Table 3.17   TROPICAL FOREST STATUS REPORT 1987

Going

Brazil	May lose 8% of remaining forest by 2000 - an area of 63 million hectares, ie two and a half times bigger than Portugal.
Colombia	May lose at least 30% by 2000.
Congo	68% of rain forest scheduled for logging.
Ecuador	May lose over 50% of remaining forest by 2000.
Ghana	May lose 26% of remaining forest by 2000.
Guatemala	May lose at least 30% of forest by 2000.
Guinea & Madagascar	May lose at least 30% of forest by 2000.
Honduras & Nicaragua	May lose over 50% of remaining forest by 2000.
Indonesia	200,000 hectares logged per year. 10% of forest existing in 1981 will be destroyed by year 2000.
Ivory Coast	Forest almost entirely logged out.
Malaysia	Peninsular Malaysian Forests resources due to be exhausted by 1990.
Nigeria	Complete deforestation feared by 2000.
Thailand	Will lose 60% of forest existing in 1981 by 2000.

Gone

Bangladesh	All primary rain forest destroyed.
China	50% loss of forest in Southern Province Xishuangbana.
Haiti	All primary rain forest destroyed.
India	All primary rain forest destroyed.
Philippines	55% forest loss 1960-85.

Continued...

Table 3.17 cont'd

Gone

Sri Lanka	All primary rain forest destroyed.
Thailand	45% forest loss 1961–85.
World	Over 40% of all primary tropical rain forest destroyed.

Source: WWF

Britain is one of the largest consumers of tropical hardwoods in the developed world: in value terms it is the largest importer in Europe; in volume terms it matches Italy and France. Britain is also the second largest importer of plywood in the world (after Japan), with 40% of supplies coming from the tropics. Some 95% of such imported wood from the tropics is estimated to come from badly managed and unsustainable sources. Thus Britain's role as an influential trade customer is being exploited by the conservation groups campaigning to "save the rain forests". The Friends of the Earth Tropical Hardwood Campaign in Britain intensified with the publication of its *Good Wood Guide* in March 1988. This lists endangered tropical wood species and alternatives and seeks to enlist both public and trade support for conservation methods (see Section 4.2). Table 3.18 provides a list of threatened tropical timbers currently in use.

Table 3.18   THREATENED TROPICAL TIMBERS IN WIDESPREAD USE 1987

Area of Origin	*Timber*
West Africa	Gaboon, okoume (*Aucoumea klainiana*)
West and East Africa	Iroko (*Chlorophora excelsa*)
West and Central Africa	Sapele (*Entandrophragma cylindricum*)
West, Central and S.W. Africa	Utile (*Entandrophragma utile*), Gedu nohor, African mahogany (*Entandrophragma angolense*)
West, Central, S.W. and East Africa	African mahogany (various *Khaya* and *Entandrophragma* species)

Continued...

Table 3.18 cont'd

Area of Origin	*Timber*
Central and South America	Brazilian and Central American mahogany *(Swietenia macrophylla)*
Florida, Jamaica, Cuba Bahamas	Spanish, Cubann, Jamaican and Central American mahogany *(Swietenia mahogani)*
Malaysia, Indonesia	Ramin *(Gonystylus bancanus)*, kapur *(Dryobanalops aromatica)*, jelutong *(Dyera costulata)*, merbau *(Intsia palembanica, I.bijuga)*
Malaysia	Kempas *(Koompassia malaccensis)*, meranti (various *Shorea* species including *S. curtisii, S. platyclados*), keruing, gurjun (various *Dipterocarpus* species including *D.cornutus. D. costulatus)*
Tropical Africa, India, Sri Lanka	Ebony *(Diospyros spp.)*
Brazil	Rosewood, Jacaranda *(Dalbergia spp.)*
Ivory Coast, Ghana, Gabon, Zaire	Afrormosia *(Pericopsis elata)*
Asia, Africa	Padauk *(Pterocarpus spp.)*

Source: FOE

Replanting

Harvesting timber is replanted on an extremely small scale, as Table 3.14 showed. Thus, to satisfy the demand for tropical hardwood, the logging industry continues to exploit virgin rain forest. Table 3.19 gives a breakdown of the comparative planting rates for hardwood and softwood. Fast growing hardwood is more popular than softwood with slow growing varieties attracting little commercial attention. Table 3.20 shows the slight increase in the establishment of *new* tropical forest plantations over 1981-85 compared with 1976-80, again with the emphasis on the fast-growing hardwood varieties.

Table 3.19   AREAS OF TREE PLANTATION 1980

000 hectares	Hardwood	
	Non-fast growing	Fast growing
Tropical America	548	2,451
Tropical Africa	588	645
Tropical Asia	1,976	2,303
TOTAL	3,112	5,399
	Softwood	All
Tropical America	1,621	4,620
Tropical Africa	547	1,780
Tropical Asia	832	5,111
TOTAL	3,000	11,511

Source: FAO/UNEP

Table 3.20   NEW TROPICAL FOREST PLANTATIONS 1976-1985

million hectares	Africa		Latin America		Asia	
	1976-80	1981-85	1976-80	1981-85	1976-80	1981-85
Slow-growing hardwood	0.17	0.23	0.29	0.25	0.63	0.45
Fast-growing hardwood	0.15	0.25	1.07	1.56	0.96	1.18
Softwood	0.15	0.14	0.69	0.86	0.51	0.56
TOTAL	0.47	0.62	2.05	2.67	2.10	2.19

Source: FAO/UNEP

Waste

Tropical loggers rarely replant. Neither are logging operations usually carried out with either care or conservation in mind. However, it is recognised that with careful logging, forests can regenerate sufficiently to be re-harvested.

Progress brings with it the means to destruction. Today's loggers have access to machinery which can reduce giant trees to shavings in a matter of moments. Huge caterpillar tractors with cable-winches and saws make light work of slicing through even the largest trees. Tree-pullers, tree-stingers and tree-rammers pull down or force up trees. With such machinery, a hectare of tropical forest (with its estimated 900 tonnes of living plants) can be cleared in two hours.

Felling a big tree nearly always causes damage to those around it. At a logging site in East Kalimantan, even selective cutting of 20 trees per hectare leads to damage to 41% of the remaining trees. Indiscriminate logging can cause lasting, sometimes irreversible damage to particular stands, of trees including absence of regeneration, soil erosion and landslides, with devastating effects on both the logging industry and the survival of forests as a whole.

The waste figures speak for themselves: for every cubic metre of wood extracted from the forests of South-East Asia, one cubic metre is left behind and a further quarter is lost in processing. Thus 100 million cubic metres are wasted in this region alone every year.

Other Rain Forest Resources

Timber is not the only product under threat as the forest resource dwindles. Tropical forests can fairly be described as a dispensary for the raw materials for modern medicines: antibiotics, heart drugs, hormones, tranquillisers, ulcer treatments and anti-coagulants to name just a few. Pharmaceuticals is an industry valued at not less than $18 billion annually.

About 70% of the 3,000 plants the US National Cancer Institute identifies as having anti-cancer properties are estimated to come from the tropical forests. For instance, the alkaloid yielded by the Rosy Periwinkle has a proven success record of improving the survival rates of children suffering from leukaemia. Other recognised tropical forest "treatments" aid hypertension, anxiety and schizophrenia. Reserpine can be commercially prepared from natural sources (the snakeroot plant from India's tropical forests) at a cost of under $1 a gram. When synthesised it costs 25% more. Native peoples have wide knowledge of the curative powers of local plants - which is often totally lost once they are displaced by the clearing of forest areas.

Other forest raw materials include fruits, game meat, fibres, resins, gums, dyes, waxes and oils - all substances used in Western industrial and manufacturing processes. In 1984 total forest product including wood contributed about $270 billion to the world economy. The trade in rattan alone is worth $1.2 billion.

Unique to tropical forests is diversity of species. A typical 4 - square-mile patch of closed broadleaved rain forest contains over 3,000 assorted species (see Part Two, *Issue: Tropical rain forest*). Of the estimated 4.5 million species of plant and animal in the world, only 500,000 have been described by the science of man, and many fewer screened for their usefulness. Yet campaigners justifiably state that over 50 different wild species a day become extinct as a result of tropical forest degradation and destruction.

The scientists' fears are not simply emotional - but loss of genetic diversity can have a serious impact on disease, pest and the inbreeding weaknesses of animals and plants.

Forestry Management

For many, the question of forest management is fundamental. It is one aspect of the major aid and development programme, Tropical Forestry Action Plan (TFAP) formulated by the FAO in 1985.

At present only 4.4% of the 76 tropical countries surveyed carry out intensive management practices in their productive broadleaved forests: 78% of these are in India, and only eight other countries (one in Tropical America, four in tropical Africa and three in Tropical Asia) have their closed broadleaved forests under intensive management on a scale other than experimental. Any long-term attempt to retain tropical forests as a sustainable yield resource must include effective intensive management involving strict and controlled logging and harvesting of other products. Table 3.21 gives estimated TFAP costs for 1987-91. That is not to say the answer necessarily lies in total protection. A forest without an industry is essentially of no financial value to its country. A sustainable industry, on the other hand, provides incentives to protect and enhance.

Table 3.21   ESTIMATED TFAP COSTS 1987-1991

$ million

Activity	Region			
	Africa	Asia	Latin America	5 year total
Land use on upland watersheds	139	682	95	916
Forest management for industrial use	167	565	584	1,316
Fuel, wood and agroforestry	439	747	390	1,576
Conservation of forest ecosystems	105	148	195	448
Strengthening of institutions	188	557	319	1,064
TOTAL	1,038	2,699	1,583	5,320

Source: FAO

The Facts About Tropical Rain Forests

The WWF has provided the following summary of information about the forests.

Extent: 2,000 million hectares. 1,200 million hectares seasonal or all-year rain forests (moist) and 800 million hectares drier, open woodland.

Loss: About 11-15 million hectares per year (larger than Austria, ie about 20 football pitches a minute). Six million hectares rain forest, remainder drier types.

Trend: All rain forest outside protected areas expected to be damaged within 30 years with no undamaged tropical forest of any type within 80 years.

Biodiversity: Tropical forests contain over half the world's species in just 7% of its land area, ie 155,000 of the *known* 255,000 plants; 80% of insects and

90% of primates. One hectare had 41,000 tree canopy insects including 12,000 beetles. Five to 20 times richer in trees than temperate forests.

Utility species: Half the world's main crops originated in tropical forests; 25% of US drug prescriptions owed active ingredients to plants, yet *under 1%* of species have yet been investigated. 1,400 forest plants may have anti-cancer potential; ten effective existing treatments may be lost due to destruction. Philippine forest people use 1,600 species for medicine/food.

Climate: Forests have unknown regulatory function. For example, 90% of Amazonian rainfall is recycled.

Soil: Erosion known to follow destruction. Panama Canal silting up.

Logging: Up to 50,000 square km closed tropical forest logged annually. Timber trade important for at least 15 exporters and worth over $8 billion annually worldwide. Over-exploitation quoted as one reason why 23 exporters are now importers of wood (cost $50 million). Estimated that developing countries' wood exports will decline to under $2 billion by end of century. Loggers extract only 4-10% of trees but leave over one-third land surface bare, compacted by heavy machinery. This is followed up by inefficient land-use and almost non-existent management (outside India only about 2% of closed forests are managed for sustained yield).

Planting: Only one hectare of plantation created for every ten hectares of forest lost to logging each year.

Export restriction: Teak log export is a capital offence in Thailand; log-export bans in force in Philippines, Malaysia (16 species) and Indonesia. Obeche export banned in Nigeria.

Importers: Principal by volume are Europe and Japan, by value Japan, the USA and the EC.

3.5 THE ATMOSPHERE

Introduction

The atmosphere, one of man's most essential renewable resources, continues to come under attack. While the harmful effects of pollutants have in some cases been recognised and at least partly acted upon (smokeless fuels, industrial "scrubbers"), there nevertheless remains a worldwide increase in atmospheric pollution.

The main causes of this deterioration are carbon dioxide, nitrous oxide, methane, chlorofluorocarbons and ozone. But of particular concern at present is the long-term effect of some of these pollutants on world climate: a condition variously known as "climatic change", "global warming" or "greenhouse effect".

Global Warming

Just as general atmospheric pollution affects industry by lowering efficiency and increasing costs, so global warming could have a serious impact on business methods and costs, even in the short term.

World scientists, meeting in Villach, Austria in 1985 to discuss global warming, concluded that climatic change must be considered a "plausible and serious probability", and that:

> Many important economic and social decisions are being made today on . . . major water resource management activities such as irrigation and hydropower; drought relief; agricultural land use; structural designs and coastal engineering projects; and energy planning - all based on the assumption that past climatic data, without modification, are a reliable guide to the future. This is no longer a good assumption.

Thus, industry calculations of trends, markets and viability may prove devastatingly inaccurate if fears of climatic change are founded.

Greenhouse gases are transparent to incoming solar radiation, which heats the earth, but their relative opacity to the longer wavelengths of radiation reflected from the earth means the heat is effectively trapped and builds up. If present trends continue, the combined concentration of CO_2 and other greenhouse gases in the atmosphere could lead to a rise in global mean temperatures.

Carbon Dioxide Levels

A doubling of CO^2 levels, predicted by the year 2030, could produce a rise in average surface temperatures of between 1.5 and 4.5°C. Warming would be more pronounced at the poles. A major fear is that this warming would lead to a sea-level rise of 25-140 cm. Coastal cities would be flooded and the agricultural and industrial activities of many countries would thus be devasted. A change in climate would also seriously affect food chains, ecosystems and many of the other fundamentals of life.

Increased CO_2 levels are directly related to the emissions from fossil-fuel burning, including gas flaring, natural gas, liquid and solid fuels, and to the manufacture of cement. A secondary, also significant, cause is deforestation. Table 3.22 shows the latitudinal distribution of CO_2 and illustrates that 95% arises in the Northern Hemisphere. The pre-industrial concentration of CO_2 was about 280 parts per million parts of air by volume. This concentration reached 340 in 1980 and is expected to double to 560 by the 2030s.

Table 3.22   LATITUDINAL DISTRIBUTION OF CO_2 EMISSIONS FROM FOSSIL FUELS 1980

000 tonnes carbon

Latitude band (degrees)	Northern Hemisphere Emissions	%	Southern Hemisphere Emissions	%
0-5	25,744	0.5	11,544	0.2
5-10	36,094	0.7	24,190	0.5
10-15	45,891	0.9	11,365	0.2
15-20	76,712	1.6	12,387	0.3
20-25	140,728	2.9	39,291	0.8
25-30	316,692	6.5	52,387	1.1
30-35	578,493	11.9	60,469	1.2
35-40	726,033	14.9	20,463	0.4
40-45	846,680	17.4	4,434	0.1
45-50	634,248	13.0	742	*
50-55	854,434	17.6	336	*
55-60	294,268	6.1	0	0
60-65	39,539	0.8	0	0
65-70	9,141	0.2	0	0
70-75	601	*	0	0
75-80	17	*	0	0
80-85	0	0	0	0
TOTAL	4,625,326	95.1	237,608	4.9

Source: UNEP
*Note: * less than 0.05%*
      totals may not add due to rounding.

Other Pollutants

Other atmospheric pollutants receiving particular attention, especially in the urban areas of both the industrialised and, increasingly, the developing world, are sulphur oxides (SOx), nitrogen oxides (NOx), carbon monoxide (CO), hydrocarbons (HC) and particulate matter. Table 3.23 breaks down emissions of the so-called "traditional" air pollutants, identifying those OECD countries emitting over 750,000 tonnes of any one pollutant. It should be noted that SOx and NOx contribute to acid rain, one of the most serious "transboundary" pollutants. Taking Britain as an example, in 1987 New Scientist identified the sources of sulphur dioxide pollution: coal-fired power stations 60.2%; other industries 17.7%; other consumers 13.3%; and domestic 8.8%. The largest single source of man-made SO_2 in the world is the copper and nickel smelting complex at Sudbury, Ontario, which annually produces 632,000 tonnes of SO_2.

Table 3.23   EMISSIONS OF TRADITIONAL AIR POLLUTANTS BY SELECTED COUNTRIES 1980

000 tonnes

	SOx	Particulates	NOx	CO	HC
Australia[1]	1,479	271	915	3,704	423
Austria	354	50 [2]	211	1,126 [2]	251
Belgium	856	267	317	839	–
Canada	4,650	1,907	1,942	9,928	2,100
France	3,558	252 [3]	2,567	5,200 [1]	2,185
Italy	3,800	196 [1]	1,550	4,036 [1]	496 [1]
Japan[4]	1,259	133 [5]	1,339	–	–
Netherlands	445	150	500	1,368	452 [6]
Spain	3,622 [7]	1,521 [7]	778	3,780	739
Sweden	483	170 [8]	328	1,250	410 [6]
Turkey	714	138	380	3,707	201
UK	4,670	442	1,932	5,127	1,954 [6]
USA	23,200	8,400	20,300	76,000	22,800
West Germany	3,200	730	3,090	8,960	1,860
Yugoslavia	815	–	–	–	–

Continued...

Table 3.23 cont'd

	SOx	Particulates	NOx	CO	HC
OECD TOTAL[9]	55,000	16,000	37,000	140,000	38,000
WORLD TOTAL	110,000	59,000	69,000	193,000	57,000

Source: OECD
Notes: [1] *1978 estimates, excluding industrial processes,* [2] *Excluding industrial processes and miscellaneous,* [3] *Excluding industrial processes,* [4] *Fiscal year 1 April - 31 March,* [5] *Stationary sources only,* [6] *Total hydrocarbons,* [7] *1979,* [8] *1978,* [9] *Estimates*

SO_2 emissions in Europe probably doubled between 1950-73, peaked 1975-78 and since then have declined in some countries and remained stable in others. In the Eastern USA emission rose from about 12 million tonnes in 1950 to about 24 million in 1965, stabilising at that level. China has estimated annual SO_2 emissions of 12-15 million tonnes and is the third largest source after the USA and the USSR.

Power stations burning fossil fuels are also major sources of NOx, but road traffic makes a substantial contribution to pollution. In Europe 30-50% of NOx emissions come from motor vehicles, compared to 30-40% from coal-burning power plants. In the USA 44% is from vehicle sources and in Canada 61%. In developing countries vehicles are usually the main SOx source.

In some countries NOx emission levels have stabilised over the past ten years although West Germany's, for example, have risen sharply. In 1980 it was estimated that 9.2 million tonnes of NOx were emitted annually in Europe, which could rise to over 11 million tonnes by the year 2000 (although this increase could be slower if reduction methods were employed). In 1980 North America produced 20 million tonnes.

The Damage and Control Costs of Air Pollution

All industries (plus the domestic fuel user) will doubtless have to pay for cleaning up the air. But some economists argue that in the long term this will be less costly than paying for pollution damage, including degraded human health, corrosion of buildings, severely damaged plant and animal life and jeopardy to political harmony between countries. The OECD has made the following estimates of costs:

1. In the Eastern USA halving the remaining SO_2 emissions from existing sources will cost $5 billion a year, increasing present electricity rates by 2-3%.

2. With NOx reduction, the additional costs could be as high as $6 billion a year.

3. Materials damage by corrosion alone cost $7 billion annually in the 17 states in the Eastern USA.

4. The annual costs of securing a 55-65% reduction in the remaining sulphur emissions in EC countries between 1980 and 2000 range from US$4.6 billion to US$6.7 billion (at 1982 US$).

5. Controls on stationary boilers, to reduce nitrogen levels 10% annually by the year 2000, range from $100,000 to $400,000 (1982 levels). These figures translate into a one-time increase of about 6% in the price of electrical power to the consumer.

6. Damage costs due to material and fish losses alone are placed at $3 billion a year, and damage to crops, forests and health will exceed $10 billion a year.

7. In 1983 the Commission of the European Community calculated that costs of emission reductions at power stations would amount to less than 10% of production costs. The annual costs of damage from acid pollution are at least comparable, if not higher.

8. The annual costs to the EC of acid deposition damage are about $50-65 billion.

Effective anti-pollution controls before, during and after combustion processes are already available; with the exception of CO_2, all pollutants produced by fossil fuels can be removed. But the debate about cost is confusing, with different bodies quoting substantially different figures and using them in arguments against emission control procedures. Observers suggest government estimates can be liable to "exaggeration". US electrical industries estimate a 30% reduction in SO_2 from 24 generating stations would consume 23-58% of total cash flow, double capital costs, treble operating costs and raise electricity costs by 5.7% over a decade.

In 1983 the British Central Electricity Generating Board (CEGB) claimed that it would face a bill of £4 billion and annual costs of £700 million if SO_2 emissions were to be reduced threefold. It also warned of a rise in electricity prices of anything from 4-10%.

These figures contrast dramatically with OECD findings in 1982, showing that average control costs should work out at about 4% of total plant capital costs, and operating costs should rise by about 2%. Improving technology could further reduce costs.

These arguments are set against statistics which show enormous and continuing costs attributed to atmospheric pollution. Examples of *annual* costs include:

(a) $500 million worth of lost crops throughout Europe;
(b) $300 million dieback of forest in Germany
(c) an atmospheric pollution-linked medical bill in USA of $2 billion;
(d) damage to buildings in the Netherlands costing $10-15 million;
(e) a corrosion bill in Europe alone of up to $6.5 billion.

This could mean that the atmospheric pollution from sulphur compounds alone is costing each person in affected countries $2-10 per year in terms of corrosion. These costs do not count the emotional and social costs of ill-health and the destruction of irreplaceable monuments.

Transboundary Pollution and International Action

One of the most important developments in the history of atmospheric pollution was the acknowledgement that pollutants recognised no boundaries. In efforts to "clean up" cities, chimneys were built higher and higher, effectively distributing poisons over a wider area.

Twenty years ago atmospheric pollution seemed only a national problem. The first public international discussion at the Helsinki Conference resulted in a convention signed by 30 countries and the European Community. In 1983 the so-called 30% Club nations agreed to reduce SO_2 emissions by 1993 by 30% on 1980 levels. There was also an agreement to reduce NOx emissions. By April 1985 there were 22 members, with notable exception of the USA and the UK which both refused to be drawn into specific reductions. Britain claimed it had already reduced its SO_2 emissions by 25% since 1980; the USA delegation said its emissions were much reduced (by 28% between 1973-83 and by 10% between 1980-83). In 1986 the British government pledged to spend £600 million on desulphurisation equipment at power stations and in July 1988 promised to double that spending.

In addition, the EC has adopted two directives: that lead-free petrol must be on sale in all member countries by October 1989; and that exhaust emissions from nitrogen dioxide, hydrocarbons and carbon monoxide must be at least halved. All new cars sold within the EC will by 1994 have to comply with the new emission controls - lean-burn engines for the smaller cars, catalytic converters for more powerful models.

Therefore it seems likely that both emissions of sulphur and nitrogen, and consequently the levels of surface ozone and methane which act together as a toxic cocktail, will be reduced, certainly in industrialsed nations, by the beginning of the 21st century.

Eventually most countries will install chemical plants to remove the sulphur from power station emissions before they reach the atmosphere. Existing processes will also be able to "clean up", using limestone (there are already fears about the "mining" of this commodity from protected areas in the UK). Vehicle emissions will also be controlled, though campaigners fear not as comprehensively as they would have liked.

The fact remains, however, that even if *all* air pollution were halted tomorrow, many of the ill-effects would linger on for years. Soils would retain their man-made acidity; acid and aluminium would continue to pollute rivers and streams and forests will continue to falter without the right balance of nutrients to promote healthy growth - all sorely needed "natural resources" used as industrial goods and services.

The Diesel Dilemma

New research into the effect of diesel vehicles on the atmosphere of Europe is leading to disquiet over the suitability of this fuel. Industry has always been pro-diesel on cost grounds, but also believed its exhaust emissions were less polluting than petrol. It now seems that although lead is not added to diesel and that gaseous pollutants are generally lower than from petrol-driven vehicles, diesel performs badly on the question of "particulate hydrocarbons" (smoke).

A diesel-filled vehicle emits ten times more smoke than an ordinary vehicle and 30-100 times more than a petrol-driven vehicle fitted with a catalytic converter. Traditionally, particulate emissions were merely synonymous with grime, but it is now increasingly believed that they could be linked with cancer, infant mortality and the aggravation of asthma and bronchitis. The USA has enacted particulate emission legislation and it is likely that similar (though probably less rigorous) standards will be set throughout Europe by 1991 (earlier for freight vehicles).

There has been a rapid increase in popularity of diesel-engined vehicles throughout Europe over the past five years. When the acid-rain-conscious West Germans acknowledged petrol cars were a major culprit they switched to diesel cars in a big way, buying more than half a million in 1985. The demand has spread rapidly and already more than 15% of all new cars run on diesel. In the UK the trend is lower: only 4% of new cars are diesel-powered, but even this shows a 50% rise in sales.

3.6 THE LAND

Introduction

The total land surface of the world is about 13 billion hectares, 10% of which is used for agriculture. One-third of this precious agricultural land will be threatened with desertification by the end of the century.

Today 6 million hectares of productive land are estimated to be lost each year to the advancing desert; another 21 million annually are estimated to be reduced to nil economic productivity. Table 3.24 gives a breakdown of land affected by erosion and desertification in OECD countries over a 10-year period.

Table 3.24   SOIL EROSION AND DESERTIFICATION IN SELECTED COUNTRIES 1970-1980

000 square km

	Erosion[1]		Desertification[2]	
	Total area affected	% total land area	Total area affected	% total land area
Australia[3]	815.0	10.7	1,364.0 [1]	17.91 [1]
Canada	510.0	5.5	35.0	0.38
France[4]	45.0	8.2	-	-
Greece	49.0	37.5	-	-
New Zealand	89.4	33.3	-	-
Portugal[5]	-	-	47.6	51.94
Spain	-	-	223.2	44.68
Turkey	571.0	74.1	-	-

Continued..

Table 3.24 cont'd

	Erosion[1]		Desertification[2]	
	Total area affected	% total land area	Total area affected	% total land area
UK[6]	2.3	1.0	-	-
USA	5,448.4	59.7	910.6	9.98
Yugoslavia	137.9	54.0	-	-

Source: OECD
Notes: [1] *Data refers to 1975 only and only to non-arid agricultural land*
[2] *Moderate, severe and very severe desertification*
[3] *Data for deserification exclude sub-humid land of South Australia*
[4] *Data for erosion refer to all potentially affected areas*
[5] *Data for desertification may include slight deterioration in sub-humid zones*
[6] *Data refer to 1975-85. England and Wales only*
[7] *Moderate and very severe erosion.*

Land loss is not exclusively a Third World problem. For instance, the USA could save up to $1 billion annually if soil compaction was avoided. Soil degradation costs Canada $1 billion a year. It is feared the USA's Mid-West agricultural zone has only 50 years of productivity left.

The intensive farming techniques first adopted by developed countries, but now increasingly used in the developing world, are turning soil into a non-renewable resource.

In the UK grain belt, soil erosion is a grave problem. Between 25 and 40 tonnes of topsoil per hectare per annum is being lost. In some of the world's more vulnerable areas, such as the tropics, the toll is likely to be several hundred tonnes of lost topsoil per hectare. Erosion is caused by poor land use - mono-cropping, over-grazing - and leads to the excessive use of potentially damaging fertilisers and a desperate exploitation of marginal land, which in turn leads to disastrous erosion.

Acidity is another problem. Throughout Europe and increasingly worldwide, air-pollution - especially that of SOx and NOx which convert to acids when transported often vast distances through the air - is deposited on the land, turning the soils acidic and less fertile; not *always* a permanent problem but one which is always expensive to rectify.

Irrigation Systems

Ironically, irrigation systems (which have offered hope for dry lands, helping to increase yield sixfold for cereals and fivefold for root crops) also cause land loss if badly managed or poorly maintained. Irrigation accounts for about 13% of all land under cultivation, and there are plans to increase this amount. However, in some regions, such as the Sahel, Iraq and Mexico, salinisation caused by irrigation is taking as much land out of cultivation as the original scheme was adding.

It is feared that 60-80% of irrigated land is in some way salinised, with between 1 and 1.5 million hectares being salinised to some extent every year.

How Salinisation Occurs

All soils contain salt, but if the level becomes too high the land cannot support plant life. When land is irrigated it is essential that the water-salt balance is maintained and water must not, therefore, be allowed to accumulate in the soil as this will lead to a rise in the water table. Where the water table has been allowed to rise, groundwaters are drawn up through the soil by capillary action. On the way up they add to their own salt levels by dissolving the existing salt in the soil. The land thus becomes waterlogged with increasingly saline water. When it reaches the surface, the water evaporates and the salts it contains are left behind to accumulate in the soil. It can leave a white salt crust on the land. Salinisation of irrigated lands is also adding to the salt levels of rivers.

The Cost of Land Loss

Land loss, for whatever reason, is expensive, especially in terms of agricultural potential. Desertification costs $26 billion *annually* in terms of lost agricultural production. World agencies claim the cost of stopping such losses by holding back the encroaching desert will total $4.5 billion annually for 20 years, $2.1 billion of which is already being spent. The UN Environment Programme has been attempting for some years to encourage both the countries affected and the international community to contribute the remaining $2.4 billion - so far without success. On these figures, the cost of neglect is five times higher than the cost of action.

The costs of land loss are being borne by the producer and user. Inefficient use of land unquestionably raises commodity prices, shrinks markets, impoverishes producers and antagonises consumers. It not only decreases productivity, it increases atmospheric dust, contributes to both flooding and drought by silting up waterways, and provokes ill-health and extinctions.

Improved land resource husbandry is likely to be encouraged in developed countries by tax incentives (and penalties) and grants (such as those already being applied for the reversion of productive land to fallow in the UK). These, and a tougher line on the production of cash crops in hungry countries, will affect Western business. Inappropriate intensive farming methods will decline in favour of "sustained" production. In addition, the political position of countries on the brink of national starvation yet growing cash crops of cotton, tobacco or coffee will be increasingly untenable.

There are already moves to give developing nations a stronger voice in their negotiations with multinational organisations. International organisations are representing their interests and ensuring a new balance in trade negotiations.

But in addition to the destructive cycles of land over-use there are threats from industry, urbanisation (Table 3.25) and even tourism. The amount of "wilderness" land protected under one or other of the national park or similar schemes (Table 3.26) is increasing, but management cannot always protect these areas from the surrounding pressures of agricultural or social need. However, carefully managed tourism can lend land a commercial value in its own right.

Table 3.25   LOSS OF AGRICULTURAL LAND TO BUILT-UP LAND 1960-1980

% of agricultural land

	1960-70 [1]	1970-80
Austria	1.8	3.6
Canada	0.3	0.1
Denmark	3.0	1.5
Finland	2.8	0.4
France	1.8	1.1
Italy	-	2.5
Japan	7.3	5.7
Netherlands	4.3	3.6
New Zealand	0.5	-

Continued...

Table 3.25 cont'd

	1960-70 [1]	1970-80
Norway	1.5	1.0
Sweden[2]	1.0	1.0
UK	1.8	0.6
USA	0.8	2.8
West Germany	2.5	2.4
Yugoslavia	–	1.4

Source: OECD
Notes: [1] *Estimates*
　　　　[2] *Estimates based on seven counties*

Table 3.26　　NATIONAL PARKS[1] IN OECD COUNTRIES 1985

	National parks		% of territory	Protected area per 1,000 inhabitants (sq km)
	Sites	Total area (sq km)		
Australia	248	192,590	2.5	1,222.6
Belgium	1	39	0.1	0.4
Canada[2]	74	229,066	2.3	902.6
Denmark[3]	1	700,000	31.6	13,690.6
Finland	18	6,553	1.9	133.7
France	6	2,704	0.5	4.9
Greece	2	88	0.1	0.9
Iceland	3	693	0.7	285.2
Ireland	3	204	0.3	5.7
Italy	3	1,270	0.4	2.2
Japan[4]	5	500	0.1	0.4
Netherlands	10	392	1.1	2.7
New Zealand	10	20,513	7.6	630.4
Norway[5]	18	19,152	5.9	461.7

Continued...

Table 3.26 cont'd

Spain	11	1,532	0.3	4.0
Sweden	15	6,179	1.4	74.0
Switzerland	1	169	0.4	2.6
Turkey	15	2,869	0.4	5.8
USA	18	227,899	2.4	95.2
West Germany	2	339	0.1	0.6
Yugoslavia	8	487	0.2	2.1

Source: IUCN/OECD
Notes: [1] *IUCN category 11 - national parks and equivalent reserves*
[2] *National classification shows 31 national parks, 170 provincial parks*
[3] *Northeast national park of Greenland*
[4] *National classification 27 national parks*
[5] *Includes Svalbard and Jan Meyen which have three national parks.*

3.7 WATER

Introduction

Worldwide, the demand for clean water from industry alone is expected to increase by a factor of 4.4 by the year 2000.

In developing countries, the lack of access to clean water is one of the fundamental causes of poor development. The UN's aim of bringing clean water to all by 1990 has long been abandoned, although it is hoped that substantial improvements will be possible by the end of the century. The cost will be at least $300 billion. In 1970-80 the number of people without access to "safe" drinking water increased by 100 million to about 1,320 million. Each month 750,000 people die of water-borne diseases, with a consequent "waste" of production and money spent on medical costs. This also produces an intolerable strain on international relations as acrimony deepens over the usage of the world's 200-plus shared watercourses.

As the developing world struggles against over-strained aquifers' diminishing reserves as water is drawn at a rate higher than the natural recharge, and drought through erosion, siltation and changing weather patterns, the developed world is also having to take a serious review of its own water resources, which are threatened in both inland and marine terms. Man-made pollution must shoulder most of the blame.

Nitrates and Heavy Metals

Britain provides a very clear example of poor resource husbandry. A major cause for concern is the alarmingly high level of nitrates and heavy metals in the drinking supply. For some time well over a million people in Britain have been drinking water which breaches EC directives on nitrate levels. In 1985 a maximum admissible concentration for nitrate at 50 mg per 100 ml of water was laid down. Areas of intensive farming are most at risk. By early 1988 the UK government had started action to reduce the excessive nitrate levels.

However, the nitrate levels being recorded now are indicative of the level of nitrogen fertiliser used on the land up to 20 years ago. Since usage has increased eightfold in the intervening period, recorded levels must be expected to increase. Since one of the most favoured methods of improving water nitrate levels is to "blend" water from two sources - one heavily, one lightly contaminated - it is likely that the quality of drinking water for millions more British people will decrease over the next decades. As well as public taste, industrial needs for water of certain standard will suffer.

The capital cost of meeting EC nitrates levels for the two most affected water authorities in Britain (Severn-Trent and Anglian) is estimated at about £70 million: water rates will rise. Treatment will involve low-density farming on a permanent basis around vital bore-holes.

Another major concern for both established industrialised nations and, increasingly, the newly industrialised nations of Asia, Africa and Latin America is the presence of heavy metals in water. These can include titanium, cadmium, mercury (all subject to EC controls) and, of most recent concern, aluminium. Although many of these substances can be traced back directly to industrial sources (the titanium dioxide process; electrolysis of alkali chlorides and cadmium as a constituent of batteries) the growing curse of acid rain is known to leach out natural metallic compounds found in soil and rock. Table 3.27 shows for selected areas the levels of sulphur and nitrogen; these convert into acid during transportation through the atmosphere. The table also shows worrying pH levels as a result of acid deposition.

Despite fears that aluminium intake by humans can lead to degradation of the brain, water authorities in Britain continue to add alum to reservoir water at a rate of 100,000 tonnes a year, and a cost of £250,000, in order to clarify the water.

Table 3.27   CONCENTRATIONS IN ACID PRECIPITATION IN SELECTED AREAS 1984–1985

Country	Area	Number of stations	pH 1984	pH 1985	SO_4 1984	mg/litre 1985	NO_3 1984	mg/litre 1985
Belgium	Offagne	1	4.82	5.61	4.95	4.62	2.79	2.92
Canada	Great Lakes	3	4.27	–	2.58	–	2.12	–
Finland	Uto, Ahtari, Virolathi	3	4.59	4.46	3.32	3.67	1.95	2.56
Norway	Birkenes	1	4.24	4.24	3.27	2.94	2.53	2.57
Sweden	Rorvik	1	4.18	4.22	4.32	4.29	3.01	3.49
UK	Inverpolly	1	5.15	5.30	1.01	0.91	0.43	0.56
	Eskdalemuir	1	4.66	4.72	1.58	1.49	1.18	0.93
USA	Great Lakes	14	4.30	–	2.73	–	1.67	–

Source: OECD/EMEP

Measuring the acidity in water

The degree of acidity or alkalinity of a liquid is measured on the pH scale. This ranges from 0-14, with 0 being the most acidic (battery acid has a pH of 1), 7 being neutral (the pH of distilled water) and 14 the most alkaline (a saturated solution of ammonia in water has a pH of 11). The scale is logarithmic, and a single-number step increases or decreases acidity by a factor of 10. Thus, a solution with a pH of 6 is ten times more acidic than one with a pH of 7, and so on.

All rain is slightly acidic because of the natural carbon dioxide content of air. Acidity is often neutralised by the soil, but higher levels become destructive. For instance, the critical pH level for most aquatic species is 6. When the pH falls below this level, the number of species, and the population of algae, animal plankton, aquatic insects, insect larvae and sensitive fish (such as salmon, roach and minnow) declines. Below 5.5 the number of snails and microscopic plant species is reduced. Below 5.2 snails disappear. Below 5.0 many microscopic animal species disappear and even the more tolerant species become rare. Between 5.0 and 4.5 no viable fishery can be maintained.

Marine Waters

Marine waters also give global cause for concern. The United Nations Environment Programme (UNEP) brings together 130 states bordering 11 shared seas in its anti-pollution/mutual benefit Regional Seas Programme.

The London Dumping Convention, which has world-wide application, was signed in 1972 and came into force in 1975. Initially it mainly comprised the "dumping" states but its 61 current members are now predominantly non-dumping. There are three levels of dumping: extremely dangerous substances - prohibited; less noxious substances - dumping permitted by "prior special permit"; all other substances, which may be dumped after general permit from national authorities.

The ocean disposal of radioactive wastes has attracted the most attention. Prior to 1983 Belgium, the Netherlands, Switzerland and the UK regularly dumped low-level wastes in the North-East Atlantic off the coast of Spain. In 1983, despite protests from these countries, there was a *de facto* moratorium, which all countries honour although some have not officially agreed to it. This was extended indefinitely in 1985.

The Law of the Sea Convention takes a tough line on pollution and requires all states to "prevent, reduce and control pollution of the marine environment from dumping".

Industry and government bodies are in the firing line of such controls. Such conventions stress that coastal states not only have a right to defend themselves against dumping in territorial seas, the 200-nautical mile Exclusive Economic Zone or the continental shelf, but they also have a *duty*. Coastal states are increasingly being encouraged to take tough measures against dumpers. Neighbourliness in shared sea situations is politically critical and is expected to become more so. Offending institutions can therefore expect to meet increasingly severe regulations in the coming decades.

A particularly good example of "neighbour" pressure arose in 1987/88 during the heated debates at the North Sea Conference in London. Britain is the only nation still dumping sewage in the North Sea, and in 1987 still dumped 5 million tonnes of sewage sludge (see Table 3.9 for earlier years). Pressure from other EC members continues to grow strongly; they claim that North Sea geography causes Britain's pollution to be "exported" to continental waters. The EC members call for a total ban on the dumping of "harmful" waste in the North Sea from 1990 and a 50% reduction in river pollution (feeding into seas) from 1995.

Along with its EC colleagues, Britain agreed at the London meeting to "drastically cut" the amount of waste incineration from ships in the North Sea within two years, with a total ban by 1995; also to implement a total and immediate ban on the dumping of "household type" rubbish from ships in the North Sea.

In November 1987 the UK government drew up a "red list" of chemicals, which restricts discharges from organisations previously able to "dilute" chemicals to officially "safe" levels. Red-list chemicals will be subject to new regulations. It is also hoped that the regulations will "encourage" new plant to include recycling potential with particular emphasis on the heavy metals and potentially dangerous organic chemicals. New restrictions on the supply, storage and use of red-list chemicals were also introduced.

Beaches

International pressure has resulted in new, higher standards of cleanliness, plus a great deal of clean-up spending, on beaches throughout Europe, including Britain. In 1976 the EC designated minimum standards of "bathing beaches". Initially Britain nominated 27 such beaches but later increased this to 389. By the end of 1987 just over 200 beaches in Britain met EC bathing-beach standards, only 17 of which were awarded the EC Blue Flag Charter for top quality. Local authorities were allocated £208 million to implement the new stricter measures. Much of the shortfall may fall to local industry, used to laxer discharge conditions. Bathing water reaching EC standards is that defined as having no more than 2,000 faecal coliform bacteria present in 100 ml of water for 95% of samples - a standard considered generous by many countries.

Table 3.28 shows that between 1980 and 1985 most reporting countries improved their performance in category D (the UK reducing from eight to four the number of such sites), although category C is still alarmingly high in some areas.

Table 3.28   BACTERIOLOGICAL QUALITY OF MARINE WATERS OF SELECTED COUNTRIES 1980/1985

%

	1980 Category				Sampling points (no.)	1985 Category				Sampling points (no.)
	A	B	C	D		A	B	C	D	
Australia	47	53	0	0	19	–	–	–	–	–
Belgium	0	40	53	7	15	–	–	–	–	–
Canada	88	5	0	7	140	79	5	0	16	43
Finland[1]	100	0	0	0	5	100	0	0[2]	0	5
France	28	32	33	7	961	84[2]	0	16[2]	0	1,555
Italy	56	33	7	3	231	60	23	17[3]	0	441
Netherlands	17	22	44	17	18	–	–	–	–	–
Norway	0	0	100	0	9	–	–	–	–	–
Portugal	0	28	33	39	18	–	–	–	–	–
UK	19	50	23	8	26	23	58	15	4	26
West Germany[4]	86	14	0	0	3	74	6	21	0	5
Yugoslavia	47	35	14	4	125	–	–	–	–	–

Categories

A: At least 95% of the measures are under 10,000 total coliforms per 100 ml and 2,000 faecal coliforms per 100 ml; *and* at least 80% of the measures are under 500 total coliforms per 100 ml and 100 faecal coliforms per 100 ml.

B: At least 95% of the measures are under 10,000 total coliforms per 100 ml and 2,000 faecal coliforms per 100 ml; *and* less than 80% of the measures are under 500 total coliforms per 100 ml and 100 faecal coliforms per 100 ml.

C: Between 5% and 35% of measures are above 10,000 total coliforms per 100 ml and 2,000 faecal coliforms per 100 ml.

D: More than 35% of measures are above 10,000 total coliforms per 100 ml and 2,000 faecal coliforms per 100 ml.

Source: OECD
Notes: [1] Data for 1982, not 1980; [2] A includes B, and C includes D
[3] C includes D; [4] One coastal zone only

PART FOUR
THE ENVIRONMENTALIST
IMPACT ON BUSINESS

4.1 INTRODUCTION

Business cannot ignore environmentalism. No aspect of management remains unaffected: there are consumers who make it a part of their buying decision; capitalists who make it a part of their investment decision; job applicants who ask about environment policy at interviews. There are local authorities that will not award a sensitive contract without first approving an environmental policy statement, and in most countries in the world there are politicians passing a steady stream of environment legislation.

The environmental movement has become extremely sophisticated. Consumers are looking for "green" products because the campaigners have realised that power comes not out of a gun but out of a purse. The ethical investment movement has appeared and grown for similar reasons. And the movement has learned that more tangible results are gained working within the system than without. Thus the mainstream environment groups have access to - indeed, are invited to make submissions by - government. Neither are environmentalists eternally outside business; many now work as consultants to industry, some occupying board positions.

Given that all this is so, could it have been achieved were there no substance to environmentalist arguments? The answer is no. Every industrialist who derides an environmental problem he secretly knows to exist simply damages long-term business credibility. The company that willingly invests in pollution abatement invests in good public relations at the same time; the publicly reluctant company spends the same money in the end but gains nothing in public relations.

Of course environmentalists can be wrong, and they can be fought. Industry has also become extremely sophisticated at defusing conflicts. Yet there is no profit in fighting environmentalists who are right: the environment itself will exact its own cost in time. But there *is* profit in exploiting environmentalism. Companies prosper when they supply the goods and services people want. Increasing numbers of people want environment-friendly goods, just as they also want the latest fashions. Why fight that? Increasing numbers of investors want some assurance of a company's ethics, just as they also want an attractive rate of return. Why not accept that investment? Increasing numbers of talented managers, who grew up in the 1960s, have a feeling for the direction of the environment movement. Why not use that talent? Conservationists have also shown how industry can actually reduce costs through saving energy and recycling materials.

These ideas are no longer controversial. Some of the world's multi-nationals and the most respected businessmen have adopted them. That is the environmentalist impact on business.

4.2 GREEN CONSUMERISM AND CONSUMER ATTITUDES

In 1972 the anti-fur-trade campaigners took the issue to the high streets of Britain and asked shoppers for their support. Within months there was a complete ban on leopard, tiger and cheetah products. This was consumer power in action. It has been increasingly harnessed by environmental groups over the past 20 years, creating a new, discriminating and powerful pressure group in its own right - the green consumer had arrived.

As businesses discovered, reluctantly at first but with an increasing intensity through the mid-1980s, these environmentally concerned consumers were creating a demand as commercially compelling as any other buying trend. There is little doubting the existence of environmental demand. It is evidenced by the increase in the "no additive" labels; in the growing number of bottle or can banks in town centres; in the policy rethinks of organisations, manufacturers and retailers over many key issues. Its increasing effectiveness has been felt and responded to by leading retail groups. In the UK, for example, retail chains often react slightly ahead of some manufacturers.
J Sainsbury was the first household-name store, for instance, to abandon its own-brand chlorofluorocarbon (CFC)-propelled aerosols after mounting pressure from environmental groups and consumers over fears that CFCs were damaging the ozone layer, giving increased cancer risk. It was followed by stores such as Tesco, Safeway and the Co-op pledging to phase out CFC aerosols. Yet not until spring 1988 did the aerosol industry itself react to pressure group campaigning and announce the discontinuance of CFC-propellants by the end of 1989. Over the following few months, many more "Ozone Friendly" stickers were being used and adverts featured more non-aerosol products.

Adverse publicity over the use of CFC-polystyrene packaging also caused some shops and fast-food outlets to change their policies. In the UK virtually all supermarkets, fast-food chains and egg packagers abandoned CFC foam by July 1988. Public opinion and political pressure had encouraged high street businesses radically to change their stand over a 12-month period. A Friends of the Earth survey showed that McDonald's, Quick, Burger King and Traveller's Fare fast-food chains had all switched or pledged to switch packaging. Sainsbury had banished CFC egg containers and was switching to a safer refrigerant. Asda, Safeway, Gateway and the Co-op were bringing in "ozone friendly" packaging and most British egg producers switched back to pulp boxes.

Where appropriate (for some countries had already banned CFC-aerosols), European shoppers were reacting with equal conviction.

Public Reaction Study

There have been innovations in commercial and industrial decision-making procedures in many European countries over the past decade. Effective policymaking appears to be almost impossible without taking into account public reactions. Participation procedures and information programmes have been introduced on a large scale in many countries. In the Netherlands, for example, a national debate was organised which aimed to involve many interested groups and also individuals. But while acknowledging the importance of consumer acceptance of a product or project, many organisations also tend to make subjective (and inaccurate) assumptions about public response.

The World Energy Conference (WEC) in its 13th Congress in 1986 studied psychological research into public perception of risks and attitudes, taking as an example large-scale energy technology. The findings, it claimed, would help decision-makers to understand public reaction and avoid misattribution through subjectivity. Looking at the characteristics of public attitudes to risks, the Congress gound:

> One of the most eye-catching results of risk perception research is the low correlation which is found between statistics of average yearly fatality rates and subjective judgements of seriousness of risk. This illustrates that lay judgements are obviously based on other factors.

> Catastrophic potential of risky activities is an important characteristic. In other words, a large number of fatalities in a short period of time is judged as more serious than the same number spread over a longer period of time.

This explains why generating electricity by nuclear power gives rise to *more* opposition than the use of coal. The public perceives nuclear power as having more potential for *disaster*; the risks of coal on the other hand are more diffused. The public also considers death by nuclear means to be more "dreadful".

A second factor contributing to public fear of accident, and therefore opposition to a project, is the feeling of controllability of a situation. Studies show that risk associated with, say, hydroelectric power station can be acceptable to the public on the grounds that it is not a mysterious process and that experts could be expected to control an accident. On the other hand, the risks of a nuclear power station are judged to be far more complex and unknown and therefore less controllable, even by experts. Technological disasters can evoke, even more than natural disasters, strong feelings of loss of control; their after-effects can therefore be stronger. These feelings of control can be manipulated. In the context of energy risk this could result in a public overestimation of expert knowledge.

The WEC conducted research into the differences in nuclear risk assessment between ordinary members of the public and experts. Lay people surveyed in Holland estimated the probability of nuclear accident as "very high", while Dutch experts rated the risk as "very low" (see Figure 4.1).

Figure 4.1   Public and Expert Attitudes to the Probability of Nuclear Power Plant Accident Poisoning Areas up to 5 km Away

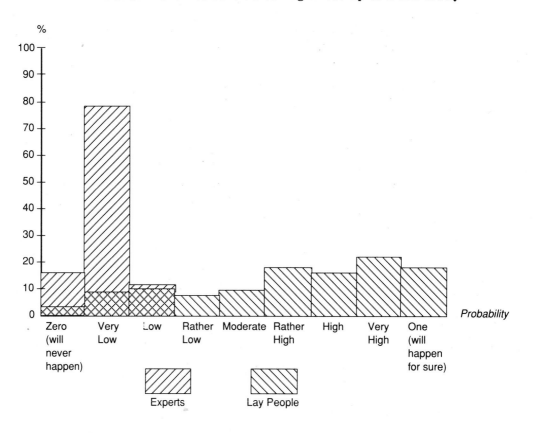

Source: World Energy Conference 1986

Lay people are often felt to hold an apocalyptic view of the consequences of nuclear accidents, whereas the experts were able to use reasoned probability estimates to present an accurate picture of attitudes towards the use of uranium. Differences between lay people and experts over the probabilities of harm arising from the use of coal are considerably smaller. (see Figure 4.2). There are larger variations both between public and experts, and among the experts themselves.

Figure 4.2   **Public and Expert Attitudes to the Probability of Acid Rain Being Caused by the use of Coal**

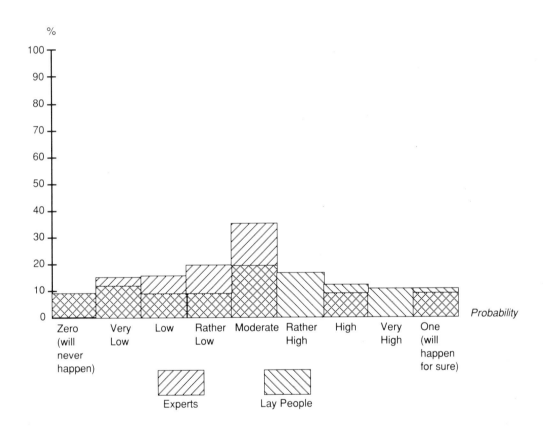

Source: World Energy Conference 1986

The WEC was told that supporters of nuclear power and coal are more ambivalent than opponents. Supporters tend to make a trade-off between risks and benefits, whereas opponents' attitudes are mainly determined by anticipated risks. Thus supporters are less involved in debate and action than are opponents.

It is often supposed that ideological differences form the main split between supporters and opponents, but studies throughout Western Europe show that this might not be the case. The organisational and structural scale of the energy supply is not considered very important by the average public respondent. The relation between attitudes toward nuclear power and toward environmental issues is blurred. While environmentalistic attitudes often go together with a negative attitude toward nuclear power, those attitudes are often based on other, unrelated beliefs. Supporters of nuclear power, on the other hand, lobby on grounds of environmental benefit. Supporters and opponents seem to vary in their estimates of the probability rather than the ideologically motivated evaluation of consequences.

The nuclear debate reveals large political differences in countries throughout Europe. The WEC study quotes the following example: "In Sweden, Social Democrats support the use of nuclear power, while Conservatives oppose it. In the Netherlands, Social Democrats oppose nuclear power and the conservative parties support it. In France, Socialists and Conservatives support nuclear power." These differences are claimed to indicate that the issue has been "embedded" in the political field, linked to consistent ideologies.

The study presents findings which, it believes, are relevant to both planned and existing siting of risk-related industry. People living near a nuclear power plant find the technology more acceptable than those living further away. Three possible explanations are suggested:

1. *Dissonance reduction*
    Residents tend to deny the risks to avoid causing disharmony among them, leading to discomfort.

2. *Familiarity*
    Residents become used to the plant after it has functioned well for many years, and get to know the personnel.

3. *Commitment*
    People develop positive attitudes because they benefit economically.

Finally, the study warns of the "serious doubts" about the possibilities of appropriate compensation for people living near nuclear power stations: "Proposals to compensate can easily be interpreted as bribery. One reason for this might be that residents view compensation as contrary to their expectations about the role of the government as protector of the population against risks." It suggests resident opposition should better be tackled by focusing on the safety issues themselves and not by introducing external compensation incentives, which "will not remove intensive feelings of threat. Extra safety precautions might offer a solution." It adds, however, that industry might come up against another form of opponent:

> There may be local representatives who do not oppose the use of nuclear power as a general policy. Usually these supporters find the risks tolerable, but strongly stress economic benefits. From their point of view, local interests would be served by counteracting siting decisions initiated on the central level; by negotiating their socio-economic benefits can be better served.

Business needs to know what concerns the green consumer. Several recent surveys have cast light on the subject.

Department of the Environment Survey

In Britain a 1986 DoE survey found that 8% of respondents mentioned "environmental problems" as a concern before even knowing the nature of the survey. The survey questioned 1,575 adults in England and Wales. Its findings (summarised in Table 4.1) included:

1. Fears about nuclear waste dumping preoccupied over half the respondents (reflecting, perhaps, public concern over the Chernobyl incident some five months before the survey).

2. Over half the sample were concerned about chemical pollution in rives. (The Sandoz major pollution accident on the Rhine was, ironically, a few weeks *after* the survey but there had been widespread publicity over river pollution in Britain including a poison spillage in Lancashire and a pollution incident in Yorkshire killing 2,000 brown trout.)

3. Acid rain attracted surprisingly low levels of concern compared with some topics, thought to be due to a number of misconceptions at the time (the public is believed to be better informed now) about the exact nature of acid rain.

Table 4.1   CONSUMER ATTITUDES TO VARIOUS ENVIRONMENTAL
              THREATS 1986

%	Very worried	Quite worried	Not very worried	Not at all worried
Chemical in rivers and sea	54	32	8	6
Get rid of nuclear waste	62	20	9	8
Destruction of wildlife	38	44	12	6
Dirty beaches and sea	37	42	13	8
Insecticides, fertilisers and chemical sprays	39	35	16	9
Litter and rubbish	30	42	20	8
Decay of inner cities and derelict land	27	42	20	11
Acid rain	35	33	16	16
Losing green belt land	26	40	19	14
Oil slicks from ships	27	37	23	12
Fumes and smoke from factories	26	37	22	15
Car exhaust fumes	23	37	26	14
Fouling by dogs	30	29	26	14
Loss of hedgerows	17	36	28	19
Neglect of old buildings and ancient monuments	12	34	34	20
Lack of access to open spaces and countryside	11	29	33	26
Ugly new buildings	13	26	32	28
Noise from traffic, radios, aircraft and lawnmowers	10	22	37	31

Source: DoE attitude survey 1986

To ascertain the level of understanding about acid rain, the DoE asked a number of extra questions, shown in Table 4.2. Over 30% were unable to give any cause for acid rain but, despite this confusion, 84% supported the idea that the government should spend more money to improve the acid rain situation.

Table 4.2   CONSUMER ATTITUDES TO ACID RAIN 1986

%

True or untrue that smoke and chemicals from power stations in this country harm lakes and forests in other countries like Norway?

	All	Male	Female	65+
True	55	61	49	46
Untrue	23	20	25	25
Don't know	23	19	26	29

Give as many causes as possible of acid rain.[1]

Factories	36
Coal and oil power stations	23
Nuclear power stations	19
Car exhausts	10
Other	20
Don't know	32

Government spending to reduce acid rain affecting other countries.

Should spend money	84
Should not spend money	12
Don't know	5

Source: DoE attitude survey 1986
Note: [1] *multiple responses*

The survey generally demonstrates a higher level of concern among women compared with men, and a higher level of concern in the 25-64 age groups. The lower social groups showed more concern for local issues such as fouling by dogs (see Table 4.3).

117

Table 4.3   CONSUMER ATTITUDES TO THE ENVIRONMENT, ANALYSED BY SEX, AGE, SOCIAL CLASS[1] AND TYPE OF AREA

% "very worried"

	Chems. in rivers	Nu-clear waste	Destruct. of wild-life	Dirty beaches	Insect-icides etc.	Litter	Decay of cities	Acid rain	Oil slicks	Factory fumes	Car exhaust	Foul-ing dogs	Hedge loss	Lack of access	Ugly new bldgs.	Noise from traffic
Sex																
Male	53	55	38	35	37	27	26	34	27	25	21	24	16	11	11	9
Female	55	68	38	38	42	34	28	36	28	26	25	36	18	11	14	11
Age																
18–24	52	62	41	35	27	21	25	24	28	22	12	14	10	9	7	3
25–44	57	64	40	35	40	27	24	36	26	29	23	27	14	11	11	9
45–64	57	68	38	43	46	37	31	42	30	29	28	35	20	12	15	12
65+	48	51	34	31	39	35	27	30	25	17	23	42	20	13	18	14
Social class																
I/II	56	63	38	35	40	29	32	35	26	26	21	30	20	9	14	9
IIIN	53	55	42	33	38	35	26	34	23	24	25	31	15	9	13	8
IIIM	54	58	36	36	42	27	23	33	28	26	22	27	15	13	12	9
IV	50	64	36	40	38	30	23	36	31	24	24	33	12	9	11	12
V	53	57	45	37	37	43	24	33	33	18	24	45	22	16	22	14

Continued...

Table 4.3 cont'd

Area	Chems. in rivers	Nu- clear waste	Destruct. of wild- life	Dirty beaches	Insect- icides etc.	Litter	Decay of cities	Acid rain	Oil slicks	Factory fumes	Car exhaust	Foul- ing dogs	Hedge loss	Lack of access	Ugly new bldgs.	Noise from traffic
Met.	54	62	32	39	39	37	33	36	25	26	27	31	13	10	13	12
Urban	57	61	36	38	36	27	24	33	26	27	23	32	15	12	11	8
Mixed	54	63	44	36	42	30	24	36	31	23	20	31	18	12	13	10
Rural	51	63	42	33	42	25	25	35	28	26	20	27	22	12	15	11
ALL	54	62	38	37	39	30	27	35	27	26	23	30	17	11	13	10

Source: DoE attitude survey 1986
Note: [1] Social Class Definition: I professional occupations; II intermediate occupations; IIIN skilled occupations (non-manual); IIIM skilled occupations (manual); IV partly skilled; V unskilled occupations

Noise as an environmental concern came last, with only 10% of respondents "very worried". This comparatively low level of concern is due largely to the wide variation in noise sources quoted and a general feeling of hopelessness about noise pollution. Although 41% of people think much could be done about noise pollution, this is a smaller percentage than for any other of the environmental concerns - for example, 85% said tougher laws would alleviate the problem of chemical pollution of rivers and seas. However, 35% feel tougher laws would help reduce noise.

Industry is widely perceived as being responsible for its own pollution. Respondents were asked who they thought ought to take charge of "doing something" about a selection of problems.

Table 4.4 shows that except for nuclear waste, almost unanimously considered a government problem, many pollution issues are blamed on industry. For instance, 42% of respondents said the polluter should be reponsible for chemicals in rivers and seas; 42% were in favour of polluters tackling their own insecticide and chemical spray problems; and 52% felt the factories themselves were responsible for their own fumes and smoke. On a local level, 36% were in favour of owners' responsibility for fouling by dogs.

Insecticides, fertilisers and chemical sprays were perceived as the most serious *business-related* local problem (Table 4.4). 45% regarding it as a problem in their area. Asked the questions "which do you feel is the most important problem usually" and which "the most important problem in Britain" the most pressing localised concerns were, again, dog fouling (20%), and litter and rubbish (15%).

It is interesting to note that over 80% felt problems in their area were better or about the same as elsewhere in Britain, with only 15% believing they were worse off (see Table 4.5). However, it is indicative of the concerns over inner-city areas that respondents felt that their local conditions were relatively worse the more urban their area. Thus 23% of those living in metropolitan areas felt environmental problems were worse than elsewhere in Britain, compared with 6% in rural areas. To confirm the growing awareness of environmental problems, over half the respondents felt their local conditions were worse than five years ago.

Table 4.4   CONSUMER ATTITUDES TO ENVIRONMENTAL ISSUES 1986: ENFORCEMENT OF POLICY, RESPONSIBILITY AND WHETHER LOCAL OR NATIONAL PROBLEMS

%	Enforcement potential*		Responsibility					Problem priority*		
	Lot can be done	Helped by tougher laws	A	B	C	D	E	Viewed as local problem	Most important local	Most important national
Chemicals in rivers and sea	84	85	47	7	42	2	2	39	4	5
Getting rid of nuclear waste	76	76	88	2	8	1	1	26	8	52
Destruction of wildlife	74	52	39	21	30	7	3	43	3	2
Dirty beaches and sea	84	69	28	49	18	4	1	27	4	2
Insecticides, fertilisers and chemical sprays	71	73	46	8	42	3	2	45	6	4
Litter and rubbish	82	57	7	60	22	9	1	66	15	6
Decay of inner cities and derelict land	77	43	54	39	3	2	2	25	5	11
Acid rain	57	53	69	2	28	2	4	27	1	3
Losing green belt land	56	41	39	50	5	3	3	47	7	3
Oil slicks from ships	61	58	48	1	48	1	2	15	–	–
Fumes and smoke from factories	64	71	32	12	52	2	2	25	4	2
Car exhaust fumes	62	56	66	4	23	4	3	50	6	2
Fouling by dogs	70	48	7	45	36	11	1	71	20	3
Loss of hedgerows	55	29	19	43	29	6	3	37	1	0
Neglect of old buildings and ancient monuments	61	27	40	49	4	4	3	23	1	0
Lack of access to open spaces and countryside	50	22	18	55	16	9	2	28	1	1
Ugly new buildings	51	26	19	63	13	2	2	23	1	0

Continued....

Table 4.4 cont'd

	Enforcement potential*		Responsibility					Problem priority*		
	Lot can be done	Helped by tougher laws	A	B	C	D	E	Viewed as local problem	Most important local	Most important national
Noise from traffic, radios aircraft and lawnmowers	41	35	42	16	31	7	4	38	8	1

Source: DoE attitude survey 1986
Notes: A = Government, B = Local council, C = Those who cause the problem, D = Those most affected by the problem,
*E = Other/don't know, * Percentage agreeing*

Table 4.5   COMPARISON OF LOCAL ENVIRONMENT PROBLEMS 1986

%

Compared with those elsewhere in Britain

			Respondents' area		
	All	Metropolitan	Urban	Mixed	Rural
Worse	14	23	12	10	6
Better	32	22	31	35	43
Much the same	51	51	53	52	49
Don't know	3	5	4	3	2

Compared with five years ago

Worse	47	48	48	49	41
Better	7	11	7	5	5
Much the same	38	33	39	38	44
Don't know	8	8	7	8	10

Source: DoE attitude survey 1986

The survey also investigated the effectiveness of legislation, the desirability of maintaining modern farming methods (an area linked with insecticides and chemical pollution questions), and whether houses should, in any circumstances, be built on green belt land (Table 4.6). It is interesting that 69% of people living in rural areas would *not* compensate farmers for having to avoid using modern farming techniques. 66% of respondents accepted it was sometimes necessary to build houses on green belt land – those in the higher social classes being slightly more likely to agree that houses should *never* be built.

Table 4.6   CONSUMER ATTITUDES 1986: LEGISLATION, MODERN
FARMING METHODS AND BUILDING ON GREEN BELT
LAND

%

Effect of laws to protect the environment (by social class)

	All	I/II	IIIN	IIIM	IV	V
Laws have helped	29	42	30	22	17	20
Laws have made no difference	53	40	51	62	68	59
Don't know	18	19	19	16	14	20

Avoidance of modern methods of farming (associated with destruction of wildlife and use of pesticides etc) (by area)

	All	Metro-politan	Urban	Mixed	Rural
Farmers should avoid using them and not be compensated financially	58	55	59	54	69
Farmers should be paid to avoid using them	28	31	28	29	22
Neither	6	5	7	8	3
Don't know	8	9	6	9	6

Building houses on green belt land (by social class)

	All	I/II	IIIN	IIIM	IV	V
Sometimes necessary	66	60	66	69	72	67
Never	30	37	30	26	23	27
Don't know	4	3	4	5	5	6

Source: DoE attitude survey 1986

The survey was interested to discover people's views on the relative importance of environmental protection when it may stand in the way of other national interests (such as economic growth), and how much people were prepared to pay for environmental improvements. Table 4.7 compares the DoE response with replies to a similar question in the EC's Eurobarometer Surveys in 1982 and 1985. The replies to the "trade-off" questions were very similar, with over 50% saying the environment should be protected, even at the risk of holding back economic growth, with a steady decrease in numbers believing the opposite.

Table 4.7   CONSUMER ATTITUDES TO ENVIRONMENT VERSUS ECONOMIC GROWTH 1982-1986

% agreeing	DoE (England and Wales) 1986	Eurobarometer (UK) 1985	1982
Government should give priority to protecting the environment even at the risk of holding back economic growth	54	57	49
Government should give priority to economic growth even if the environment suffers as a result	29	32	41
Neither	7)	11	10
Don't know	10)		

Source: DoE attitude survey 1986/EC Eurobarometer Surveys 1982, 1985

Table 4.8 shows respondents' views on who should pay for environmental improvements. While 36% felt that local and national government should cut spending in other areas (a predictable response), the amount people were prepared to pay from their own pockets was astonishing. Of those surveyed, 68% were willing to contemplate an extra 16p on petrol prices and 59% felt that an additional 50p a week on the average electricity bill, to reduce pollution, was a good idea.

Table 4.8   PUBLIC WILLINGNESS TO PAY FOR ENVIRONMENTAL
IMPROVEMENTS 1986

% agreeing

Fairest ways of finding money

Government and local councils should cut back on other areas of public spending	36
Industry should charge higher prices for any products we buy that cause pollution when they are made	27
Higher taxes and rates	15
Nothing should be spent because Britain cannot afford the money	3
None of these	9
Don't know	9

Suggested price increases

	16p on a gallon of petrol	50p per week on average electricity bill
Good idea	68	59
Bad idea	25	34
Don't know	7	7

Source: DoE attitude survey 1986

The Friends of the Earth Survey

The DoE findings were echoed in a Friends of the Earth/MORI survey of 1,965 adults throughout Britain, conducted shortly before the 1987 general election. Respondents were given a choice of measures to reduce pollution (Table 4.9). The proposal to add 2p a gallon to the price of petrol to help reduce air pollution and acid rain caused, in part, by exhaust fumes received most support (41%, increasing to 43% when the question was confined to car owners). Analysed by social class, just under half the ABs supported the measure for more expensive petrol, but fewer than a third of DEs.

Almost as many (34%) favoured a 1p in the pound increase in income tax to pay for environmental protection (43% of ABC1s said yes to this compared with 28% of C2DEs, and 38% of those with jobs compared with 30% of those without). Family health was the motivation behind the option of a 5% increase in the food bill to ensure freedom from pesticide residues (supported by 26%, a clear sign that many no longer consider washing and peeling fresh food to be an adequate safeguard).

Table 4.9   CONSUMER ATTITUDES TO ENVIRONMENT
            IMPROVEMENT METHODS 1987

% of respondents agreeing

An extra 2p per gallon on petrol to help reduce air pollution and acid rain caused by some of the gases emitted by car exhaust fumes	41
An increase in income tax by 1p in the pound to pay for measures to protect the environment and conserve natural resources	34
An increase in your food bill of 5% to pay for fresh fruit, vegetables and other foodstuffs which were guaranteed to be free of pesticide residues	26
Stop buying wood products made from trees such as teak and mahogany unless it could be guaranteed that they come from countries which were protecting their forests	25
An extra £5 per annum on electricity bills to help reduce acid rain	18
None of these	15
Don't know	10

Source: FoE/MORI survey 1987

A fairly low 18% chose to consider a £5 per annum increase in their electricity bills to help acid rain problems. The response to government action over acid rain spending (Table 4.10) shows that only 8% of respondents believe the government should give the problem no special priority.

Table 4.10   CONSUMER PERCEPTION OF GOVERNMENT POLICIES
FOR ACID RAIN 1987

%

Acid rain: which if any of these policies the government could adopt comes closest to your view?

Provide money for more scientific research into acid rain before taking action to reduce sulphur pollution	39
Provide money for changes to existing coal-fired power stations to reduce pollution given off	28
Provide money for new coal-fired power stations to be built over the next ten years	13
Give no special priority to acid rain	8
None of these	3
Don't know	9

Source: FoE/MORI survey 1987

It is indicative of the British consumer's growing unwillingness to tolerate what are increasingly acknowledged as poisonous chemical residues in water and food that 85% of respondents to FoE survey supported the adoption of strict maximum levels (see Table 4.11). After many months of consumer and environmental group pressure, the UK government has now agreed to meet EC water purity directives.

Table 4.11   CONSUMER ATTITUDES TOWARDS SELECTED
ENVIRONMENTAL ISSUES 1987

%	A	B	C	D	E	F	G
Government should fix maximum levels of pesticides and residues in food and drinking water	43	43	10	3	1	86	4
Proposals for the shallow burial of nuclear waste should be immediately withdrawn pending further research into other options for its storage	52	30	12	5	1	82	6
Government should give much higher priority to protecting the environment	32	49	13	5	1	81	6
Government should provide funds to help finance local authority waste recycling schemes such as for glass and paper	30	50	12	7	1	80	8
Recent government decision to allow development on farming land seriously threatens traditional British landscape and wildlife	27	67	40	16	13	17	4
The present level of financial support from government for Britain's bus and rail service is inadequate	22	37	21	17	3	59	20
UK government should help Third World to develop their economies in a more environmentally responsible way	19	39	22	14	6	58	20
Lower speed limits should be introduced into residential areas to reduce number of accidents	28	28	11	26	7	56	33

Continued...

Table 4.11 cont'd

	A	B	C	D	E	F	G
Tax on artificial fertiliser and pesticides would cause less farm over-production and reduce food mountains	14	38	24	19	5	52	24
The destruction of tropical rain forests is something which will directly affect me in the future	23	29	27	17	4	52	21
More effective controls on artificial fertiliser and pesticides would make no difference to the quality of Britain's drinking water	5	19	24	35	17	24	52
No need for tighter controls on loads carried by heavy lorries in Britain	5	15	14	38	28	20	66

Source: FoE/MORI survey 1987
Notes: A = Strongly agree
B = Tend to agree
C = Neither/no opinion
D = Tend to disagree
E = Strongly disagree
F = Total agreeing
G = Total disagreeing

The FoE survey, like the DoE survey the year before, found a high level of concern about nuclear energy, with 82% of respondents agreeing that proposals for shallow burial of nuclear waste should be withdrawn until further research had been carried out. Local authority recycling schemes found much support (80%), probably because recycling is perceived as a household contribution to a healthier environment.

Another similarity of the two surveys is the strength of environmental concern felt within the middle (25-44) age range, although on the residues question males (87%) as opposed to females (84%) showed the most concern.

Other Surveys

Addis

Specific research on the question of rubbish recycling has been carried out by the housewares manufacturer Addis, which produced its "rubbish" survey in 1985. Some 289 "housewives" from all over Britain were telephoned by Nielsen Consumer Research. Of these 43% experienced guilt feelings about the amount of rubbish thrown away, and a substantial 89% (a similar proportion to the FoE survey) felt local authorities had a strong responsibility to undertake waste recycling programmes. An astonishing 94% of respondents were willing to sort rubbish at home to aid recycling.

OECD

Similarly strong environmental feelings are being expressed worldwide. An OECD survey in 1987 demonstrated unanimous preference for environmental rather than economic governmental priority (see Table 4.12). Particularly strong environmental support comes from France (56%), and Denmark and Italy (both 55%) - all countries with strong green parties.

Table 4.12   WORLDWIDE CONSUMER ATTITUDES TO ENVIRONMENTAL PROTECTION VERSUS GROWTH 1987

%	Priority to environmental protection	Priority to economic growth	Both are possible	Don't know
Belgium	35	8	49	8
Denmark	55	3	30	12
Finland*1	47	11	35	7
France	56	11	29	4
Greece	47	12	23	18
Ireland	40	23	26	11
Italy	55	6	32	7
Japan*2	28	11	41	20
Luxembourg	65	6	28	1
Netherlands	45	9	40	6

Continued...

Table 4.12 cont'd

	Priority to environmental protection	Priority to economic growth	Both are possible	Don't know
Portugal	38	11	33	18
Spain	47	12	17	24
UK	48	11	32	9
USA*[3]	62	28	na	10
West Germany	50	3	41	6

Source: OECD Environment Survey 1987
Notes: na = question not asked
  * slightly different form of question asked
  [1] 1983 data
  [2] 1981 data
  [3] 1984 data

The OECD survey also wanted to gauge consumer reaction at three different levels: locally, nationally and internationally. As Table 4.13 shows, strongest local concerns tended to be waste disposal (Greece 22%, Italy 18%, Portugal 14%). National environmental concern ranges fairly equally between accidental damage to the marine environment, industrial waste disposal, and water and air pollution. Questions on nuclear waste disposal were not generally asked, although the USA (69% in 1984) and Finland (50% in 1983) were "very concerned". International problems were identified as the extinction of plants and animals (58% "very concerned" from Luxembourg), depletion of forests and natural resources (46% from Spain) and possible climate change brought about by carbon dioxide (48% from Luxembourg).

Eurobarometer

A Europe-wide survey of environmental questions was carried out in March/April 1986. Respondents were asked whether they saw pollution as an urgent and immediate problem. Across the 12 member states, 72% found it just that, with Italy, Greece, Luxembourg and West Germany showing the most concern in almost all areas. On environmental protection, all member states recorded "immediate and urgent problem" answers of over 55% to the question: "Protection of the environment is . . ." (see Figure 4.3).

Table 4.13   CONSUMER CONCERN ABOUT LOCAL, NATIONAL AND INTERNATIONAL ENVIRONMENT PROBLEMS 1987

% very concerned

	Local problems							National problems				International problems		
	A	B	C	D	E	F	G	H	I	J	K	L	M	N
Belgium	6	8	10	5	6	10	8	28	34	30	32	28	27	28
Denmark	2	2	4	2	3	4	3	52	55	51	43	47	44	44
Finland	2	na	14	–	7	17	7	48	46	26	21	38	41	29
France	5	10	12	8	7	8	8	45	44	41	38	42	30	36
Greece	16	11	18	22	11	20	17	48	40	39	46	35	33	38
Ireland	2	3	5	11	4	3	2	37	42	35	32	21	22	30
Italy	12	12	20	18	16	13	13	57	59	56	56	45	40	46
Japan	na	na	10	28	na	12	24	16	18	31	31	11	33	16
Luxembourg	3	10	22	9	5	15	11	48	47	52	50	58	36	48
Netherlands	3	4	9	8	3	4	4	49	54	47	51	47	33	28
Portugal	9	8	10	14	8	11	12	43	44	44	40	40	37	42
Spain	13	11	16	9	14	13	10	47	45	51	46	51	46	43
UK	4	6	9	7	4	4	5	41	49	36	30	43	40	37
USA	6	12	15	na	11	9	8	54	64	52	46	na	na	na
W Germany	4	4	8	3	4	8	6	38	39	34	36	38	26	32

Source: OECD Environment Survey 1987

Notes: na = Question not asked

Finland data 1983, Japan and USA data 1984

A = Loss of access to open space, B = Loss of good farmland, C = Deterioration of landscape, D = Waste disposal, E= Quality of drinking water, F = Air pollution, G = Noise, H = Accidental damage to marine environment, I =Industrial waste disposal, J = Water pollution, K = Air pollution, L = Extinction of some plant or animal species in the world, M = Depletion of world forests and natural resources, N = Possible climate changes brought about by carbon dioxide

Figure 4.3   European Consumers' Environmental Protection Priority 1986

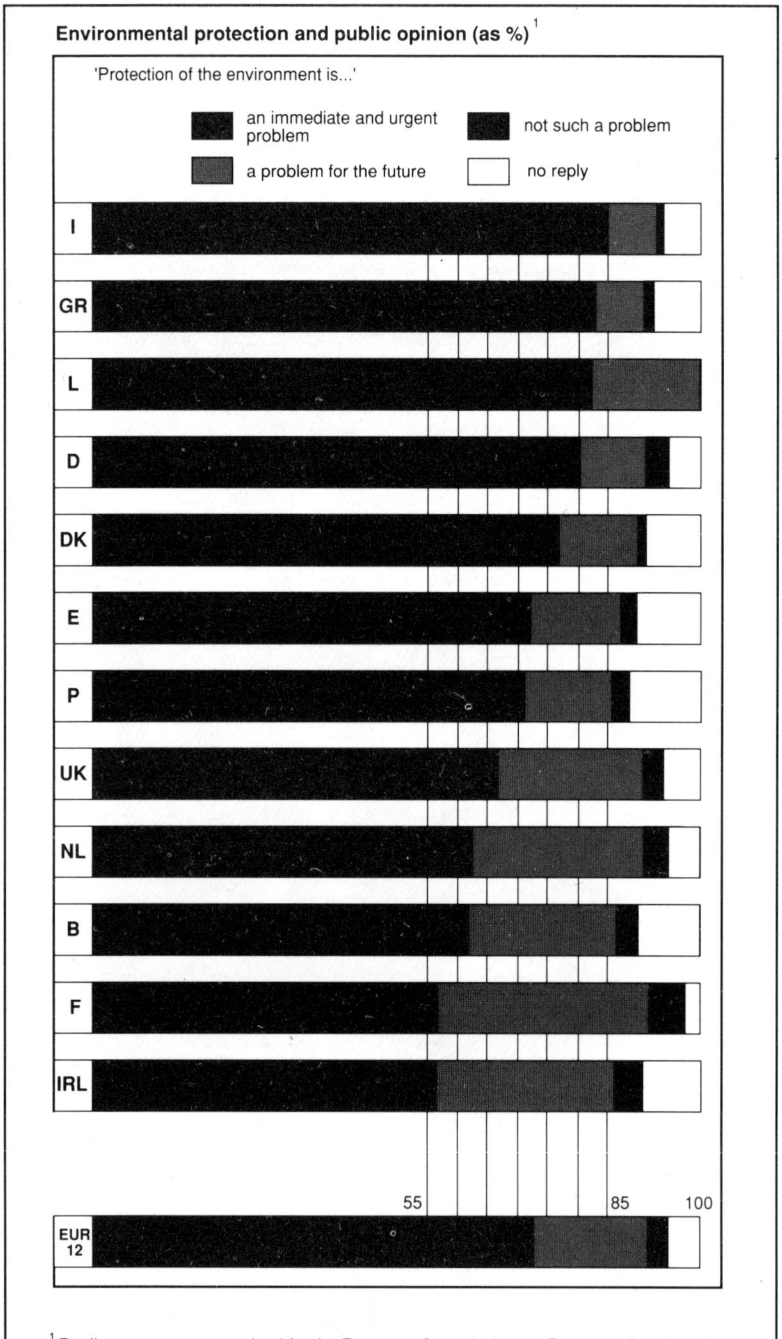

Environmental protection and public opinion (as %) [1]

'Protection of the environment is...'

- ■ an immediate and urgent problem
- ■ not such a problem
- ▨ a problem for the future
- □ no reply

I

GR

L

D

DK

E

P

UK

NL

B

F

IRL

55   85   100

EUR
12

[1] Replies to a survey organized for the European Commission by 'European Omnibus Survey' (11,840 people questioned throughout the Community in March-April 1986).

Who are the Green Consumers?

There are about 1,400 environmental groups in the UK, most of them acting as pressure groups to governments. Up to 3 million British people belong to one or more of these, so statistics are difficult to convert into trends. What is certain, however, is that paid-up membership of these organisations is growing fast. Greenpeace, for instance, reports that its membership (100,000) doubled in 18 months.

Britain's favourite conservation group is the National Trust, with 1.4 million members; the National Trust for Scotland has 150,000. The Royal Society for the Protection of Birds has 427,000 plus 102,000 young members. The Royal Society for Nature Conservation has 180,000 and the Worldwide Fund for Nature (previously the World Wildlife Fund) has 110,000 UK members. Friends of the Earth has 28,500+ members in the UK.

Environmental groups have long complained that although membership in the concerned 25+ age group is strong and getting stronger, there is a disappointing weakness in younger groups. Just what are the new generations, set firmly in their consumerist ways by their middle teens, thinking? How do their general attitudes affect their environmental concern?

The Youth Survey

Advertising agency McCann-Erickson updated a previous European youth attitudes study in 1987 by looking specifically at New Wavers (15-19s) and Baby Boomers (20-35s). The survey was conducted throughout Britain by Carrick James Market Research and 985 young people were questioned.

New Wavers are a very differently motivated group from their older brothers and sisters. Undeniably consumerist, when their responses to the survey are compared to those made ten years ago by the Baby Boomers (when *they* would have been the new generation), it is clear that today's group generally appear to believe more in the ideals of free market forces than in the more liberal concepts of the 1970s. For instance, New Wavers are much less inclined towards state control than their older colleagues either today or in 1977 (25% compared with the Baby Boomers' 33% in 1987 and 30% in 1977). Baby Boomers also care more for environmental protection (61% compared with 54%).

Over half the young people surveyed showed an awareness of the importance of healthy eating (Table 4.14), a major change from ten years ago. However, it seems to be a topic which can be pushed *too* far, with 54% of males claiming: "There's too much talk about healthy eating - I ignore it."

Table 4.14   YOUNG CONSUMERS' ATTITUDES TO HEALTHY EATING
1987

% agreeing

	Males	Females
If you don't pay attention to what you eat, you'll endanger your health	67	71
I tend to eat snacks, not main meals	49	46
I try to avoid additives	33	46
There's too much talk about healthy eating - I ignore it	54	35

Source: McCann-Erickson Youth Study 1987
*   base: 985 15-35 year olds*

Generally, it seems clear that the strong growth of the environment movement will attract forthcoming generations - but only if it appeals to them in terms the survey shows they understand best: money, goods, and style.

Environmental Campaigns

Campaigners are aware that the green consumer has highly developed demands and, coupled with a well-informed and efficiently presented basis for concern, these can be harnessed most effectively.

Environmental consumer campaigns have included the following.

Anti-Fur Trade

In 1973 anti-fur-trade campaigners took the issue into the high streets of Britain and Europe, picketing shops and distributing leaflets. This resulted in a total ban on tiger, leopard and cheetah products.

Save the Whale

A worldwide save-the-whale campaign also enlisted the support of the British shopper. As a result, in 1982 the EC banned the trade of whale products. (The impact and long-term effects of the subsequent worldwide whaling ban are dealt with in detail in Section 3.2.)

The Dirty Dozen

An international dangerous pesticides campaign was organised by the Pesticides Action Network (PAN) with support from Friends of the Earth. A list of the world's 12 most toxic agrochemicals was prepared, with details of their immediate and feared long-term effects on health. Shoppers were urged to boycott suspect substances and lobby for more comprehensive testing, restriction and, where appropriate, banning.

Food Additives

A long-running campaign urges consumers to reject any foodstuffs with unnecessary additives, and to question closely suppliers of fresh foods about possible chemical residues. The growing commitment to organic produce is now recognised by two organic standards systems.

Good Wood Guide

Friends of the Earth is working with its international sister organisation to bring consumer power to bear on the intensifying crisis facing the world's dwindling rain forests. It issues a list of wood product outlets using alternatives to endangered wood species and also has a "black list" of offending retailers. The British National Association of Retail Furnishers co-operates fully and the International Timber Trade Federation has approved in principle a code of conduct. Conservation groups around the world have helped WWF establish the International Tropical Timber Association, which has a primary aim of conserving and encouraging the sustainable use of tropical forests.

CFC Aerosol Boycott

This is claimed to be one of the most recent FoE campaign success stories. At the end of 1987 the organisation published 20,000 leaflets listing CFC-free and therefore "safe" UK aerosol products. It earned enormous publicity and attained a very high profile with consumers.

As far reaching scientific evidence about the damaging effects of CFCs on the ozone layer increased pressure during the early part of 1988, the UK government agreed to sign the Montreal Protocol, limiting production through the 1990s. A number of aerosol products started carrying "Ozone Friendly" and "No CFC" labels. In February 1988 Britain's eight largest aerosol manufacturers pledged to phase out CFCs by the end of 1989. The consumer awareness campaign continues, with other CFC products such as fast-food foam packaging and refrigerants coming under the microscope. There are political moves both to speed up and extend the Montreal Protocol requirements to attempt to reduce or even eliminate CFC use as soon as possible.

Environmental campaigns have a proven record against industry but, invariably, become major issues only when there has been a breakdown in communications between the environmentalists and industrialists. But confrontation is no longer acceptable business practice. There is instead growing acknowledgement of the benefits of working with the environmentalists, at the very least in tandem with if not ahead of the green consumer.

4.3 GROWTH OF ETHICAL INVESTMENT

In May 1987 the value of "socially screened" US securities was put at over $350 billion. In addition to private investors, 23 states, 91 cities and counties, 140 universities and colleges and an unknown number of foundations were applying screened investment policies.

Elsewhere in the world the ethical investment movement is only just beginning. In the UK the seminal ethical unit trust movement was worth around £100 million at the start of 1988. To this figure must be added the investment funds of individuals operating under their own personal ethical constraints and the huge sums controlled by religious and charitable organisations. The Church Commissioners of the Church of England, for example, have total assets in excess of £2 billion, while the Central Board of Finance of the Church of England runs three funds, of which the investment fund (investing directly in company shares) alone was worth £210 million at the end of 1986.

Banks will become increasingly involved, from the World Bank down to the high street. On 5 May 1987 Barber Conable, president of the World Bank, made a speech in which he said that "sound ecology is good economics". He admitted that environmental critics of the World Bank had often been right, conceded that the Bank had "stumbled" and mentioned the now notorious Polonoroeste project in Brazil as an example. In the high street pressure has already begun. The Ethical Investment Fund (£2.7 million in October 1987), for example, will not invest in banks: "All banks are excluded as their main business is to take deposits in order to lend money in return for interest. We are unable to obtain sufficient information on the companies, organisations or institutions to which banks lend money."

So far, the ethical movement may be small - and the environmental movement only a tiny part of that - but just as bull and bear markets tend to be self-fulfilling, so the leverage exerted by an ethical constraint on finance can be out of all proportion to the size. Thus of the many channels through which environmental pressure is building on companies, finance is potentially the most muscular.

There is an irony in the fact that the ethical investment movement has accelerated through the South Africa issue, a few companies' intransigence over which has led to the scrutiny of many on a wider range of issues. Much of the US socially screened investment represents divestment from South Africa, but environmental criteria have been added. The Calvert Social Investment Fund, for example, specifically avoids nuclear power and seeks protection of the natural environment. The New Alternative Fund is primarily interested in investment in alternative energy such as solar cells, conservation systems, solar architectural products and natural gas. Nuclear power and oil companies are avoided because they are not considered profitable.

Table 4.15 shows the size of some US mutual and money market funds at the end of 1986. A growing number of investment managers and brokers are also beginning to offer clients research into the ethical position of corporations.

Table 4.15   ETHICAL MANAGED FUNDS IN THE USA 1986

$ million assets at 31 December

Mutual funds	
Calvert Social Investment	121.5
Dreyfus Third Century	153.5
New Alternatives	2.4

Continued...

Table 4.15 cont'd

Mutual funds

Parnassus Fund	3.3
Pax World	53.8
TOTAL	334.5

Money market funds

Calvert Money Market	59.8
South Shore Bank Development Deposit Portfolio	46.0
Working Assets Fund	96.6
TOTAL	202.4

Investment managers and brokers

Barlett & Co	31.4
Franklin Research	107.5
Shearson Lehman	38.0
US Trust	280.0
Smaller investment managers	163.6
TOTAL	620.5

Source: Ethical Investment Fund

UK Funds

In some cases the ethical position of a company is its prime attraction to investors. In the UK, for example, Traidcraft plc's first share issue in 1984 was oversubscribed despite the "commitment to just trading and to the well-being of the weak and disadvantaged, rather than profits" and to dividends "restricted to no more than 5%" in its business of importing goods made by Third World groups. In 1987 Traidcraft's second public share issue, for 1 million non-voting shares at £1.15 each, was oversubscribed.

In the case of Traidcraft, charitable feeling was uppermost but Table 4.16 shows the US Trust Company finding that its socially screened accounts performed roughly as well as its other accounts.

Table 4.16   PERFORMANCE OF US TRUST COMPANY SOCIALLY
              SCREENED ACCOUNTS 1984-1986

% growth	1984	1985	1986 [1]
Socially screened accounts	9.5	27.6	13.1
Discretionary balanced accounts	11.8	28.3	14.1
Dow Jones industrial average	1.4	33.7	18.8

Source: US Trust Company
Note: [1] *First quarter only*

Indeed this newly perceived profitability of environmental investment must lead to its growth. In *Socially Responsible Investment* author Sue Ward sets out the financial argument: "A socially responsible portfolio, for instance, will possibly not include companies that pollute the atmosphere or manufacture products that carry health risks, and so well might not be vulnerable to massive court cases for damages when society catches up with these concerns." There are a growing number of companies whose alleged or proven damage to the environment has seriously impacted their performance and their attraction to investors. In the US Manville, the asbestos manufacturer, has been obliged to set up a $2.5 billion trust fund, requiring up to 20% of profits; the full penalty of the Bhopal disaster on Union Carbide has yet to be determined; in the UK the share price of Turner and Newall fell suddenly after a television programme about the company's involvement with asbestos was screened.

Stewardship Unit Trust

Indeed, Friends' Provident emphasises the performance of its Stewardship Unit Trust (Figure 4.4) as much as its effort "to avoid investing in companies that are involved in any way with armaments, gambling, alcohol or tobacco or have interests in countries with oppressive regimes or dictatorships". The Trust seeks funds on the basis that it "has consistently out-performed traditional forms of savings such as banks and building societies" and beaten the Financial Times Actuaries All-Share index. Where does it invest? "In companies with a proven track record in good labour relations, with healthy attitudes towards the environment, pollution control, use of natural resources and whose products and services provide a real contribution to society both here and overseas."

Figure 4.4   Stewardship Unit Trust Performance 1984-1987

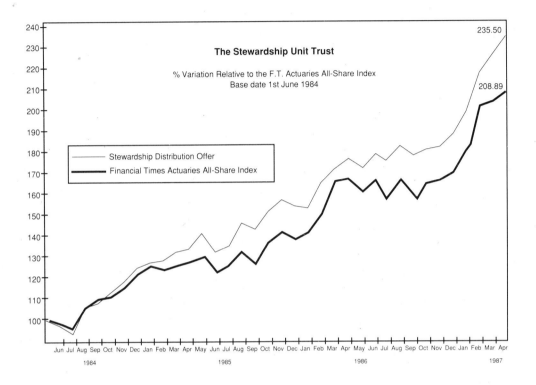

Source: Friends' Provident Unit Trust Managers

The Stewardship Unit Trust was the first socially screened account and remains the largest in the UK (Table 4.17). Although not specifically environmental it has a definite environmental bias. Second in importance at the end of 1987 was Fidelity Famous Names Trust, a "single issue" fund which avoids tobacco companies "because of the widespread concern within the medical profession regarding the harmful effects of smoking on health". Again, Fidelity is not specifically environmental but there are many who do see tobacco as an environmental as much as a health issue. David Simpson, director of ASH, calls it one of "the most important environmental issues of our time" (see Part Two, *Issue: Smoking*).

Table 4.17   ETHICAL FUNDS IN THE UK 1987

	Established	Size (£ million)
Stewardship Unit Trust	1.6.84	70.0 [1]
Fidelity Famous Names Trust	24.6.85	16.9
Ethical Investment Fund	January 1986	2.7
Fellowship Trust	7.7.86	4.3 [1]
Ethical Personal Equity Plan	15.9.87	–
Ethical Trust	3.10.87	3.6 [1]
Conscience Fund	9.10.87	5.0
Stewardship Income Trust	2.11.87	–
Stewardship North American Trust	2.11.87	–
Target Global Opportunities	6.11.87	–
TOTAL		102.5

Source: Ethical Investment Research Service (EIRIS)
Note: [1] *Following stock market crash of 19 October 1987*

Conscience Fund

The trust that was most specifically environmental by the end of 1987 was the Conscience Fund, significantly perhaps third in size at around £5 million although the seventh to be launched in the UK. The idea of a more environmental fund was floated by the Conservation Foundation, the charity headed by David Bellamy, and taken up by NM Schroder. The Conscience Fund:

> looks for companies that are aware of the environment and actively help to look after it . . . also those companies that are involved in community welfare, look after their employees properly, participate in local enterprise, give money to charity . . . We avoid companies who produce tobacco, alcohol, armaments, do research on live animals, promote gambling or who are closely linked to oppressive regimes.

The Fund has a validation panel which, at the end of 1987, consisted of David Bellamy, James Rowland, ex-Oxfam and accountant of New Internationalist Publications, and Steve Robinson of the Commonwealth Institute. Several other funds operate advisory boards or ethical committees as well. While often reluctant to publicise the names of companies that have been ruled unethical, all the funds publish their portfolios and thus perhaps cause some knock-on effect.

Questions Posed for Business

For the businessman the ethical investment movement raises a number of questions:

1. Can influential bodies like unit trusts and pension funds legally "black" my company?
2. Will anybody know whether business is "ethical" or not?
3. As a private company, surely I'm divorced from "ethical" pressures anyway?
4. Given all the ethical ambiguities, the problems of balancing portfolios and the overriding desire to make money, will the ethical investment movement really become significant?

Some of these questions have already been touched on but deserve more detailed consideration.

The Legal Position

Individuals can obviously invest their money as they wish. The real question mark hangs over pension funds and similar types of investment on behalf of others (trusts). In this the 1984 case concerning the Trustees of the Mineworkers' Pension Scheme seems to exemplify the general position. In his judgement, Sir Robert Megarry had this to say:

> I am not asserting that the benefit of the beneficiaries which a trustee must make his paramount concern inevitably and solely means their financial benefit, even if the sole object of the trust is to provide financial benefits. Thus if the only actual or potential beneficiaries of a trust are all adults with very strict views on moral and social matters, condemning all forms of alcohol, tobacco and popular entertainment, as well as armaments, I can well understand that it might not be for the "benefit" of such beneficiaries to know that they are obtaining rather larger financial returns under the trust than they would have received if the trustees had invested the trust funds in other investments. The

beneficiaries might well consider that it was far better to receive less than to receive money from what they consider to be evil or tainted sources. "Benefit" is a word with very wide meaning and there are circumstances in which arrangements which work to the financial disadvantage of a beneficiary may yet be for his benefit.

The Mineworkers' case did not change the law in Britain but this statement of the legal position is the one on which environmentalists increasingly rely, even though other aspects of the judgement were less favourable to them. What seems beyond dispute is that trustees can always favour an ethical investment over an equivalent non-ethical investment. In the case of ethical unit trusts, the fund managers are, of course, specifically instructed to favour even those giving a *lower* rate of return.

The Ethical Investment Research Service (EIRIS) has recently published guidance on trust deeds and suggested that legal complications would not arise if the example of the Christendom Trust is followed, namely that trustees be given "the same full and free unrestricted powers of investment and of changing and transposing investments as if they were absolutely entitled to the trust fund beneficially".

In respect of charities, the National Council of Voluntary Organisations in the UK has consulted the Chief Charity Commissioner, Denis Peach, and been given the opinion that trust law allows trustees to set aside purely financial considerations in investment matters if they would otherwise lose support.

For investors there are often undoubted legal complications, but public limited companies should simply be aware that there are many cases in which groups as well as individuals can restrict their investment on ethical grounds.

Who knows if the Business is Ethical?

The answer to this question comes in two parts. First, companies that feel their environmental record is good are proclaiming it in advertising and public relations. The mere failure to project a positive environmental image may of itself be counterproductive in a competitive environment.

Furthermore, companies' environmental performance is coming under increasingly detailed scrutiny from campaigning organisations, which then feed that information back to trade unions, consumers and consumer organisations, validation panels and legislators. In many countries information is easily available about companies' charitable and political donations made by companies, their involvement in South Africa, defence contracts, nuclear power, animal experiments, tobacco and in specific environmental problems such as pesticides, CFCs and tropical hardwoods.

The ethical funds have their own methods, sometimes probing very deep when stung by public criticism, more usually simply relying on a company's own published reports. The Conscience Fund, for example, employes two in-house researchers; others rely on "close contacts with the trade union movement" or "contact with Labour Research Council and Friends of the Earth". Many charities as well as ethical funds rely on EIRIS, which was established in 1983 with the financial support of the Joseph Rowntree Charitable Trust, the Joseph Rowntree Social Service Trust, the Methodist Church World Development Fund, the Society of Friends (Quakers), the Church of England Board of Social Responsibility, the Presbyterian Church in Ireland, the Church in Wales and Oxfam.

The range of issues currently examined by EIRIS includes animals (meat production and sale, leather/fur manufacture and sale); arms and sales to military purchasers; nuclear power (fuel, components and construction of plants); South Africa/Namibia; tobacco. EIRIS reports on "major UK companies and each individual factsheet gives basic details of the company's involvement in the areas outlined". The environment as a specific issue will be covered in the future; meanwhile major investors can request it as a bespoke service.

Individuals can also use EIRIS. Alternatively, they can increasingly obtain ethical information from their own stockbrokers, especially portfolio managers such as Lancashire & Yorkshire.

Another more recently set up ethical research service is the Pensions and Investment Resource Centre (PIRC), established in 1986 by a number of local authorities. Local government superannuation funds amount to £13 billion.

In the USA research is even easier to come by, begun as a result of the Vietnam war and fuelled by South Africa. Not only is there a wide range of ethical unit-linked investments and ethical portfolio managers (like Franklin Research and Development Corporation) but also an organisation to promote ethical investment: the Social Investment Forum, set up in Boston in 1985. Membership includes analysts, advisers and banks as well as the full spectrum of investors from individuals to profit-making corporations to charities.

Franklin Research and Development was founded in 1981 and its stance is seen very much as seeking opportunities that are, if anything, enhanced by being socially responsive. By contrast, the Interfaith Center on Corporate Responsibility puts primary emphasis on ethics, its areas of research including pesticides and pharmaceuticals, nuclear weapons, energy and specific problems related to investment in Asia and Latin America. The long-established Council for Economic Priorities researches and publishes reports on the human impact of corporate and government activity. Its special areas of interest include air and water pollution, toxic waste disposal, nuclear energy and the behaviour of US companies overseas.

i *Small Companies*

Small companies generally tend to be insulated from specific investigation since their shares are not publicly quoted or traded and the legal requirements on disclosure of information are less far-reaching. As the green movement develops, however, so the old system of prioritising national and international issues by leading activists diminishes and is replaced by more locally generated, grassroots concerns. Small companies will increasingly become the target of local groups.

Is Green Investment Significant?

EIRIS has few illusions about the impact of its work so far. "Companies are not the slightest bit bothered." Those choosing to ignore the ethical investment movement do so on several grounds. They believe, first, the level of feeling is low; second, that no effective mechanism exists to translate such feelings as there are into action; third, that financial considerations will always outweigh ethical feelings.

There are signs, however, that these feelings are giving way to recognition that green investment could become a force to be reckoned with. Several ethical funds now report approaches by companies omitted from the approved investment list

The first cause for concern is the profile of the ethical investor. Investors in an active sense (as opposed to life assurance etc) tend to be those who are also more likely to be concerned about environment issues. The Ethical Investment Fund, for example, conducted a survey of existing investors and enquirers (see Tabel 4.18) and found that two-thirds lived in the prosperous South of England and a further 10% overseas, as opposed to less than 30% from the more depressed North.

Table 4.18   PROFILE OF ETHICAL INVESTMENT FUND INVESTORS
1987

	Existing investors	Enquirers
Residence (%)		
South England	64.5	60.7
North England	22.7	28.1
Overseas	12.8	11.0
Sex (%)		
Male	26.2	
Female	41.8	–
Couples	31.9	
Age (%)		
75+	10.0	
65–74	24.0	
55–64	30.0	–
45–54	23.0	
35–44	33.0	
34 and under	21.0	
Average investment (£)		
Male	7,990	
Female	8,101	–
Couples	8,782	

Source: Ethical Investment Fund

The only major difference from a profile of UK investors in general is the higher percentage of female investors (58% including couples), reflecting what is generally considered to be women's greater concern about ethics and the environment.

A 1987 profile of FoE members in the UK (Table 4.19) reveals a similar level of investment potential. Some 49% were in the 35–64 age groups and 13% over 65; 70% have received tertiary education. The biggest single identifiable group is teachers/lecturers at 16%.

Table 4.19   PROFILE OF FRIENDS OF THE EARTH UK MEMBERSHIP
1987

Ratio of women:men	50:48
Age (%)	
65+	13
55-64	7
35-54	42
25-34	29
17-24	9
Tertiary education (%)	70
Teachers lecturers (%)	16
Guardian readership (%)	54
Observer readership (%)	47

Source: FoE/BJM Research

In his preface to *Socially Responsible Investment*, Michael Norton concludes that "a lot of radical groups are involved, [but] a lot of the more conservative groups are too - particularly church organisations and some charities". On the topic of groups, Norton continues: "One investor can have very little impact. Acting together, concerned investors can achieve change."

Tower Hamlets International Solidarity and Tower Hamlets Trade Union Council took much the same view in 1985 in their pamphlet "Pulling Out from Apartheid: A Guide for Action":

Individually our powers are limited . . . As members of groups, however, as trade unionists, *subscribers to pension funds*, members of voluntary or church organisations or as ratepayers and voters, our voices are amplified. In such capacities we have the chance to question and direct the way organisations with much larger resources use and direct them . . .

Socially Responsible Investment presages an increase in shareholder action: "Companies should expect investors to show concern. Indeed, as we enter an era of people's capitalism through wider share ownership, they should not be surprised if some wish to exercise their democratic rights as shareholders by questioning on occasion what the company is doing."

In the USA it is calculated that in 1986 shareholder action on ethical issues resulted in 60 major corporations being lobbied at their annual general meetings. All the UK ethical funds say that they listen seriously to representations by concerned investors. The Ethical Investment Fund's stance was the most dynamic of all: "The issue will be reviewed that day and if valid against our criteria will be sold immediately."

The EIRIS Church of England Study

Many companies take comfort from the belief that it is not possible to have a portfolio that is both ethical and balanced. Consequently they believe major investors like pension funds must necessarily eschew ethical considerations. EIRIS has done much to dispel this myth. In 1987 it published *Ethical Investment Dilemmas: The Church of England as a Case Study*. At that time the Church Commissioners and the Central Board of Finance were between them investing £700 million in UK equities.

In its paper GS Misc 259 the Central Board states that it has since 1958

> excluded on ethical grounds certain categories of investment (breweries, tobacco, gambling, armaments, S. Africa) from which it was felt that it would not be appropriate for church trusts to draw income . . . This policy was justified in legal terms because these exclusions amounted to only a small part (about 10%) of the available UK equity market. It was considered that this would not affect long-term financial growth and it was therefore acceptable within the trust law principle of the best financial interests of the beneficiaries.

The Central Board believes the exclusion of 10% on ethical grounds does not constrain prospects. But it *has* warned of going beyond that proportion:

To make further disinvestments of major holdings would:

a) reduce diversification
b) unbalance the portfolio
c) inhibit the ability to generate increased income in future years and
d) limit the marketability of the assets of an open-ended fund which has to meet monthly withdrawals.

EIRIS calls this "a City-eye view of an ethical problem" and contends that any investor can go well beyond 10%. In avoiding South Africa, it should be pointed out, the Central Board had excluded only "direct investment in South Africa . . . and companies with a significant proportion of their income (profits) coming from South Africa".

EIRIS set out to quantify the cost of lost opportunities by making major ethical exclusions and concluded that it was negligible: the expected loss would be no more than 0.08% a year, taking both income and capital gain into account. However, the model assumed that companies excluded were "neither particularly better nor particularly worse" than others. EIRIS points out that ethical investments may actually perform better than average, and cites the Stewardship Unit Trust - placed 18 out of 80 general unit trusts for the three years to 1 June 1987.

Table 4.20 shows the companies that the Central Board is believed to have already specifically withdrawn from or excluded. On the EIRIS figures it could also exclude the 34 companies in which it was investing at 31 October 1986 which had South African interests, without loss of financial performance. South Africa is not seen as an environment issue, and is not therefore strictly within the scope of this book. EIRIS does point out, however, that its study looks at "what happens when large investors are concerned about an ethical issue . . . many of the points made could be translated very easily into a debate about other ethical or social issues".

Table 4.20   COMPANIES THE CENTRAL BOARD IS BELIEVED BY EIRIS TO HAVE EXCLUDED ON ETHICAL GROUNDS FOR INVESTMENT 1987

	Probable reason	Percentage Stock Exchange (2.4.87)
FT Breweries Sector	Alcohol	4.37
Northern Engineering Industries	South Africa	0.06
Ferranti	Armaments	0.14
British Aerospace	Armaments	0.44
Delta Group	South Africa	0.10
Babcock International	South Africa	0.07
Ladbroke Group	Gambling	0.29

Continued...

Table 4.20 cont'd

	Probable reason	Percentage Stock Exchange (2.4.87)
BAT Industries	Tobacco	2.19
Rothmans International	Tobacco	0.17
Rio Tinto Zinc	South Africa	0.70
Consolidated Goldfields	South Africa	0.55
TOTAL		9.08

Source: EIRIS

Privatisation

The issue of privatisation in the UK shows exactly what can happen when an industry insulated from the need to raise commercial investment faces the full glare of investor scrutiny over the environmental implications of its policies.

At the end of 1987 the UK government announced its thinking on the privatisation of the electricity industry. Energy Secretary Cecil Parkinson was said to favour compelling a privatised industry to produce 20-25% of its electricity from nuclear sources, leading the *Guardian*'s Energy Correspondent John Hooper to write that:

> The Energy Secretary knows as well as anyone that no businessman, left to his own devices, would put his shareholders' money into nuclear power. Even leaving aside the vast cost of building a reactor, the historically high risk that it will not be completed on schedule and to budget, the unknown cost of dismantling it when it reaches the end of its life and the ruinous debts his firm would incur if it blew up, the fact is that - in Britain - nuclear power has not delivered the cheap energy it promised.

The link between the environment and investment, then, is not merely one of ethics. It is often equally a matter of profit. Investors may increasingly come to believe that sound environmental management and sound business management are inextricably linked.

The Banks

What, though, of other sources of finance open to companies? Investors may be becoming progressively greener but what of banks?

As has already been mentioned, not even banks are immune to green pressure, which they in turn transmit through their lending policies. The International Bank for Reconstruction and Development (the World Bank) has recently been at some pains to improve its environmental image. It remains to be seen how profound a change there will be in reality - many environmentalists believe the World Bank to have been the most destructive force the world has yet seen.

Two examples will illustrate why environmentalists feel as they do and why the World Bank has therefore felt obliged to revise its policy. In the early 1980s the Bank approved six loans totalling $443.4 million for the Brazil Northwest Development Programme (Polonoroeste), involving the construction of a 1,500 km highway and 39 settlements in the Amazon basin. As a consequence, the rate of deforestation has been the highest in Brazil, some Indian tribes face extermination through introduced disease and a huge but unquantifiable number of plants and animals have been made extinct.

In Indonesia the World Bank, together with the Asian Development Bank, has lent more than $1 billion to transmigrate millions of people from the inner to the once densely forested outer islands. The impact on the outer islands is, once again, deforestation leading to species extinction, soil erosion and flooding.

Even the Bank's hydro projects have often proved themselves damaging to the environment and in the longer term ineffective, leading to salinisation of irrigated land, climatic changes and the spread of waterborne diseases.

At the opposite end of the banking spectrum, some new-style financiers are emerging, such as Mercury Provident, described as "a financial channel to encourage and facilitate socially beneficial enterprises", and Industrial Common Ownership Finance, through which "people can lend financial support to the development of worker co-operatives". In the USA in 1987 Edward Feighan introduced a Bill to Congress to convert 10% of US overseas aid into low-interest loans for human-scale projects, the model being the so-called "village banking" in El Salvador. The latter is a joint initiative of the Arizona-based Foundation for International Community Assistance and the Save the Children Fund, providing small loans for local enterprises. In the four years to 1987 a bank in Dominica financed 2,700 projects averaging $300 each to help poor people start small businesses.

Organisations such as co-operative societies are particularly vulnerable to grassroots pressure. In 1979 the environmental body M-Fruhling was set up to attempt control of the 1.3-million-member Migros co-operative, Switzerland's biggest retailer. In 1987 the 16,000 members of M-Fruhling and their supporters received 20% of the votes. In 1988 the association was planning a further attempt on Migros in eastern Switzerland, aiming to "take over the majority of seats in the directing board and in the co-op's council". If successful M-Fruhling would aim to reverse the trend towards fewer, larger outlets, in order to reduce traffic, and would introduce a buying policy that paid attention to "the environment, the third world, animals, small farmers, public health, pollution, waste and other socially and ecologically oriented propositions".

4.4 THE ENVIRONMENTAL EMPLOYEE

Four environment-related issues in particular consistently preoccupy sections of the workforce in many countries: peace, and especially the use of nuclear weapons; nuclear power; hazardous wastes; pesticides.

Peace

The peace movement is one of the most intriguing in its implications because it involves a group of employees generally dissociated from militant trade union activity - that is, scientists, electronics engineers and programmers. In Britain the focus for the disaffected in the eletronics and computer industries is Electronics and Computing for Peace, together with its associated employment agency Exchange Resources, which was set up in 1986 for non-defence work. Director Tony Wilson says the aim is to "bring together like-minded people and businesses who want to operate outside the military-industrial complex".

Is peace an environmental issue? According to Mostafa Kamal Tolba, Executive Director of UNEP, the answer is emphatically "yes". In his 1982 statement to the UN General Assembly Special Session Devoted to Disarmament he spelt out what he saw as the environmental impact both of the use of weapons and of the manufacture of weapons:

> Wars of the past have had both direct and indirect effects on the environment. They changed agriculture, shifted the margins of deserts and grossly disturbed the balance of ecosystems . . . Chemical and biological weapons involve deliberate pollution by the release of toxic chemicals or harmful microorganisms . . . In Vietnam, chemical

154

herbicides completely destroyed 1,500 square kilometres of mangrove forest and caused some damage to a further 15,000 square kilometres; natural recovery is proceeding at a disturbingly slow rate . . . Even if not one single bullet was to be fired in anger, the arms race would still be causing damage to the environment. The Stockholm Conference recognised, and the Nairobi conference endorsed the view that the gravest threat to our environment is posed by poverty resulting from underdevelopment . . . With a reversal of priorities, it would become possible to deal with the appalling poverty, scarcities and environment degradation so prevalent in the world today. Real security can only come when nations co-operate to exploit equitably, wisely and sustainably this planet's dwindling treasure of natural resources.

Neither Electronics and Computing for Peace, which had a membership of around 400 at the end of 1987, nor Exchange Resources could be described as substantial. However, there is evidence that they are the visible tip of a more significant "ethical employment" movement in Britain.

In January 1986 *Electronics Times* published a questionnaire on ethics. There were 150 responses, undoubtedly weighted towards the peace movement. However, the results (Table 4.21) are still thought-provoking, suggesting a significant feeling against defence work by those in the electronics industry. Of the respondents, 45% said they would reject military sector employment on moral grounds and 30% said they had actually refused a job because of its military content; 57% said they would prefer their companies to have no defence work. Nearly half the respondents identified themselves as aged 20-30, 30% were aged 30-40 and only 6% were over 50; 59% worked in companies with 200-5,000 employees, and 57% had a BSc/BA.

Table 4.21   EMPLOYMENT AND THE PEACE MOVEMENT 1986

%

If you were looking for a job, and were offered
a post with favourable conditions in the military
sector, would you:

Accept?	29
Accept if no offer outside military?	26
Reject on moral grounds?	45

Continued...

Table 4.21 cont'd

Have you ever refused a job because of:
a)   Its military content?

Yes	30
No	55
Depends on exact nature of job	11

b)   Other ethical considerations?

Yes	6
No	72

Which of the following would you be prepared
to work on?

a) Nuclear and other weapons	22
b) Other military systems such as aircraft	41
c) Non-military systems such as police computers and civil nuclear work	76

Should British companies become involved with work
that is connected with the Strategic Defence Initiative?

Yes	39
No	56

Does your company have a significant defence business?

None	44
Under 10%	20
10-25%	13
25-50%	7
50-100%	14

How much would you like it to be?

None	57
Under 10%	9
10-25%	11
25-50%	9
50-100%	6

Source: Electronics for Peace Newsletter following publication of questionnaire
        in Electronics Times

Tony Wilson is convinced that there is a clear trend towards ethical consideration among job hunters. "Many graduates don't want to go into anything not socially useful," he believes. "I have worked for companies doing

MOD contracts. My experience is that half the people in defence don't like what they're doing."

Pesticides

The ability of any trade union to mobilise its members on environment issues is controlled by perceptions of both short- and long-term employment impact. It seems that many would rather risk their health than their jobs.

In Britain the Transport and General Workers Union has long been active on the pesticides issue, yet has taken a very soft approach. According to the TGWU Health and Safety Specialist Peter Hurst: "Clearly there is contradiction between the members' need for employment and possible environmental practices but in reality this is not irresolvable as practical co-operation on the pesticide issue has shown." The document *The Trade Union Perspective On Pesticides*, prepared by Peter Hurst, demonstrates the dilemma unions believe themselves to be in:

> Banning pesticides, restricting their manufacture, use, export, the promotion of alternative crop production systems such as organic farming, "low input" agriculture, integrated pest management, biotechnological pest control etc - all these factors clearly have job implications.

> The danger is that if the question of alternatives is not tackled sensitively and in a non-threatening way, then unions and their members - especially in areas such as pesticide manufacture, formulation and even use - may well mistakenly adopt a purely defensive attitude to proposals for alternative production and jobs and say - "you're threatening our jobs". This would make it much harder for groups campaigning for the phasing out of pesticides to win their case.

It would seem, then, that on a straight environment versus jobs issue, employers have little to fear from the unions. However, such an assumption overlooks, first, the growing belief that tighter environment controls will increase employment in the longer term and, second, the more subtle campaign the unions are adopting. Paragraph 4 of the TU Perspective continues:

> As well as treating pesticide control in organisational terms - perhaps a traditional role of trade unions - there has been a growing emphasis on trade unions widening their perspective to see themselves as part of a wider pesticide campaign. The aim here being to influence and enlist public opinion and support to improve pesticide safety standards not

only in the work place but in the wider community and environment as well. Indeed to help break down the arbitrary division between a "union member" and "member of the public" as though they are two distinct beings. This has meant demonstrating that the trade union perspective is not solely concerned with their own members' health and safety but also with the general health of the environment; with problems faced by communities with pesticides factories in them or a rural community affected by crop spraying; with the problem of pesticide residues in food and water and in the food chain generally; with the disastrous effects of uncontrolled pesticide exports to developing countries, and with the need to campaign for full freedom of information on pesticides.

Other unions involved in the Perspective are the GMB, NUPE, ASTMS and USDAW while UCATT (members using wood preservatives in building and construction) and the Fire Brigades Union (members dealing with pesticides fires and spillages) are also affected.

While farm workers in Britain see themselves as particularly vulnerable to job losses - *Directions for Change: Land Use in the 1990s*, published by the National Economic Development Office, predicts a contraction of the agriculture industry - the labour movement in general is increasingly susceptible to the environment argument.

Environmental Controls and Employment

In January 1987 Labour MP David Clark produced his second interim report, "Jobs and the Environment", and concluded that 200,000 additional jobs would be created if Britain were to adopt similar environment policies to the Netherlands and the USA. These jobs could come over a two-to-three-year period, half in the pollution control field (especially combating acid rain) and the remainder in a variety of fields including energy conservation, cleaning up rivers and beaches, urban environment improvements, rural tourism and the enhancement of wildlife and the landscape in the countryside.

As far back as 1983 the Association for the Conservation of Energy and Environmental Resources published a study suggesting that a programme of loft insulation, draught-proofing, wall insulation and double glazing could create between 50,000 and 128,000 jobs over a ten-year period. The investment was estimated at between £10 and £24.5 billion with consequent energy savings of between £1.4 and £2.8 billion a year. In nature conservation (and in related education/publishing) the Dartington Institute for the NCC estimates that 14,250 jobs could be created.

All this tends to support the David Clark view, although critics have pointed to weaknesses. The UK Centre for Economic and Environmental Development, an organisation which aims to act as a bridge between environmentalists and industry, observes that pollution control technology is already dominated by the USA and by Japan, making a late UK attack difficult. The CBI's Environment Committee also remains unimpressed.

Dr Malcolm MacGarvin, who worked with Clark, was also the author of the 1987 Greenpeace report, *Will Environmental Measures Force Companies Abroad?*. That report concluded that such fears were "groundless", largely because the costs of waste disposal were already much higher in many alternative countries than in the UK. The report also noted that where environmental controls are greater than in the UK, the economic benefits have outweighed the losses.

The American Experience

Figure 4.5   Impact on US Unemployment of Different Environment Policies 1970-1987

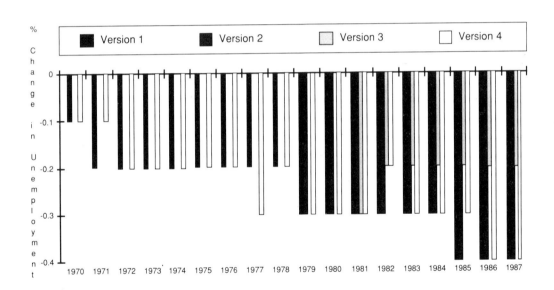

Source: *"Impact of Environmental Measures on Growth, Productivity, Inflation and Trade"*
Notes: *Version 1 - High profile environment policy*
        Version 2 - Alternative high profile environment policy
        Version 3 - Loosening environmental controls from 1981
        Version 4 - Tight fiscal policy

The USA has some of the best and longest-based data on the relationship between environmental protection and jobs.

Over the period 1971-83, the Environmental Protection Agency found that 33,000 workers were dismissed in 155 factory closures in which anti-pollution controls were implicated. The evidence for job creation, however, overwhelms this. *Cost and Impact of Environmental Control Investments* by Management Information Services, Washington (1986), says that 167,000 jobs have been created in pollution abatement, an industry said to be worth $70 billion in 1985.

"Impact of Environmental Measures on Growth, Productivity, Inflation and Trade" (OECD, 1984) examined the impact of environmental measures on the US economy between 1970 and 1980 and made forecasts for 1981-87 based on four different policies. The data in Figure 4.5 suggest that any relaxation of environmental controls would have a *detrimental* impact on US unemployment. Environmental controls would seem to be capable of reducing unemployment by 0.4%, representing more than half a million jobs.

The European Experience

In West Germany the Clark paper estimates that around 250,000 jobs have been gained through the manufacture of pollution control systems. There are, however, clear signs that companies and countries that have gone too far ahead of the pack could suffer. In 1987 a delegation of West German industrialists visited Britain to study Britain's environment practices and to lobby for harmonisation of environment legislation across the EC at the West German level. The German industry body, the BDI, fears that Germany will begin to suffer a competitive disadvantage if other countries do not match its level of environmental investment.

Table 4.22 shows how that investment has grown over the years, from DM5.3 billion in 1971 to DM16.4 billion in 1986. It is estimated that Germany will have to spend a further DM30-40 billion by 1995 to meet new air pollution control targets alone.

Table 4.22   ENVIRONMENTAL PROTECTION COSTS FOR WEST
GERMAN INDUSTRY 1971-1986

DM billion

1971	5.3
1972	5.8
1973	6.2
1974	6.7
1975	7.0
1976	7.2
1977	7.2
1978	7.3
1979	7.3
1980	8.1
1981	8.6
1982	9.6
1983	10.2
1984	10.4
1985	13.7
1986	16.4

Source: BDI
Note: Capital costs and operating expenditure for environment protection

BASF, one of the big three German chemical companies, spent DM1.4 billion on environmental protection at its Ludwigshafen plant between 1970 and 1986. Over that period, operating costs for environmental protection rose by 1050% yet the company's total sales revenue increased by only 285%. Like others, the company fears its international competitiveness may be harmed.

The Netherlands has already modelled the employment impact of having higher standards than other countries. Figure 4.6 shows that its environment protection will have increased unemployment unless other countries follow suit.

Within the EC as a whole it is believed that 1.5-2 million people are employed in various aspects of the environment industry. The balance between different countries within the EC, however, suggests that unions in some will find themselves constrained by potential job losses. In countries where protection is at a low level, though, the unions will have more flexibility. That, in many sectors, will be the position in the UK.

Figure 4.6   Impact on Dutch Employment of Environmental Protection Policies in Other Countries 1979-1987

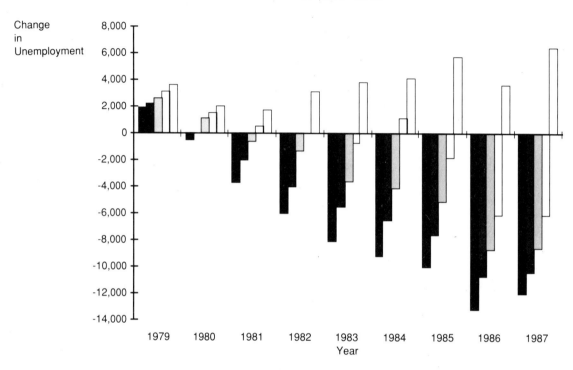

Source: "Impact of Environmental Measures on Growth, Productivity, Inflation and Trade"
Note: Versions 1-5 range from other countries doing nothing to improve environmental protection up to all countries adopting the same high level as the Dutch. Only if other countries follow the Dutch (5) will employment prospects improve

Hazardous Waste

There are issues where jobs have been put fairly directly at risk. The National Union of Seamen, for example, banned the dumping of nuclear waste at sea in 1983, a stand subsequently taken up by other transport unions worldwide. Jim Slater, president of the NUS at the time, believed that there was widespread enthusiasm for the ban among members. Attention has now turned to toxic waste.

162

Indeed, transport unions are in a key position when it comes to turning environmental policy into action. In 1988, for example, both the NUS and the National Union of Railwaymen were involved in an incident concerning spent radioactive nuclear fuel from Switzerland bound for Sellafield, both unions refusing to handle it. And at Liverpool the NUS, this time together with the TGWU, blacked a consignment of treated uranium because it had originated in Namibia.

The most immediate impact of trade union organisation, however, will come within the workplace. According to the Trades Union Congress, 700 workers in the UK die every year in work accidents, 275,000 are injured and there are some 900 notified deaths from industrial diseases. The TUC adds: "The true extent of occupational ill health however is very much greater but remains largely uncharted. As many as 50,000 people are expected to die over the next ten years from past exposure to asbestos alone."

The TUC is calling for increased inspection and tougher enforcement of health and safety regulations, and for the abolition of the immunity from such regulations enjoyed by the National Health Service, the Prison Service, the Civil Service and government establishments generally.

In its document, *Health and Safety at Work: The Way Forward* (1987) the TUC identified specific areas of risk:

> Evidence continues to emerge which raises concern about the extent and consequences of hazards to human reproduction from a wide range of physical, chemical, biological and psychological factors encountered at work. These can affect both men and women and include both ionising and non-ionising radiations, teratogenic and mutagenic substances and stress.

> Microbiological hazards pose a growing risk to workers, for example AIDS, hepatitis B, and dangerous pathogens encountered in certain occupations including medicine, laboratories, agriculture, sewerage and waste disposal.

The same statement, adopted by the 119th Annual Trades Union Congress in September 1987, also specifically covered risks to the environment, "including the control of major hazards and the adoption of best practicable environmental options for the control of pollution". The statement called for further steps to be taken to extend trade union involvement in environmental issues, and for the government to "give top priority to establishing a permanent advisory body on environmental protection" and to "extend public accountability and involvement in major areas of environmental concern - for example radioactive waste and hazardous waste management". The TUC also expressed concern about "hazards which are no longer acceptable in developed countries" being "exported to newly industrialised nations".

It would be wrong, of course, to pretend that the initiative is entirely with the factory floor, the trade unions and a small minority of disaffected managers. The Confederation of British Industry (CBI) "commends the following principles to members and to business generally".

1. Establish policies to secure openness in safety, health and environmental information, and make adequate arrangements for their application in practice.

2. Provide the local public with sufficient appropriate information to enable them to understand the nature of potential risks and the arrangements that exist for their safety.

3. Wherever possible, agree to requests from regulatory authorities for consent to disclose to the public information previously supplied to such authorities.

4. Support the disclosure of information to the general public sufficient to enable them to be well informed and reassured about the extent and efficiency of the controls which regulatory authorities operate on their behalf.

5. Handle all specific requests for information quickly and politely and, in the event that information cannot be disclosed, reasons should be given. Information necessary to protect the safety or health of the public or an individual should always be disclosed.

6. Withhold safety, health and environmental information on grounds of confidentiality only if genuinely satisfied that confidentiality is justified for commercial or personal privacy reasons.

7. Keep representatives and spokesmen for the local community - local councillors and officials, MPs and MEPs and the media - regularly informed of site activities and proposed developments of future events that concern the public.

4.5   THE COST OF ENVIRONMENTAL DAMAGE AND RISK
MANAGEMENT

Mismanagement of environmental risk is becoming increasingly costly both for companies directly involved and, through insurance and other mechanisms, for the business community generally. Historically, company accounts have taken little or no account of environmental damage, or of any contingent liability for its effects. Increasing acceptance of the "polluter pays" principle, however, a growing body of legislation and a greater willingness of employees and the public to sue require a new approach to risk management and to accounting.

Sometimes environmental damage is the inevitable and continuous consequence of the way industrial processes are carried out: many, perhaps all, landfills do leak. On other occasions environmental damage is the result of an accident. In that case it is generally categorised as either man-made, as at Chernobyl, or natural.

Companies are increasingly aware of and ready for the financial exposure to man-made accidents. What they are less aware of, and less ready for, is the link environmentalists are now making between so-called natural disasters and industrial and commercial activity. There is a fairly clear link, for example, between deforestation and landslides. Environmentalists (for example, in Italy) have recently been taking action to try to make those responsible for tree clearing financially accountable for subsequent earth movements. Other connections between industrial activity and "natural" disasters are also being drawn. The environmentalists' position is that this is not an attack on business. Rather, they say, pollution and environmental mismanagement is itself an attack on business.

Some examples will serve to illustrate the environmentalist view.

It has long been believed by some scientists that high nitrate levels in drinking water pose a threat to human health. Indeed, the World Health Organisation has stated that "nitrate is toxic when present in excessive amounts". In 1985 the EC passed a directive setting a maximum admissible concentration (MAC) of 50 mg of nitrate per litre of water. In Britain neither the government, the water authorities nor the farming community - responsible for the pollution caused by the use of nitrogenous fertilisers - took any action until legal proceedings were commenced by the EC. The 1988 decision to comply came at a point when nitrate levels in the ground were already so high that their slow percolation into groundwater will eventually cause pollution levels in some areas to reach 200 mg. The options for tackling the problem include water treatment, blending with low-nitrate sources and less intensive farming methods round aquifers. If no action were taken, some scientists forecast an increase in stomach cancers and blue-baby syndrome, resulting in additional costs to the health services. The conclusion is that the use of fertilisers has not been properly costed.

Acid rain provides an even clearer illustration, a phenomenon related to emissions from vehicles and coal-fired power stations. West German forests, for example, are estimated to be worth at least $50 billion but to be suffering dieback induced by acid rain at a rate of $300 million a year. According to the Ministry of the Interior, property damage is running at $1 billion a year. In Sweden forestry provides 100,000 jobs and is the country's largest export earner, but damage is assessed as extensive; the cost of water pipe erosion alone is put at $120 million. In France a study published in 1984 found that 35,000 hectares of the Vosges were affected by acid rain. In the Netherlands 85% of all woodlands are affected, according to the Dutch Forestry Service. Without corrective action annual losses due to acid rain for all sectors in the Netherlands are put at up to $190 million, while total capital losses in forestry have been put at $1.9 billion. The list is worldwide. Again the conclusion is that industrial processes leading to emissions of nitrogen oxides and sulphur dioxide have not been properly costed. If the forests of Scandinavia and the coal-fired power stations of Britain were owned by one company, it is clear that the savings from not fitting flue gas desulphurisation to the power stations would be more then wiped out by the losses of the forestry division.

In its nuclear generating capacity, the electricity supply industry provides an even more dramatic illustration of the issue of pollution costs. Reactors containing natural or slightly enriched uranium fuel could not explode like a nuclear bomb but breeder reactors do have that potential. Even accepting that a nuclear explosion is so remote a possibility as to be ignored, there is far too much hard evidence of other environmental risks. In 1957 one of two plutonium-producing atomic piles at Sellafield, Cumbria, caught fire and released a cloud of radioiodine across Europe. In March 1975 an electrician carrying a candle set fire to cables under the control room of the Brown's Ferry nuclear power station in Alabama, disabling all five emergency core-cooling systems on one reactor - fortunately not needed during the hours it took to control the fire and make repairs. In 1977 at Three Mile Island, Pennsylvania, there was a partial core melt-down. Fortunately the concrete containment was not breached and the release of radiation was considered small. Even so, more than 17,000 personal lawsuits have been filed as a result of Three Mile Island and by 1985 well over $300 million had been paid out in various compensations. In addition, the clean-up cost $1 billion.

Russia had already suffered one nuclear disaster before Chernobyl, the 1957 explosion at Kyshtym. Thirty villages had to be evacuated. Estimates of the damage caused by the Chernobyl disaster vary considerably. The Swedish Radiological Protection Board has predicted a total of 8,000 cancers, the US

Lawrence Livermore Laboratory 52,000, the UK Political Ecology Research Group 100,000. Some other business impacts have been more tangible. In August 1987, more than a year after the accident, the UK government had to introduce new measures controlling the movement and slaughter of sheep in Wales and Scotland on farms previously designated safe. In July 1988 the House of Commons Agriculture Select Committee announced that lamb irradiated after the Chernobyl disaster "probably" entered the food chain. In Japan, a year after the accident, a consumer co-operative was banning a range of European products, including Italian spaghetti.

Before Chernobyl the risk of a serious nuclear accident was put by some as low as one in a billion years of operation. In fact, Chernobyl came after only 4,000 years of worldwide reactor operation. The reality is that a major nuclear accident is uninsurable. Business can insure against other environmental risks, of course, but the rising cost of that insurance, without proper risk-management methods, should not be forgotten.

Man-made disasters

Tables 4.23 and 4.24 list some of the major industrial accidents and oil spills of recent years. Of non-nuclear incidents, Bhopal is the most infamous. The indisputable facts of Bhopal are that on the night of 2 December 1984 a six-inch-thick concrete wall fractured, allowing highly toxic methyl isocyanate to escape. There is controversy over the cause of the accident and the precise number of deaths and injuries will never be known. But of the 800,000 inhabitants of Bhopal it is estimated that some 200,000 inhaled methyl isocyanate and that at least a quarter of those were seriously injured. The official death toll is between 2,000 and 5,000; unofficial observers have placed it even higher.

Table 4.23   MAJOR INDUSTRIAL ACCIDENTS[1] INVOLVING CHEMICALS AND EXPLOSIVES 1980-1986

Year	Description	Impact
1980	India, Mandir Asod, factory explosion	50 dead
	India, factory explosion	40 dead
	Spain, Ortuella, explosion	51 dead
	Thailand, armament explosion	54 dead

Continued...

Table 4.23 cont'd

Year	Description	Impact
1980	UK, Barking, factory fire involving sodium cyanide	3,500 evaculated, 12 injured
	USA, Somerville, rail accident involving phosphorus trichloride	23,000 evacuated 300 injured
1981	Venezuela, Tacoa, explosion	145 dead, 1,000 injured
1982	USA, Taft, explosion involving acrolein	17,000 evacuated
	USA, Livingston, rail accident involving fuel oil	3,000 evacuated
	Canada, rail accident involving hydrofluoric acid	1,200 evacuated
1983	Venezuela, fuel oil explosion	640+ dead
	Nicaragua, oil explosion	23,000 evacuated
	USA, gas explosion	70 dead
1984	Brazil, pipeline explosion	90 dead
	India, Bhopal, methyl isocyanate leak	2,500+ dead, 50,000+ injured, 200,000 evacuated
	Mexico, gas tank explosion	452 dead, 4248 injured, 300,000 evacuated
1985	China, factory explosion	82 dead
	China, coalmine explosion	53 dead
	Japan, coalmine explosion	62 dead, 24 injured
	USA, factory explosion	21 dead
	Mexico, sulphuric acid leak	5,000 evacuated

Continued...

Table 4.23 cont'd

Year	Description	Impact
1986	USSR, Chernobyl, nuclear reactor fire	31 immediate deaths, unknown long-term deaths, 135,000 evacuated

Source: Office of the UN Disaster Relief Co-ordinator (UNDRO)/ UNEP/OECD
Note: [1] *Those which involved more than 50 deaths, 100 injured or 1,000 evacuated*

Table 4.24   MAJOR ACCIDENTAL OIL SPILLS[1] FROM TANKERS
1979-1985

Year	Ship	Country affected	Quantity spilled ('000 tonnes)
1979	*Betelgeuse*	Ireland	27.0
	Antonio Gramsci	Sweden, Finland, USSR	6.0
	Messlaniki Frontis	Greece	6.0
	Kurdistan	Canada	7.0
	Gino	France	42.0
	Aviles	Gulf	25.0
	Atlantic Express	Tobago	276.0
	Ionnis Angelicoussis	Angola	30.0
	Chevron Hawaii	USA	2.0
	Burmah Agate	USA	40.0
	Independenta	Turkey	94.6
1980	*Princess Anne Marie*	Cuba	6.0
	Irenes Serenade	Greece	102.0
	Tanio	France	13.5
	Juan A Lavalleja	Algeria	40.0

Continued...

Table 4.24 cont'd

Year	Ship	Country affected	Quantity spilled ('000 tonnes)
1981	*Jose Marti*	Sweden	6.0
	Ondina	Germany	0.5
	Cavo Cambanos	France	18.0
1983	*Castello de Belver*	South Africa	255.5
	Sivand	UK	6.0
	Feoso Ambassador	China	4.0
1984	*Assimi*	Oman	51.4
	Pericles GC	Qatar	46.6
1985	*Neptunia*	Iran	60.0
	Nova	Iran	71.1

Source: Secretariat of the International Maritime Organisation/International Oil Pollution Compensation Fund/Advisory Committee on Pollution of the Sea/Institut Français du Pétrole/Tanker Advisory Center
Notes: [1] *Over 25,000 tonnes or over $5 million insurance cost*

In 1986 the Indian government began legal proceedings against Union Carbide, claiming $5 billion compensation. The main product of the plant was carbaryl, a pesticide usually sold under the name sevin, for which methyl isocyanate is an intermediary product. Carbaryl is a suspected carcinogen, a suspected teratogen, a skin irritant and a danger to fish and wildlife. In 1989, Union Carbide made an out-of-court settlement of US$470 million.

Only months after Bhopal, the West Virginia plant of the parent company suffered an accident leading to evacuation of local residents.

Prior to Bhopal, Seveso had been the most frightening word in terms of industrial accidents. In 1976 a valve jammed in the ICMESA factory in the northern Italian town, causing an explosion which released 500 kg of toxic vapour, the main constituents of which were trichlorophenol and dioxin TCDD. In the year prior to the accident there was only one malformed birth in the towns closest to the plant; in the year after there were 23. In 1978 one researcher put birth defects for the area at 53 per thousand compared with an average of five per thousand for Lombardy as a whole. In the early 1980s the level of miscarriages for Seveso was still above the national average.

170

In 1984 liquid gas storage tanks exploded in Mexico City, killing 452 people. Thousands more were made homeless.

In 1986 came the Sandoz warehouse fire at Basle, Switzerland, causing hundreds of tonnes of chemicals to be washed into the Rhine. There were massive fish deaths, damage to drinking water supplies and pollution was measured all the way to the Netherlands. Three weeks later BASF dropped 1.7 tonnes of 2,4-D herbicide into the Rhine from its Ludwigshafen plant. In the glare of post-Sandoz publicity, it was a costly error for BASF, already a big spender on environmental protection, causing the replacement of the continuous monitoring units on the 13 cooling water discharge points by a far greater number of monitors at all major discharges into the cooling water system. And the goodwill from $750 million spent on previous environmental protection measures was lost.

Natural disasters

There is increasing evidence that so-called "acts of God" are sometimes man-made and frequently exacerbated by industrial activity. According to the 1986 State of the Environment Report published by UNEP:

> Even so-called "natural disasters" are often ultimately bound up with environmental and development factors. They, too, are frequently aggravated by inappropriate development or lack of development - or both. We are accustomed to calling floods, earthquakes and storms "acts of God" but their impact is often, at least in part, determined by the activities of man.

What evidence is there that this is so? A comparison of the numbers of people killed each year in "natural" disasters during the 1960s and 1970s (Table 4.25) certainly suggests that there is an increase which is disproportionate to population increase alone.

Table 4.25   DEATHS FROM NATURAL DISASTERS 1960s/1970s

'000s

	1960s	1970s
Earthquake	0.2	1.2
Tropical cyclones	2.5	2.8
Flood	5.2	15.4
Drought	18.5	24.4

Source: E El-Hinnawi, "Environmental Refugees", UNEP 1985

Hurricanes

Hurricanes might particularly be considered to have little or nothing to do with human activity, yet studies by the Center for Meteorology and Physical Oceanography at the Massachusetts Institute of Technology show a direct link between increased atmospheric carbon dioxide and the destructive potential of hurricanes. The amount of carbon dioxide in the earth's atmosphere has varied since long before man but there is now known to be an annual increase of 1.5 parts per million (ppm), substantially due to human activity. In 1987 the level stood at 348 ppm; during the last ice age it is believed to have stood at around 200 ppm.

Over the relatively short time span considered in Tables 4.26 and 4.27 it is difficult to discern a pattern of increase in cyclone activity. But Kerry Emanuel at MIT has concluded that: "While better estimates of tropical cyclone intensities must await more sophisticated modelling efforts, the present analysis suggests that predicted climate changes associated with increased atmospheric carbon dioxide will lead to substantially enhanced tropical cyclone intensity."

Table 4.26   HURRICANES, TYPHOONS, CYCLONES AND TORNADOS
              1980-1985

Year	Description	Location	Deaths	Impact
1980	Hurricane	Australia		
	Hurricane	France		
	Hurricane	USA		
	Tornado(3)	USA		
1981	Hurricane	Bangladesh		2 million homeless
	Hurricane	USSR		Thousands homeless
	Typhoon	Philippines(2)	350	400,000 homeless
	Tornado	USA(2)		
1982	Hurricane	Guatemala/ El Salvador	1,000	
	Hurricane	USA(2)		
	Hurricane	Japan	44	
	Hurricane	Vietnam		200,000 homeless
	Cyclone	India	163	Hundreds missing
	Tornado	USA(4)		
1983	Hurricane	Cuba		
	Hurricane	NW Europe		
	Hurricane	USA		
	Typhoon	Hong Kong	18	
	Typhoon	Japan	30	
	Typhoon	Vietnam	500	
	Cyclone	India	50	6,000 homeless
	Tornado	China	340	
	Tornado	USA(5)		
1984	Hurricane	USA		
	Typhoon	Philippines	1,000	Thousands homeless
	Tornado	USA(8)		

Continued...

Table 4.26 cont'd

Year	Description	Location	Deaths	Impact
1985	Hurricane	USA		100,000 evacuated
	Typhoon	China	177	1,400 injured
	Typhoon	Japan	19	1,380 homeless
	Typhoon	Vietnam	670	Thousands homeless
	Typhoon	Philippines	39	100,000 evacuated
	Tornado	USA/Canada	88	

Source: UNEP/OECD

Table 4.27   TROPICAL CYCLONE[1] ACTIVITY 1971-1984

	Number of tropical cyclones	% deviation from 1958-84 average
1971	97	+21
1972	87	+ 9
1973	74	- 8
1974	74	- 8
1975	76	- 5
1976	85	+ 6
1977	67	-16
1978	87	+ 9
1979	76	- 5
1980	80	0
1981	83	+ 4
1982	79	- 1
1983	79	- 1
1984	96	+20
Average *1958-84*	80.1	+ 7

Source: UNEP
Note: [1] *Those with sustained low-level winds greater than 17 m/s and also hurricane and typhoons (maximum sustained winds equal to or greater than 33 m/s)*

Specifically the MIT model suggested that if atmospheric carbon dioxide doubled there would be a 40-50% increase in the destructive potential of hurricanes. That would have meant a marked increase since the beginning of the 20th century and there will be a further significant increase over the next 50 years.

Floods

Another well-published climatic effect of increased carbon dioxide is global warming, leading to melting of the ice caps and the flooding of low-lying areas. Even before any such potential is unleashed it is possible to see an increase in floods (Tables 4.28 and 4.29) and their impact through hydro schemes. The Indian National Commission on Flood Control, for example, estimates that despite spending $1 billion on controls between 1953 and 1979, the area ravaged by floods has doubled in the past 30 years. The 1978 floods in West Bengal and 1983 floods in California were directly linked with the construction of dams.

Table 4.28   FLOODS 1980-1986

Year	Location	Deaths	Observations
1980	USA	36	
1981	Australia	-	
	China	1,500	1,130,000 homeless
	France	-	
	India	3,000	500,000 homeless
	Portugal/Spain	16	
	Somalia		60,000 homeless
	South Africa	150	
	USA	30	
	USSR		Thousands homeless
1982	China		1.5 million homeless
	France		
	India	700	
	Japan	275	

Continued...

Table 4.28 cont'd

Year	Location	Deaths	Observations
1982	Peru	2,500	5,000 homeless
	Spain	43	
	UK		
	USA	30	
1983	Ecuador/Peru	250	
	France		
	India	1,600	
	Japan	30	
	Portugal	9	1,000 homeless
	Spain	42	
	USA	11	
1984	New Zealand		
	Korea	139	200,000 homeless
	USA	10	
1985	Benin	30	200,000 homeless
	Argentina	14	50,000 evacuated
	Brazil	1	10,000 evacuated
	China	50	24,000 homes destroyed
	Ethiopia		8,000 homeless
	India	237	
	Puerto Rico	50	
	Saudi Arabia	32	
	Venezuela	26	8,000 homeless
1986	Bolivia		2,000 homes destroyed
	India	230	
	Indonesia	1	30,000 evacuated
	Peru	7	25,000 homeless
	Sri Lanka		300,000 evacuated
	USA		10,000 evacuated

Source: UNEP/OECD

Table 4.29   DAM BURSTS 1965-1985

Year	Location	Impact
1965	Chile	400 deaths
1967	India	75 deaths
	Indonesia	138 deaths
1972	Philippines	2 million homeless
1976	Mexico	400 deaths
	USA	11 deaths
1977	USA	39 deaths
1978	Japan	
1979	India	3,000 deaths
1985	China	48 deaths
	Italy	260+ deaths

Source: Office of the UN Disaster Relief Co-ordinator/UNEP/OECD

Earthquakes

Table 4.30 gives details of earthquakes occurring between 1971 and 1985. Although man's activities can be linked to few of them, the pressure of water on geological structures at dams is believed to have been a component in earthquakes in 1962 at Hsingengkiang, China (6.1 on the Richter scale), in 1963 at Kariba in what was then Rhodesia (5.6), in 1966 at Kremesta, Greece (6.3), and in 1967 at Koyna, India (6.5).

Table 4.30   EARTHQUAKE OCCURRENCE 1971–1985

Year	Epicentres indentified	"Felt and damaging"	Principal destructive
1971	4,757		13
1972	4,661		9
1973	5,160		11
1974	4,893		12
1975	5,318		23
1976	6,308	1,468	13
1977	5,775	1,340	7
1978	6,428	1,603	7
1979	7,162	1,575	14
1980	7,348	1,615	7
1981	6,829	1,272	7
1982	7,747	1,616	6
1983	9,842	1,983	9
1984	10,496		
1985	13,114		

Source: International Seismological Centre, UK/UNESCO

Drought

The link between human activity and drought is more easily established. According to the WCED:

Desertification is caused by a complex mix of climatic and human effects. The human effects, over which we have more control, include the rapid growth of both human and animal populations, detrimental land use practices (especially deforestation), adverse terms of trade, and civil strife. The cultivation of cash crops on unsuitable rangelands has forced herders and their cattle onto marginal lands. The unfavourable international terms of trade for primary products and the policies of aid donors have reinforced pressures to encourage increasing cash-crop production at any cost.

Deforestation often leads to wind and water erosion of the soil and certainly to changed rainfall patterns. A mechanism of drought has even been described where there has been no change in rainfall at all - degraded soil loses much of its water-retaining capacity.

Some 35% of the earth's land surface is now suffering desertification, of which about one-sixth is classified as "extremely severely desertified". Nearly one billion people live in these areas, almost a quarter of them affected by severe desertification.

Table 4.31 shows areas of the world suffering drought occurrence between 1980 and 1984 on the basis of measured failure of normal precipitation. The true picture is much larger and getting worse. Some 870 million hectares in South America, Asia and Africa are now classed as severely desertified while the annual rate of growth of desert-like conditions is put at 6 million hectares and that of land providing no economic return at 21 million hectares.

Table 4.31   DROUGHT OCCURRENCE 1980-1984

Year	Countries affected
1980	Kenya/Tanzania/Uganda; Morocco/Canary Is; Rwanda; Senegal; Greater Antilles; Chile; Ecuador; Mexico; Peru; China; South India; Mongolia; Pakistan; Sri Lanka; Australia
1981	Oceanic Is; Tunisia; Canada; Chile; USA; China; North India; Pakistan; Italy/Malta
1982	Mozambique; Senegal; South Africa/Botswana/Swaziland/ Lesotho; Sudan; Zambia/Malawi/Zimbabwe; USA; Mongolia; Poland; Spain/Portugal; Australia; Brunei/Indonesia; Pacific Is (East)
1983	Benin; Burkina Faso;Ghana; Guinea; Kenya/Tanzania/Uganda; Ivory Coast; Liberia; Mali; Mauritania; Morocco/Canary Is; Niger; Oceanic Is; Senegal; South Africa/Botswana/Swaziland/ Lesotho; Sudan;Togo; Zambia/Malawi/Zimbabwe; Greater Antilles; Argentina; Bolivia; Brazil; Canada; Chile; Colombia/ Venezuela; USA; China; Spain/Portugal; Brunei/Indonesia; Pacific Is (East and West); Sri Lanka

Continued...

Table 4.31 cont'd

Year	Countries affected
1984	Algeria; Central African Republic; Guinea; Kenya/Tanzania/ Uganda; Liberia; Mali; Mauritania; Niger; Senegal; South Africa/Botswana/Swaziland/Lesotho; Sudan; Togo; Zambia/ Malawi/Zimbabwe; North India; Pakistan; Saudi Arabia/ Kuwait; USSR; Pacific Is (West)

Source: World Meteorogical Organisation
Note: Table shows countries with less than 60% of normal precipitation for 50% or more of the area; countries in which drought can only be inferred from data of surrounding countries have not been included

Landslides and avalanches

There is an equally clear link between human activity and landslides and avalanches. Loss of tree cover is frequently to blame, resulting from deforestation by pollution and by clearing for housebuilding, roadbuilding, firewood, and construction of ski runs and other "unnatural causes". Table 4.32 shows some of the major incidents betwen 1980 and 1986, resulting in death, injury and homelessness. There have been many more, less severe.

Table 4.32   LANDSLIDES AND AVALANCHES 1980-1986

Year	Location	Type	Deaths	Observations
1980	Indonesia	L	100	
	Turkey	L	60	
	Yugoslavia	L	70	
1981	Colombia	L	65	14,000 homeless
	Indonesia	L	23	
	Indonesia	L	500	3,300 evacuated
	Japan	L	40	
	Peru	L	70	
	Puerto	L	26	

Continued...

Table 4.32 cont'd

Year	Location	Type	Deaths	Observations
1982	Bolivia	L	25	
	Colombia	L	30	
	Indonesia	L	50	
	Taiwan	L	19	
1983	Brazil	L	13	40 injured
	China	L	277	
	Colombia	A	150	
	India	L	67	
	Indonesia	L	21	
	Italy	L	–	4,000 homeless
	Italy	L	17	3,000 evacuated
	Japan	L	70	
	Lebanon	L	20	
	Mexico	L	32	
	Nepal	L	21	
	Pakistan	A	95	
	Papua New Guinea	L	45	
	Peru	L	245	300 missing
1984	Argentina	L	10	
	China	L	100	
	Indonesia	L	11	
	Japan	L	14	
	Peru	L	13	
1985	Peru	L	150	4,000 homeless
	Philippines	L	300	
	Japan	L	20	
1986	Japan	A	13	
	Peru	L	13	
	Sri Lanka	L	40	

Source: UNEP/UN Disaster Relief Co-ordinator/OECD

Volcanoes

Volcanoes may still be classed as entirely acts of God, but failure to take proper account of their potential has undoubtedly cost lives (Table 4.33).

Table 4.33   DESTRUCTIVE VOLCANIC ERUPTIONS 1980-1986

Year	Location	Site	Deaths
1980	USA	Mt St Helens	62
	Zaire	Nyamuragira	
1981	Indonesia	Semeru	252
	Philippines	Mayon	100
1982	Indonesia	Gulunggang	35
	Mexico	El Chichon	287
1984	Cameroon	Lake Monoun	37
1985	Colombia	Ruiz	20,000
1986	Cameroon	Lake Nyos	1,600

Source: UNESCO/OECD/Scientific Event Alert Network (SEAN)

In Natural Disasters and Vulnerability Analysis, the Office of the United Nations Disaster Relief Co-ordinator (UNDRO) concluded that:

The nature and violence of most volcanic phenomena make it practically impossible to reduce the vulnerability of human life and property to below 100%. The only way to mitigate the risk is therefore to reduce the elements at risk either, on a long term basis, by restricting human settlement and investment in hazardous zones or, on a short-term basis, by evacuating populations and movable goods from such zones during periods of increased hazard (ie periods of actual or predicted eruptive activity).

There nevertheless remain certain possibilities of reducing vulnerability to some volcanic phenomena such as ash falls, lapilli showers etc. Sloping roofs are less liable than flat roofs to collapse under layers of ash; windows of houses may be boarded up to reduce the risk of fires....

Insurance cost

Table 4.34 gives the insurance cost of some major environmental disasters between 1980 and 1986. The figures relate only to "natural" disasters but, as has been argued, acts of God are often more accurately "works of man" or exacerbated by man. Over such a short period and from such incomplete figures it is impossible to discern any pattern. It is enough only to say that the cost, together with the cost of direct industrial pollution and damage is consderable, and borne by all the business community through the insurance mechanism.

Table 4.34   INSURANCE COST OF SOME MAJOR ENVIRONMENTAL DISASTERS 1980-1986

$ million

Year	Description	Cost (US$ million)
1980	Flood, USA	500
	Earthquake, Azores	400
	Landslide, USA	500
	Volcano, USA	2,700
1981	Flood, Australia	230
	Flood, France	166
	Earthquake, Greece	800
	Hail storm, USA	125
1982	Flood, UK	175
	Flood, France	152
	Flood, USA	200
	Landslide, Italy	700
	Snow storm, USA	220
	Storm, UK	100
	Storm, France	1,000

Continued...

Table 4.34 cont'd

Year	Description	Cost (US$ million)
	Snow storm, USA	243
	Tornado, USA	100
	Tornado, USA	100
	Hail storm, USA	113
1982	Typhoon, Japan	137,000 [1]
	Hurricane, Hawaii	137
1983	Flood, France	599
	Flood, Spain	223
	Flood, USA	100
	Storm, Denmark	350 [2]
	Storm, France	5,000 [3]
	Storm, USA	82
	Hurricane, USA	675
	Snow storm, USA, Canada, Mexico	510
1984	Flood, USA	98
	Flood, USA	94
	Flood, USA	277
	Flood, USA	75
	Tornado, USA	204
	Tornado, USA	92
	Tornado, USA	79
	Tornado, USA	98
	Rain, USA	94
	Tornado, USA	277
	Thunderstorm, Germany	1,500 [4]
	Tornado, USA	75
1985	Flood, USA	79
	Hail, Australia	100 [5]
	Storm, USA	400
	Cold, France	1,000 [3]
	Tornado, USA	90
	Storm, USA	80
	Tornado, USA/Canada	321
	Typhoon, Japan	19,951 [1]
	Hurricane, USA	543
	Hurricane, USA	419

Continued...

184

Table 4.34 cont'd

Year	Description	Cost (US$ million)
1986	Flood, USA	125
	Flood, USA	76
	Storm, USA	75
	Heatwave, USA	1,500 +
	Hurricane, USA	80
	Rain, Australia	100 [5]
	Typhoon, Japan	16,500 [1]

Source: Bulletin of the Swiss Reinsurance Company/UNDRO
Notes: [1] *million yen*
 [2] *million krone*
 [3] *million francs*
 [4] *million Deutschmarks*
 [5] *$ Australian million*

Financial Exposure

All businesses should have a sound environmental risk policy. The first step is to identify the hazards; the second to assess the degree of risk in terms of probability and severity; the third to eliminate or control the risks. What cannot be eliminated or sufficiently controlled will have to be insured. Generally that insurance will fall into one of the following categories:

1. Property
2. Consequential loss
3. Employer's liability
4. Public liability - injury to third parties
5. Public liability - third party property
6. Transit/marine.

The system of litigation and insurance is in a sense a market mechanism for controlling pollution. Those who believe they have suffered from pollution can sue - and this is increasingly happening. Two other market mechanisms are also gaining favour, though neither necessarily precludes recourse to litigation by those who consider themselves harmed. One is the emission charge and the other - already in use in the USA - the marketable permit.

The objection some economists make to the more usual system of emission standards is that industries have different costs in meeting those standards. It might be more efficient, so the argument goes, to let one company create a great deal of pollution yet another company hardly any. The emission charge is one way of permitting that flexibility. Companies would create, and pay for, pollution in accordance with the profitability of their processes. The objection to this is that no authority could be certain what impact any given level of charges would have on emissions.

The marketable permit overcomes that particular problem. The authorities set a total quantity of pollution to be permitted. Permits are then issued for that quantity of pollution and, as a further refinement, sold or auctioned to industry using a mechanism which would also allow companies to trade in permits between themselves. Company X, for example, in possession of a permit to create a certain quantity of sulphur dioxide, might instead sell the permit at a profit to Company Y, who can more cost-effectively carry out a process of which sulphur dioxide is the pollutant by-product.

Attractive as this may sound to many entrepreneurially minded people, and practical as it may be in a few cases, it would seem to overlook the more general position of *local* pollution. While some airborne emissions from high stacks may disperse widely, so that the concept of total emission level is relevant, many other toxins remain in a confined location. Given that, it could never be permissible to offset zero emissions in one location against a high level of emission in another.

Table 4.35 compares various market options for nitrogen dioxide emissions in Chicago. It suggests that a uniform emission charge would not necessarily achieve environmental objectives, due to the flat nature of the curve beyond 300 tonnes per day. In other words, to achieve the 1980 Los Angeles standard of 350 tonnes per day through the price mechanism of a $470 emission charge could equally result in emission as high as 450 tonnes per day.

Table 4.35   COST OF CONTROLLING SULPHUR DIOXIDE IN LOS
             ANGELES

$	Emission charge per tonne of SO_2	SO_2 emission resulting per day (tonnes)
	2,000	150
	850	200
	750	250
	560	300

Continued...

Table 4.35 cont'd

Emission charge per tonne of SO_2	SO_2 emission resulting per day (tonnes)
470	350
470	400
470	450

Source: Adapted from calculations in "Barriers to Implementing Tradable Air Pollution Permits", by RW Hahn and RG Noll, Yale Journal of Regulation, Vol 1, 1983

Note: At an emission charge of $470 per tonne per day, the abatement cost curve is horizontal, such that anything from 350 to 450 tonnes of sulphur dioxide emission could result

Table 4.36 looks at the problem of nitrogen dioxide emissions in Chicago in a simulated study. It is inconclusive, at least using the assumptions of the authors. All the strategies meet the federal standard but the uniform charge, for the greatest cost to industry, also gives the greatest reduction in emissions, while on a least-cost basis there is not a great deal to choose between the imposition of standards and the setting of an emission charge policy.

Table 4.36   ALTERNATIVE STRATEGIES FOR REGULATING NITROGEN DIOXIDE IN CHICAGO

Type of policy[1]	No. of sources to be controlled	Emission reduction[2](%)	Total cost[3] ($ million)
Setting emission standards by:			
State implementation plan[4]	472	21	130
Least-cost control	100	3	9
Source category standard	472	18	66

Continued...

Table 4.36 cont'd

Type of policy[1]	No. of sources to be controlled	Emission reduction[2](%)	Total cost[3] ($ million)
Emission charge policies of:			
Least-cost charge	100	3	13
Uniform charge	534	84	719
Source category charge	472	18	155

Source: *Adapted from information in "An Empirical Analysis of Economic Strategies for Controlling Air Pollution", by EP Seskin, RJ Anderson Jr. and RO Reid, Journal of Environmental Economics and Management, June 1983*

Notes: [1] *All methods would meet federal standards*

[2] *Emission reduction is for area-wide point sources*

[3] *The total cost (to polluters) would comprise either the annual control costs or the annual charge payments or a combination of both*

[4] *The state implementation plan is the traditional emission standard approach; a source category charge involves imposing charges related to the nature of the source of pollution (coal-fired burners, gas-fired burners etc)*

The likelihood is that most countries will not use market mechanisms to control pollution, leaving industry to meet standards set down with the threat of litigation for failure. Whether government standards are met or not, the potential for legal action by third parties over possible harm is clearly on the increase.

To date, one of the biggest disasters for the insurance industry has been asbestos. The ultimate liability is assessed at not less than $10 billion. It could easily reach $50 billion.

4.6 ENVIRONMENTALISM AND EFFICIENCY

Industry has always accepted the need to build health and safety measures into its costings; this is neither controversial nor new. The problems now are that science has begun to discover risks to health that were previously unknown, and the scale of human activity has begun to exceed the earth's capacity to process waste products.

In 1986 Du Pont revealed that out of $10 billion of capital investment in the chemical industry from 1975 to 1985, $3 billion was for pollution, including noise control. It also claimed that 10-20% of new capital cost was typically for environment protection, which gave "no direct return to the company". But environmentalism does have its positive effects on costs, most clearly illustrated in the energy field.

Energy

Energy is a central concern for environmentalists. They worry about the depletion of finite resources, about the local environmental impact of power stations, about long-range and long-term pollution, about acid rain and changes in climate. Many businessmen disregard their views but others already find themselves wrestling with the very *business* problems that the environmentalists predicted - forestry damaged by acid rain, agriculture damaged by the greenhouse effect and by radioactive fallout, claims for damages to health. In time most businessmen will have to address the energy issue from the environmental standpoint. The environmentalists have simply been ahead of their time and ahead of most businessmen.

As to the alternatives to conventional energy generation in the developed world, the environmentalists argue even among themselves. One faction proposes wind power, another points to the damage to the visual environment. But all environmentalists agree that the first priority is to stop *wasting* energy.

Figure 4.7 sets out the environmental problems posed by various forms of energy generation (see also Section 4.7, *Opportunities Through Environmentalism*). All those represented have *some* environmental impact, even solar and geothermal power. Of those not represented, hydro schemes pose a threat of flooding, disruption of water environments and the spread of waterborne diseases such as bilharzia; wave and tidal power may disrupt estuaries and seashores; wind turbines are noisy, take a lot of land, are ugly and may pose some safety problems.

All environmentalists and businessmen should be able to agree on a policy of conservation. In 1979 the IIED published *A Low Energy Strategy for the UK*, and concluded that no fixed relationship existed between energy consumption and economic growth, as conventional energy forecasting had maintained. Indeed, IIED found that, using known energy-saving methods and discounting any future breakthroughs, it would be possible for GDP to treble between 1973 and 2025 with no more than a 10% increase in energy consumption by the turn of the century and a return to the 1975 figure of 330 million tonnes of coal equivalent (mtce) by 2025. By contrast, official figures produced by

Figure 4.7   Environmental Impact of Various Energy Sources

		Coal	Oil	Gas	Nuclear Fission	Nuclear Fusion	Solar Photo-voltaic	Methyl & Ethyl Alcohol	Geothermal
Exploitation of Raw Materials	1	★	o	o	★	o	o	o	
	2	★	o	o	★	o	★	o	
	3	★	o	o	★	o	o	o	
	4	o	o	o	o	o	o	o	
	5	★★	★	★	★	o	★	★★	
	6	o	o	o	o	o	o	★	
	7	o	o	o	o	o	o	o	
	8	★★★	★	★	★★	★	★	★★	
	9	★★★	★	★	★	★	★	★★★★	
Transportation Storage & Transformation of Raw Materials	1	★★	o	o	o	o	o	o	
	2	★	o	o	★	o	o	o	
	3	★	o	o	★	o	o	o	
	4	o	★★	o	o	o	o	★★	
	5	★★	★★	o	o	o	o	★	
	6	★	★	o	o	o	o	o	
	7	o	★	o	o	o	o	o	
	8	★★★	★★	★	★★	o	o	★★	
	9	★	★	★	o	o	★	★★★	
Construction, Demolition of Electric Power Plants	1	★	o	o	o	o	o		
	2	o	o	o	o	o	★★		
	3	o	o	o	★★	★	o		
	4	o	o	o	o	o	o		
	5	★	★	o	★	★	★		
	6	o	o	o	o	o	o		
	7	o	o	o	o	o	o		
	8	★★	★	★	★★	★	★★		
	9	★	★	★	★	★	★★		
Energy Generation	1	★★★	★	★	o	o	o		o
	2	★★	★	o	o	o	o		★★★
	3	★	o	o	★★	★★	o		★★
	4	★	★★	★★★	o	o	o		★★
	5	★	★	★	★	★	★		★★★
	6	★★★	★★	★★	o	o	★★		★
	7	★★★	★★★★	★	o	o	o		★
	8	★★★	★★	★	★★	★★	★★★★		★★★
	9	★★	★	★	★	★	★★		★★
Waste Disposal	1	★★★	o	o	o	o	o	o	
	2	★★	★	o	o	o	★	o	
	3	★	o	o	★★	★	o	o	
	4	★	★	o	o	o	o	★	
	5	★★	o	o	★	o	o	o	
	6	o	o	o	o	o	o	o	
	7	o	o	o	o	o	o	o	
	8	★★★	o	o	★	o	o	o	
	9	★	o	o	★	★	o	o	

Environmental Effects

1 – Particulates
2 – Stable Toxic Elements
3 – Radioactive Elements
4 – Carcinogenic & Toxic Compounds
5 – Water Pollution & Hydro-Geological Alterations
6 – Climatic Alterations
7 – Acid Rain
8 – Territorial Impact
9 – Connected Risks

Extent of Effects

o	Negligible
★	Small
★★	Substantial
★★★	Great
★★★★	Very Great

Source: Le Scienze, 5/1981, No. 153

the UK Department of Energy at about the same time forecast that energy requirements for that level of economic growth would reach 570 mtce by the year 2000.

Since there are certain to be breakthroughs in energy technology over the next few decades, the IIED figures could no doubt be bettered. This was the standpoint of a study by Earth Resources Research, which forecast on the basis of more radical conservation measures although it could not, of course, take account of any developments not presaged at the time. That study concluded that a consumer society with a high standard of living - termed the Technical Fix society - could still reduce primary energy use by 30-40%. A so-called Conserver Society with an emphasis on recycling and reuse of materials could reduce energy consumption by 55-65% over 50 years, as illustrated in Figure 4.8

Figure 4.8   The Conserver Society in the UK 1975-2025

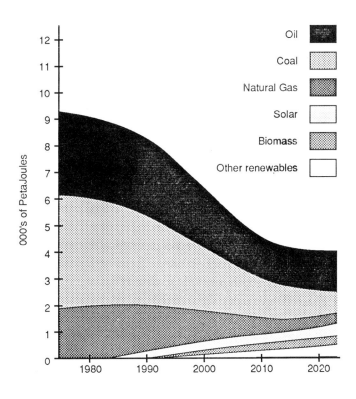

Source: Earth Resources Research

Energy Conservation

In the year before the 1973 oil crisis Denmark derived 93% of its energy requirements from oil, mostly imported from the Middle East. Following the crisis, the country initiated a review of energy supply and demand and, in 1976, the Danish government published an energy policy with six major objectives, including:

1.   To curb the growth of the gross energy consumption - totally and in specific sectors.

2.   To bring about a reduction in the speed at which non-renewable energy resources are exhausted.

3.   Constantly to adapt to experiences gained from energy-saving measures, from the introduction of new forms of energy and from the results of research and development.

In 1979 the Danish Parliament approved two Acts concerning energy, Natural Gas Supply (concerned with transmission from North Sea wells) and the Act of Heat Supply, aimed at reducing heat demand and promoting a move from oil in the space-heating sector and towards natural gas, surplus heat, straw, wood, waste and other resources. A further steep rise in oil prices that year led to some adjustments in strategy and the publication of Energy Plan 81, which not only affirmed the need for lower costs and reduced vulnerability of supply but, once again, "to reduce the growth of the energy requirement in relation to the economic growth of the society".

With experience, further adjustments were made in 1984/85, including a higher priority for indigenous energy resources, such as natural gas, and local renewable fuels including straw and biogas (from the end of 1989, the burning of surplus straw in the fields is forbidden). Parliament also decided that nuclear power should no longer be part of energy strategy; safety and environmental risks were given as the reasons. Implicit in this no-nuclear decision was recognition of the potential of combined heat and power stations (CHPs).

How successful has the strategy been? Undoubtedly the oil price rises alone would have brought about a less wasteful use of energy, but developments between 1976 and 1985 have indeed reflected the strategy laid down. At the start of the period gross energy consumption (GEC) was growing at 6% a year, yet by 1985 it was actually 3% lower than in 1976. Oil consumption fell 37%, its overall importance thus declining from 83% of energy consumption to 54%.

In space heating the results have been even more spectacular. GEC in the sector fell by 25% between 1976 and 1985, while the proportion derived from oil fell from 93% to 65%. The contribution of CHPs to the district heating system rose from 34% to 49%.

Individual companies have followed the national example. For instance, the multinational chemical company DSM, based at Heerlen in the Netherlands, first formed an energy committee with executive powers in 1976. The main objective of the committee was to draw up and co-ordinate energy-conservation strategies. The company has some 25 plants producing fertilisers, plastics, yarns and fibres, and its energy bills have reached 700 million Dutch guilders a year.

The company's first task was what it calls "good housekeeping", energy conservation through improved maintenance - reducing steam leakage, regular cleaning of heat exchangers - and minor plant modification, such as reducing the size of pump impellers and improving thermal insulation. The company also introduced energy accounting to identify and tackle wasteful use of energy through, for example, start-ups and process upsets.

DSM's next targets were process analysis, energy recovery - through a study of the latest technological developments - and use of optimisation models for steam and power generation, affording the most cost-effective response to fluctuations in steam and electricity demands. The company has been through four successive process generations for polymers: solution processes, suspension processes using solvents, suspension processes using monomers and, finally, gas-phase processes. Table 4.37 shows how the energy requirements for the production of high-density polyethylene and polypropylene have fallen with each new process.

Table 4.37   ENERGY CONSUMPTION FOR DSM's PRODUCTION OF
             HDPE AND PP USING DIFFERENT PROCESS METHODS

Gigajoules per tonne

Process generation	Type of process	Energy consumption PP	HDPE
First	Solution	–	11.3
Second	Suspension in solvent	14.2	10.5
Third	Suspension in monomer	8.4	–
Fourth	Gas-phase	7.3	9.8

Source: DSM
Notes: PP = polypropylene
*   HDPE = high-density polyethylene*

One of the more radical techniques employed by DSM has been product substitution. The company aims to replace existing products by others that fulfil the same needs but which require less energy, always provided there is economic justification and that consumers will accept the substitution. The mainstay of the DSM approach, however, is simply energy monitoring, requiring no significant capital investment. The company considers that on top of the savings brought about by physical changes in production methods, monitoring can save of the order of a further 10%.

> When in 1982 the number of profitable energy saving projects began to decline, the emphasis shifted more and more towards energy monitoring. In this context, a centrally co-ordinated campaign was started with the aim of reducing the annual energy consumption by 10% in the period from January 1983 through January 1986 . . . all the signs are that this has been accomplished . . . a considerable decrease of the average energy consumption can be obtained without extra capital investment but simply with some extra attention by the operators.

Figure 4.9 shows the impact of DSM's energy saving methods at Geleen from 1976 to 1985.

**Figure 4.9   Production, Energy Consumption and Specific Energy
Consumption for the DSM Facilities at Geleen 1976-1985**

Unit: Gigajoules

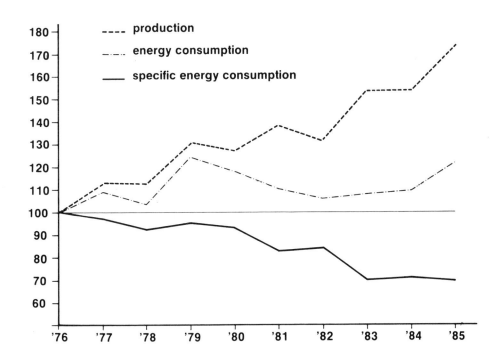

Source: DSM

Combined Heat and Power in Industry

Combined heat and power stations (CHPs) have a long track record in
Scandinavia. In the Netherlands, too, since the late 1970s there has been an
emphasis on CHP by industry. According to the Netherlands' experience,
conventional large-scale electricity production reaches 40% conversation
efficiency, or 45% in certain special processes. For gas turbines the efficiency

is put at 25-35%, for gas-fired combustion engines 30-38% and for mass produced combustion engines in motor vehicles, only 15-20%. But, through the combined production of heat and power, that is to say, utilising the waste heat from energy production, overall efficiencies of 80% or even 90% are possible.

A paper presented to be 13th WEC Congress stated: "An important trend in the industry is that more savings are realised in heat use than in power use, which leads to lower average heat/power ratios. As an example, between 1977 and 1984 steam consumption decreased by 16% where industrial output increased by 12%; but in the same period electricity consumption rose by some 16%." The key to decision-making seems to be the heat requirement for which the flue gases will be used. If the waste heat cannot be fully utilised the efficiency of CHP may drop to unacceptable levels.

CHP is also becoming widely used for office and apartment blocks, shopping centres, hospitals, swimming pools and hotels. By 1986, 1,000 gas engines for CHP had been installed in the Netherlands with a total power capacity of around 120 MW. Surplus electricity is supplied to the grid. By the same date only some 200 mini-CHP installations, known as minichips, were working in the UK. The installed cost is around £500 per kilowatt of electricity, which compares favourably with conventional generating plant. The proponents of CHP put the efficiency of minichips as high as three times that of conventional generating plant and speak of paybacks of three to five years.

Waste as Energy

Most forms of collected refuse are cost effective now against national investment criteria; even those at the higher end of the supply cost range could achieve a 3 year pay-back by 1990. The use of collected refuse is now at the deployment stage and the main problems are to demonstrate this cost effectiveness and to establish commercially reliable routes from supplier to user. The resource has the potential to make an important contribution to UK energy supplies - 12 to 14 million tons of coal equivalent a year.

That assessment was made by the UK Department of Energy's Energy Technology Support Unit at Harwell. Energy from waste brings obvious indirect benefit to industry, but what of direct and immediate cost-saving? In fact, quite small companies in some sectors can utilise their own waste. Schofields, a department store in Leeds, has installed a boiler fired by store waste. The waste is fed into a shredder from which it passes to a granulator and then to a silo which feeds the boiler. Anticipated savings are £24,000 a year on energy costs and £15,500 on waste disposal costs.

196

The viability of waste as energy obviously varies from business to business. Table 4.38 shows the energy content of an average dustbin in the UK. Coal has an average calorific value of 26,000 kilojoules per kilogram while oil for heating produces 43,500 kilojoules per kilogram. At an average calorific value of 10,500 kilojoules per kilogram (after allowing for a moisture content of 20-30% by weight) it takes approximately 5 tonnes of rubbish to equal 2 tonnes of coal of 1 tonne of heating oil. Nevertheless, the 30 million tonnes of rubbish produced in the UK each year could save some 6 million tonnes of oil or 12 million tonnes of coal. Rubbish could provide space and water heating for nearly 2.5 million UK families.

Table 4.38   THE ENERGY CONTENT OF A DUSTBIN

Composition	% by weight	Average calorific value[1]
Fine dust	13	9,600
Paper and board	27	14,600
Vegetables and putrescibles	28	6,700
Textiles	3	16,300
Plastic	5	37,000
Glass	8	nil
Metals	8	nil
Unclassified (wood, shoes, etc)	8	17,600

Source: Department of Energy
Note: [1] *Measured as received kilojoules per kilogramme. Allowing for moisture content (typically 20-30% by weight), good quality raw refuse has an average calorific value of 10,500 kj per kg. 1 kj per kg = 0.43 BTU per lb.*

Within the EC, Denmark leads in energy recovery from rubbish. The same level of rubbish efficiency throughout the Community is estimated to correspond to 17 1,000-MW-capacity nuclear power stations.

Worldwide, despite this knowledge, there are little more than 1,000 purpose-built refuse combustors taking largely unsorted refuse as feedstock. The alternative is first to sort and process the rubbish to create refuse-derived fuel (RDF) in the form of pellets or flock. RDF can be used in the same way as other solid fuels, 1.5 tonnes having the same calorific value as 1 tonne of coal or just over half a tonne of heating oil. By cost rather than weight, however, the figures are more favourable to RDF. At current prices RDF can produce heat at little more than half the cost of coal and a quarter that of heating oil.

Using specially designed boilers and combustors, therefore, an industrial company might significantly reduce costs by utilising RDF, which, combined with coal, might also be used for industrial process firing, such as for cement manufacture. RDF does, however, pose some environmental problems, even though its flue gases have much lower acid-rain emissions than coal or oil. Table 4.39 shows that for both sulphur dioxide and nitrogen oxide, raw refuse and RDF are cleaner, but other dangerous emissions are possible if raw rubbish is not carefully sorted.

Table 4.39   SULPHUR DIOXIDE AND NITROGEN OXIDE EMISSIONS FROM RUBBISH

	SO_2 (%)	NOx (ppm)
Raw refuse	0.2-0.5	100-130
Refuse-derived fuel (RDF)	0.3	120
Coal	1.5	500-700
Oil	3.5	150-300

Source: The Warmer Campaign

Cleaner Energy

The environmentalist case becomes more controversial when it moves to cleaner energy. Energy conservation means *lower* costs; cleaner energy appears to mean *higher* costs: but does it? Most businessmen accept the dictum, "No such thing as a free lunch". It follows that there cannot be free pollution. Pollution means damage and damage must be paid for.

Historically, the polluter has seldom had to pay directly for pollution costs. But with the "polluter pays" principle (PPP) gaining ground the connection is more clearly established. Even so, how does that have any impact on the industrial user of energy from a polluting source?

Pollution cost works its way though to energy users in a variety of ways, direct and indirect. The most direct impact will fall on those businesses that are affected by the pollution. While environmentalists talk of damage to *nature* there seems to be little connection with *industry*. But nature *is* business, often very big business. Power station pollution is damaging fisheries and forestry while the greenhouse effect, caused by waste gases in the atmosphere, will damage - perhaps already is damaging - agriculture in many parts of the world. These impacts can in turn work their way through to other related industries. No fish means no canning, no sale of angling equipment, no tourism; damage to forestry damages all industries using timber.

Further, the emergence of the "polluter pays" dictum could in the future involve massive claims for damages by those industries immediately affected by the pollution. Meeting those claims will in turn spread the burden to all the users of the energy. Were a Chernobyl-type disaster to occur under a PPP system, the costs to the power station operators would be almost beyond comprehension - hence the problems for energy privatisation in the UK.

IBM and 3M

In the early 1970s, IBM had already perceived that its profitability was to be linked with minimising environmental impact. The company had always encouraged its engineers to plan for minimum wastage, but from the early 1970s IBM went on to attack energy costs, water control, pollution and the siting of installations. Behind the approach lay the clear belief that what was good for the environment was also good for profits. Figure 4.10 reproduces the 1973 policy statement.

IBM in the UK estimates that it saved £3 million on energy costs between 1971 and 1984 (compared with a total electricity bill of £11 million by 1984). Since 1983 the company has had a full-time energy conservation officer. Energy-saving methods include the use of waste heat from computers, converted into hot water, plus lower levels of background light combined with high-level "task lighting". The switch to volumetric charges (ie metering) for water has encouraged a similar discipline to that for electricity, including computerised recording and reporting. The use of a sewage tariff based on uptake of water (what goes in must come out) has further encouraged recycling, and sites at North Harbour, Havant, Hursley and Greenock have their own filtration and treatment plants for industrially used water.

Figure 4.10   Statement of IBM Environmental Protection Policy 1973

IBM will reduce to a minimum the ecological impact of its activities. Management in IBM is expected to be continuously on guard against adversely affecting the environment and to seek ways to conserve natural resources.

Although IBM is not in a business which creates severe pollution problems, IBM is committed to:

1.   Meet or exceed all applicable government regulations in any location.

2.   Establish stringent standards of its own where government regulations do not exist.

3.   Attempt to utilize nonpolluting technologies and to minimise energy consumption in the design of products and processes.

4.   Work toward a 1979 goal to minimise dependence on terminal waste treatment through development of techniques to recover and reuse air, water and materials.

5.   Assist government and other industries in developing solutions to environmental problems when appropriate opportunities present themselves and IBM's experience and knowledge may be helpful.

Source: IBM

The sense of IBM's pollution control strategy was underlined by the Silicon Valley problems exposed at the end of 1981. Two companies, Fairchild Camera and Instruments and Intel, were forced to admit to leakages of 1,1,1 Trichloroethane and Trichloroethylene. The inherently clean image of high technology was dramatically and immediately dispelled, and allegations of links between groundwater contamination, miscarriages and birth defects followed. As a result, new regulations were introduced for the 1,400 electronics companies in the region. IBM, however, had been monitoring groundwater since the mid-1970s, discovering groundwater pollution ranging from a few parts per billion up to 10 parts per million, and had invested in remedial measures. More significantly, the company had already looked for less-polluting methods and for recovery processes rather than the "conventional, and more costly, abatement techniques". The 1981 revelations therefore left IBM in a much better competitive position than many of its rivals.

The company with the best-known policy of preventing pollution at source, rather than coping with it later, is 3M, which in 1975 introduced its Pollution Prevention Pays strategy. The awards and incentives for employees who contribute pollution-prevention ideas are only one part of the approach; more significant is the recognition that prevention must be built into processes at the planning stage.

By 1987 3M had activated some 1,900 3P projects said to have brought savings of around $300 million. The projects cut solid waste and sludge by 275,000 tonnes, air pollutants by 110,000 tonnes and water pollutants by 13,200 tonnes, while saving 1.5 billion gallons of waste water.

New Economics: An Introduction

It is an old business adage that if you lay all the economists in the world end to end they will not reach a conclusion. Of course, the same applies to the new economists, but some generalisations can be made. The new economists aim to "put a proper value on human needs, social justice and ecological sustainability". One of the bodies active in developing this new thinking is The Other Economic Summit (TOES); another is the New Economics Foundation (NEF).

Despite the idealism of the new economics, many businessmen also believe that it provides a more realistic basis for life in the 21st century, where the world is no longer big enough for cause and effect to be separated. Section 4.5 details some of the costs of environmental damage; the new economics requires these costs to be accounted for.

In conventional economics, for example, it is sensible for products to wear out or become obsolete very rapidly, thus maintaining the market for replacement products. In the new economics it makes better sense for products to last a long time; the consumer can then have *two different* products, the one he bought last year which still operates satisfactorily plus a new product. Under the old economics the consumer still had only one product since the item he bought last year ceased working and had to be thrown out.

The new economists see many anomalies. For example, if pure water can be obtained from a stream, it has no value under conventional economics; but if it is polluted the expenditure on a water treatment plant creates wealth and economic growth. Yet all the new economist sees is the same water to drink, probably less satisfactory in reality than the pure water from the stream.

W David Hopper, senior vice-president of policy, planning and research at the World Bank, gave the 1988 UK World Conservation Lecture, in which he pointed to this paradox in conventional economics. (The World Bank says that Hopper's comments "should not be interpreted as the views of the World Bank" but solely his personal opinion.)

> Towards the end of February 1978 I recommended to the Board . . . the financing of an irrigation project in a South Asian nation. I had been in the Bank a little over a month and this project severely tested my principles. As a researcher and agriculturist with more than ten years of living and working on agricultural development issues in India, I had seen too many acres become useless from waterlogging and salinity. Irrigation projects ignored the necessary investments in drainage, water hungry and inexperienced farmers over-irrigated their lands, and the hot summer sun and short rainy seasons parched the soil, wringing-out the surface and sub-surface moisture, depositing the earth's salts in the root zones to sicken and kill future seeds.

> I promised then that if ever I had the chance, I would see that no irrigation investment would be unaccompanied by appropriate drainage, and that no irrigation project would be without its component of farmer demonstration and education.

> The project I sent forth in February was without drainage, without demonstration, without farmer education. Yet I sent it forward. I protested to my staff . . . and they, rather wearily, explained . . . that the project in question barely met the test of a 10% economic rate of return and that if drainage or demonstration or eduction were added, the extra cost would make the project uneconomic and, thereby, eliminate it from the lending program. Reviewing the data on drainage, it was obvious that they were right. Proper drainage would have tripled the cost of the investment. I found that delaying the smooth course of the project processing irritated not only my staff but also the officials and politicians in the borrowing country who . . . wanted to implement it as quickly as possible . . .

> It was a few months later that I sent to the Board another project to add drainage to irrigated land now waterlogged and saline from decades of farming with little water control. This time the investment met the economic rate of return because unproductive acres were to be returned to productive use. But the costs were higher, much higher, than if the

202

investment had been made concomitantly with the initial irrigation project; an investment that would have insured the long term, sustained, productive use of the land.

The peculiar anomaly of this story is the fact that the accepted economic justification for proceeding with the investment was certain to lead to a degrading of the resource base, and there was no acceptable justification for protecting those resources from destruction. It was ironic that later that same technique of economic justification provided an acceptable rationale for making a much more substantial investment in the reclamation of the resources degraded by the earlier project . . .

The challenge is to assure that development conserves, even ameliorates the human and natural resource base integral to its sustenance. There is no development unless the environment within which development takes place is left with an enhanced or, at minimum, unimpaired capacity to sustain over time the new activities that intrude upon it.

This simple but central concept has not been easy to convey to development professionals. This new vision of the course of economic change and growth must become part of a way of thinking about development projects and about the course of economic expansion.

The business of the World Bank is sustainable development.

4.7 OPPORTUNITIES THROUGH ENVIRONMENTALISM

Environmentalism is simply a consumer preference like any other, be it for a particular colour, a particular look or for the latest technology. It can boost saturated markets for durables by, for example, the demand for low-energy versions and it can differentiate products from otherwise virtually identical rivals - "natural" as against "artificial" cosmetics. Moreover, consumer concern translates directly into new industrial technology, plant and services. In reality, environmentalism is a positive opportunity for business. Indeed, "green" and "environmentalist" are terms recently applied to products which have long existed but been differently regarded. Tourism is perhaps the clearest example.

Tourism

Tourism can be regarded as the desire to experience new environments. Clearly, not all of the tourism industry relies upon "natural" environments but a substantial percentage does - visits to national parks and game reserves, fishing, bird watching, trekking, tribal cultures. Moreover, most of the remainder relies upon the protection of either semi-natural or man-made environments from such problems as acid rain (which destroys ancient monuments) and sewage pollution.

The scale of the world tourism industry is shown by the fact that there were over 1 billion visitor arrivals annually between 1982 and 1985, creating receipts of more than $100 billion each year. This represents an average of some $23 for each member of the world's population, ranging from $1.5 per capita in South Asia to as much as $77 in Europe. Many individual countries are much more dependent on tourism, Austria deriving as much as $672 per capita in 1985.

In 1985, 28 countries derived more than $1 billion from tourism (which total grew to 31 in 1986). The USA was the "richest" with receipts of $11.6 billion and a total of 118.4 million arrivals; expressed in per capita terms the USA was only 20th with $49. Singapore was the second most dependent on tourism, which contributed £648 per capita. For the UK the figure was $123, for Japan a mere $9. Table 4.40 lists the 28 "tourism billionaires".

Table 4.40   WORLD TOURISM BILLIONAIRES 1985

Order		Receipts from tourism ($ billion)	Visitor arrivals (million)	Tourism receipts per capita ($)	
1	USA	11.66	118.4	49	(20)
2	Italy	8.35	56.6	146	(9)
3	Spain	8.15	43.3	211	(7)
4	France	7.94	58.7	144	(=10)
5	UK	6.99	18.6	123	(13)
6	West Germany	5.90	128.0	97	(17)
7	Austria	5.08	68.7	672	(1)
8	Mexico	3.60	66.2	46	
9	Switzerland	3.14	101.5	482	(3)
10	Canada	3.10	35.9	122	(14)
11	Hong Kong	1.83	3.5	338	(4)
12	Brazil	1.74	2.1	13	
13	Singapore	1.66	3.5	648	(2)

Continued...

Table 4.40 cont'd

Order		Receipts from tourism ($ billion)	Visitor arrivals (million)	Tourism receipts per capita ($)	
14	Netherlands	1.50	43.2	103	(16)
15	Turkey	1.48	3.5	30	
16	Greece	1.43	8.5	144	(=10)
17	Belgium	1.41	20.5	143	(12)
18	Denmark	1.33	19.8	259	(6)
19	Sweden	1.33	7.6	160	(8)
20	China	1.25	17.8	1	
21	India	1.20	1.7	2	
22	Thailand	1.17	2.6	23	
23	Portugal	1.14	12.4	111	(15)
24	Japan	1.14	2.7	9	
25	Israel	1.10	1.5	260	(5)
26	Australia	1.09	1.2	69	(19)
27	Yugoslavia	1.05	24.4	45	
28	Saudi Arabia	1.00	1.4	80	(18)

Source: WTO
Note: The figures in parentheses give the top 20 placings in per capita receipts

The travel industry is relatively young, with a growing customer base. The impact of environmental damage on the industry is therefore not easy to see at first - the supply of first-time and less sophisticated travellers has generally more than kept pace with the disillusioned who have abandoned the over-developed in favour of the more remote and unspoilt.

According to the WTO, international arrivals increased more than tenfold between 1945 and 1980, from some 25 million to around 280 million. Including internal arrivals, the level is now over 3 billion per year. In those countries affiliated to the WTO, receipts standing at $6.9 billion in 1960 had broken the $100 billion barrier by 1982. The WTO forecasts growth at around 5% per year, which means that by the year 2000 demand will be twice what it was in the mid-1980s.

Two types of environmental damage impact tourism: that caused by the tourist industry itself and that from other sources. Tourist-based industries which fail to tackle both of these will suffer. According to UNEP:

Such a growing and enormous trade in tourism was bound to have (and has had) far-reaching environmental and social consequences. Generally in the past, tourism was not particularly well planned or managed, much of it having been allowed to develop ad hoc, with facilities, including hotels, restaurants, water supply and electricity having been hastily erected or brought in as demand rose. Too often the inflow of tourists, coming en masse during a short holiday season, would overload the system, leading to water shortages, sewage problems, electricity cuts and overcrowding . . . But with the development of competition and choice the tourist has tended to become more discerning . . . Less and less therefore will the tourist accept overcrowded beaches, shoddy hotels, inadequate facilities, noise and pollution.

"Carrying capacity" has become an established part of tourism management. In the 1960s recommended beach densities were 5-25 square metres per user; a 1973 study at Brittas Bay, Ireland, concluded that a density of 10 square metres per user would not be considered overcrowded by many. And as UNEP's *Industry and Environment* magazine has observed: "Clearly far higher densities are tolerated, perhaps even sought, by the gregarious tourists who flock to the beaches of the Riviera each summer."

There are, however, other less subjective constraints on carrying capacity such as sewerage, roads, water supply, electricity, beach erosion, degradation of marine habitat, destruction of coral reefs through shell collecting, spear fishing, mooring and reef-walking, footpath erosion, wildlife displacement and so on.

The tourism industry is equally vulnerable to environmental damage from non-tourism development. Acid rain alone has damaged forests in ten European countries, fish stocks and aquatic plants in lakes from Sweden to Canada, eroded the gold roof on Krakow's cathedral, the Taj Mahal, the Coliseum, the Acropolis, the Statue of Liberty and many other monuments and historic buildings, is causing Europe's 100,000 stained-glass windows to fade and is directly linked with the corrosion of transport infrastructure including bridges and railway lines. The implications of this for tourism are obvious - anglers will go where there are fish, and so on.

An incident in the USA in the summer of 1988 illustrates how immediate and direct environmental damage can be where tourism is concerned. As the *Guardian* for 9 July reported:

Americans . . . are suddenly being confronted with an invasion of medical detritus, including used syringes and at least 145 phials of blood. To the most health-obsessed nation on earth, blood means Aids nowadays. And the dread word yesterday scattered most of the defiant few still lolling on Long Island's golden Atlantic shore. It all started on Wednesday when the beaches of the Robert Moses State Park, which bring relief for the perspiring millions of nearby New Yorkers, were closed and swimmers evacuated when the first wave of surgical gloves, first aid kits, cracked vials and the rest were spotted. Beaches opened again on Thursday only to be closed when helicopters spotted slicks of medical garbage floating off the 26-mile stretch of beach.

Business implications As with many consumer products, tourism will increasingly feel the spending-power pressure of an environmentally demanding market. Clean water, safe beaches, unpolluted air, healthy surroundings and traditional culture will be important. Environmentally concerned travel companies are already identifying themselves.

Pollution Abatement

In the USA the pollution abatement industry is believed to be worth some $75 billion. Within the EC it is estimated annual spending on pollution control and environmental protection is 30 billion ECU. In 1985 9,000 EC companies were involved in the export of air pollution control and waste-water treatment equipment, valued at 10 billion ECU, of which air and water purification equipment alone amounted to 730 million ECU, with imports of some 177 million ECU (Table 4.41).

Table 4.41   EC TRADE IN POLLUTION ABATEMENT EQUIPMENT
             1985

million ECU	Exports	Imports
Air purification equipment	177.3	76.1
Air purification parts	112.0	41.3
Water purification equipment	303.8	18.0
Water purification parts	137.7	41.9
TOTAL	730.8	177.3

Source: European Commission

In employment terms it is estimated that between 1.5 and 2 million people in the EC work in the environment industry.

Vehicle Emissions

In 1984 the House of Commons Environment Committee was "appalled" that the motor industry, in giving evidence on acid rain, had shown "an almost total lack of awareness" of the role of vehicle emissions in acid and ozone pollution.

The EC agreed stricter exhaust emission standards should stabilise the immediate position, but findings by the oil industry environmental body CONCAWE suggest that additional measures will be needed if emissions are not to rise with increased ownership and mileages in the 21st century.

As Figure 4.11 illustrates, there would have been a steady rise in hydrocarbon emissions from vehicles if the EC had taken no action. The current ECE "04" standard has ensured the containment of emissions to the year 2000 but not beyond. The latest "05" standard will significantly reduce emissions in the short but not the longer term. The CONCAWE figures suggest that only the use of large carbon canisters will greatly reduce hydrocarbon emissions in the longer term and therefore make a contribution to reduced acid pollution. Canister costs are estimated at $20-80.

Meanwhile, Johnson Matthey, already producing around 1.5 million catalytic converters at its Royston, Hertfordshire, plant, is investing £9 million in a new catalyst manufacturing plant in Belgium, with an initial planned output of 1.5 million units per year, increasing to 4.5 million units later.

Business implications It is difficult at this stage to predict what future action will be taken on vehicle emissions but it is certain that a new industry will grow up around the environmental problems posed by vehicular pollution.

Alternative Energy

Energy alternatives to so-called primary sources (oil, coal and gas) are predominantly renewable resources, such as solar, geothermal, wind, wave and biomass (the production of energy from organic matter). Some of these form established industries, others are still viewed as experimental. The theoretical potential of alternatives is well known, and around the world research and development has been progressing over the years, but so far only the surface of this resource pool has been scratched, with technical and financial problems hindering most projects.

Although having some reservations about the less desirable side effects of alternative energy processes (unsightly wind turbines, socially disruptive hydroelectric schemes, potential toxins from waste incineration etc), environmentalists complain that government support is too little and may well prove too late. Indeed, with a few exceptions, it is clear that alternative energy resources receive only low priority in government expenditure, victims, it would appear, of complacency about primaries.

Figure 4.11   Hydrocarbon Emissions from Cars in Western Europe 1970-2010

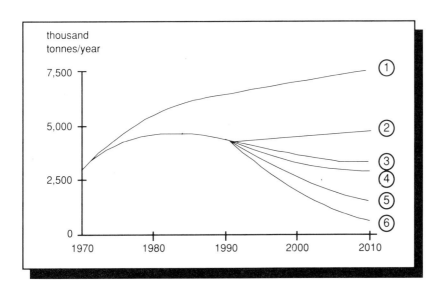

Source: CONCAWE
Notes: [1] *Hydrocarbon emissions if there were no EC controls*
  [2] *Hydrocarbon emissions under the ECE 04 standards*
  [3] *Hydrocarbon emissions under the latest ECE 05 standards*
  [4] *Hydrocarbon emissions if ECE 05 were to be combined with maximum practicable reduction in petrol volatility and with stage 2 equipment to recover fuelling losses at petrol stations*
  [5] *Hydrocarbon emissions if the ECE 05 standard were to be supplemented by the use of large canisters*
  [6] *Hydrocarbon emissions if large canisters were combined with catalytic converters on all cars*

Research and product development opportunities for industry exist in all the alternative energy fields and in the modernisation of existing techniques. Servicing and fitting will also be significant, industrially and in domestic premises.

Table 4.42 shows the world use of primary and leading alternative energy sources. Table 4.43 details the country by country sources of both primary and alternative energies.

Table 4.42   RELATIVE IMPORTANCE OF WORLD FUELS 1983

%

Oil	45.1
Coal	30.2
Gas	20.7
Geothermal	0.03
Hydroelectric	2.6
Nuclear	1.3

Source: UN Statistical Office

Table 4.43   ENERGY REQUIREMENTS BY SOURCE 1985

million tonnes oil equivalent

	Solid fuels	Oil	Gas	Nuclear	Hydro/ geothermal/ solar
Australia	35.4	27.7	11.5	0.0	3.3
Canada	34.6	71.4	49.4	13.5	67.9
Denmark	8.0	10.9	0.6	0.0	0.0
Finland	8.6	10.2	0.8	4.3	2.7
France	25.2	84.5	25.1	50.1	14.4
Iceland	0.1	0.5	0.0	0.0	0.9
Italy	16.5	81.9	27.7	1.6	10.6

Continued...

Table 4.43 cont'd

	Solid fuels	Oil	Gas	Nuclear	Hydro/ geothermal/ solar
Netherlands	6.7	21.2	33.0	0.9	0.0
Norway	1.9	8.1	1.1	0.0	15.4
Spain	19.6	39.0	2.2	6.3	7.4
Sweden	8.2	17.8	0.1	13.1	16.0
Switzerland	1.3	12.5	1.3	5.0	7.4
UK	61.8	78.3	47.5	13.7	1.6
USA	491.9	713.4	423.0	90.9	66.0
West Germany	82.8	112.0	41.5	28.1	3.9
WORLD TOTAL	1,942.7	2,852.1	1,362.9	331.3	557.8

Source: OECD

Hydroelectric Power

Hydroelectric power (HEP) is probably the most developed form of "alternative" energy production. The value of exploiting HEP is not in question; much of its potential is already tapped in some countries. In Europe, for example, about 80% of HEP potential is already exploited; in the USA 60%. Table 4.44 lists the possible generating capacity certain countries might install, and estimates potential output. The output per Megawatt of installed capacity varies because of the different flow characteristics of rivers. It will also be seen that regions poor in coal and oil, such as South America, Africa, and South-East Asia, have major water power resources; only 20% of these have already been developed.

Table 4.44   WORLD HYDROELECTRIC POTENTIAL 1974

	Theoretic capacity (usable MW)	Theoretrical annual output (GWh)
China	330,000	1,320,000
USSR	269,000	1,095,000
USA	186,700	701,500

Continued...

Table 4.44 cont'd

	Theoretic capacity (usable MW)	Theoretrical annual output (GWh)
Zaire	132,000	660,000
Canada	94,500	535,200
Brazil	90,200	519,300
Madagascar	64,000	320,000
Colombia	50,000	300,000
India	70,000	280,000
Burma	75,000	225,000
North Vietnam and Laos	48,000	192,000
Argentina	48,100	191,000
Indonesia	30,000	150,000
Japan	49,600	130,000
Ecuador	21,000	126,000
Papua New Guinea	17,800	121,700
Norway	29,600	121,000
Cameroon	23,000	114,800
Peru	12,500	109,200
Pakistan	20,000	105,000
Sweden	20,100	100,300
Mexico	20,300	99,400
Venezuela	11,600	98,000
Chile	15,800	88,600
Gabon	17,500	87,600
All other nations	514,800	2,011,800
TOTAL	2,261,100	9,802,400

Source: WEC
Note: Average flow conditions assumed

Building HEP stations is a long-term, high-cost business. In developed countries it is more a question of plant modernisation, overcoming major location and technical difficulties for the expansion of suitable watercourses and applying new technology to exploit new areas. However, the problems in vastly under-exploited developing countries are very different: initial enthusiasm for HEP has, to some extent, cooled as international financing has pulled back; there are fears that the indiscriminate generation of electricity does not necessarily benefit the poor and needy of the Third World. On the contrary, if a high level of electricity consumption presupposes a level of wealth sufficient for people to purchase and use electrical appliances, the low and highly selective consumption in poverty zones must lead to frustration, inequality and, of course, wasted capital.

Thus developing countries are looking carefully at any hydropower proposals, not because they doubt the efficacy of the natural and renewable resource, but to assess details of timing and scale. The construction of a full-scale HEP plant can cost billions of dollars and take decades to complete. Serious environmental problems need to be taken into account. The flooding of large areas for dam projects has caused great distress to native peoples, dispossessed and disoriented when their land is flooded in the name of HEP. There are also fears about the effects on fish and animals, indeed whole ecosystems, as a result of interruption and manipulation of large bodies of water.

In 1987 the World Bank (WB) and the International Development Association (IDA) approved loans totalling millions of dollars for hydroelectricity projects. These included:

Chile: WB loan of $95 million Construction of the 500MW Pehuenche hydroelectric power plant will help meet the country's growing demand for electricity. A training programme for staff of the executing agency will strengthen their capacity to manage the plant, while a national environmental programme will develop professional expertise for an awareness within Chile of the importance of environmental management.

China: WB loan of $140 million Economic growth in East China and Fujian province will be supported through development of a major hydroelectric site on the Min River.

India: WB loan of $330 million Power shortages in the southern region are to be alleviated by exploiting indigenous hydro resources. The Sharavati (Karnataka State) hydropower staion will be renovated and transmission capacity augmented, thus reducing power losses.

Turkey: WB loan of $312 million Financing is to be provided for the 283.5 MW Sir hydropower station on the Ceyhan River, thus supporting efforts to develop the country's indigenous energy resources and bring about greater involvement of the private sector in energy development.

Western Samoa: IDA loan of $3 million The government's policy to reduce dependence on imported fuel is to be supported through help in developing the country's hydro resources to replace high-cost diesel-generated energy.

World HEP capacity in existing installations is 490,000 MW, about 22% of potential. The output has grown at an annual rate of about 3.5% over the past ten years. If all the world's potential were harnessed, it would supply the equivalent of 33% of the world's current energy consumption. However, full exploitation is considered unlikely due to political and social pressures.

Business implications Major growth of HEP is likely to be focused more on small specific projects that the giant developments of the past. Developing countries will call on the expertise of experts from developed countries, but decreasingly so, and more political attention will be paid to local training of both engineers and labour.

The potential still exists for more specialist HEP projects in developed countries, particularly as social and technical difficulties are overcome. There is interest, for instance, in underground development (both of piping and installation) and of less disruptive lake and river-tapping technology.

Wind Power

The amount of wind-powered energy created for commercial purposes in the world has grown substantially during the past decade. Installations peaked in the USA and Europe in 1985 and there are now more than 14,000 wind-turbine generators, with a power capability of 1,100 MW. The UK has potential wind-power capacity of up to 45 billion kilowatt hours each year on land (ie almost 20% of current UK electricity use) and up to three times this amount offshore. The UK is beginning to show an active interest in large-scale wind-power generation.

The CEGB Richborough wind turbine should be able to generate enough power unders its 1,000-kW operating capacity to meet the electricity demands of 1,000 homes. The 3,000-kW machine built at Burgar Hill, Orkney, for the North of Scotland Hydro-Electric Board and the Department of Energy, at a cost of £8 million, should supply the electricity needs of 2,000 homes. There are two other medium-size generators on this site. Other installations include a 50-kW machine on the Isle of Lundy, one on Shetland, one on the Fair Isles and several on mainland Britain connected to the national grid.

The UK government is under pressure to establish wind farms as a next step from individual or small collective systems. These farms, like those operated in the USA and some European countries including Denmark and Holland, could each generate up to 10 MW. Environmentalists fear wind farms will be socially and scenically unacceptable, so the debate between small and economically preferred systems or wind-turbine giants continues.

Meanwhile the number of wind farms in Europe increases. Denmark has three established farms; two have between them 13 100-kW machines and 20 55 kW machines, the third five 750-kW machines. In Holland a farm at Sexbierum has 18 300-kW units. More farms are planned in a 150-million-guilder Dutch government investment programme. There are believed to be more than 400,000 suitable wind-farm sites in the EC, capable of developing 3.4 million kW hours of wind-generated electricity each year.

Wind-turbine manufacturers in Denmark had exported more than 5,000 wind turbines to California by the end of 1986. By the end of 1985, 20 small companies were manufacturing wind turbines and employing around 3,000 people. Sales exceeded $200 million. The UK market is also developing. The traditional smaller companies are being joined by large consortia such as the Wind Energy Group, formed by British Aerospace and Taylor Woodrow Construction, and industry giants such as McAlpine and GEC.

There is great confidence in the future of wind-generated energy on a large, national scale - for instance, the US utilities alone expect to be using some $20 billion worth of wind-generated energy between 1990 and 2000. In the UK the large-scale future of wind farms could lie at sea, in supposedly environmentally acceptable clusters disturbing neither shipping, fishing, nor bird migration habits. Plans are being formulated for such a development for Eastern Electricity.

At the other end of the scale, there is a reported upswing in demand for small, independent wind turbines aimed at customer or small company use. Greater environmental awareness and resistance to both fossil fuels and nuclear power have led to demand for machines in the 3-kW range which can be purchased and installed for under £4,000, such as Energy Services Ltd's 3-kW Curlew wind turbine (Figure 4.12 gives its annual energy output and electricity costs). The potential market is the rural community - smallholders and crofters with suitable remote and windy sites, and the 300,000 or more small farms and market gardens in the UK.

Business implications The market for renewable energy technology is growing, partly as a result of heightening public awareness of fossil-fuel pollution and nuclear hazards. There is a danger of the UK lagging behind the USA and the rest of Europe in export markets in the light of poor government support of manufacturing technology. As Table 4.45 shows, renewable resources as a whole received grants of £14 million in 1984/85, 6% of the amount allocated to the nuclear research and development programme. UK companies need to tap into the export market for developing countries, which are increasingly opting for renewable resource systems.

Figure 4.12   Annual Energy Output and Average Cost of Electricity of the Curlew 3-kW Wind Turbine 1986

(a) Annual energy output

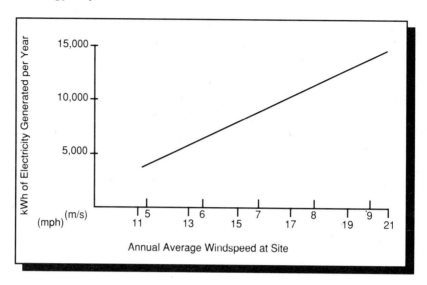

(b) Average cost of electricity

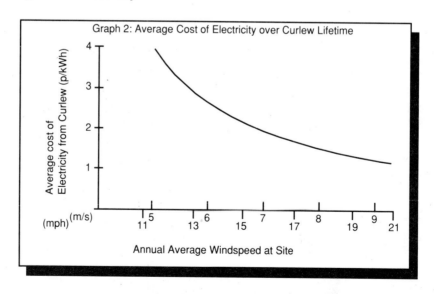

Source: Energy Services Ltd

Table 4.45   UK DEPARTMENT OF ENERGY EXPENDITURE ON RENEWABLE ENERGY RESEARCH AND DEVELOPMENT 1979-1985

£ million	1979-80	1980-81	1981-82	1982-83	1983-84	1984-85	1985-86	1986-87 estimate	Budget provision 1987-88
Wind	0.6	0.8	0.9	2.5	2.5	4.8	5.4	3.7	3.2
Wave	3.0	3.3	4.4	3.1	1.0	0.4	0.4	0.1	0.1
Geothermal aquifers	1.3	1.7	2.6	1.5	1.8	1.1	0.3	0.1	0.2
Geothermal hot dry rocks	–	0.6	5.6	3.0	2.9	4.6	3.5	3.5	3.2
Solar	1.2	0.9	0.7	1.4	0.9	0.5	0.7	0.8	1.1
Biomass	0.1	0.3	0.4	0.7	0.3	1.1	0.8	1.3	1.3
Tide	0.6	1.4	0.4	–	–	0.3	0.1	0.1	1.0
Energy Technology Support Unit	1.4	2.2	2.3	2.0	1.9	2.1	2.0	2.3	2.1
TOTAL	8.2	11.2	17.3	14.2	11.3	14.0	13.2	11.9	12.2

Source: Energy Technology Support Unit(ETSU)

Solar Energy

The midday intensity of solar energy on a clear day in the tropics can exceed 1 kilowatt per square metre. This level of energy falling on an 8-km square is equivalent to the output of the whole of the UK's electricity generating system. Solar energy collecting systems currently harness only a tiny amount of potential, usually employing flat-plate solar collectors. These can provide hot water for domestic and small-scale business needs, particularly in countries with guaranteed amounts of sunshine such as Australia, Japan, Israel, Turkey and the southern USA. In 1984 Israel had 700,000 such domestic collectors, the USA 550,000, and Japan 300,000 - rising to 3 million in 1987.

Unfortunately, in less sunny countries the economics of domestic solar systems make them generally unattractive, and despite a research boom in the 1970s, no scientific breakthrough improving this situation seems likely in the near future. In the UK a household solar panel system, costing over £3,000 in 1988 including installation, might provide about a third of domestic hot water requirements. In Denmark a similar installation costs in the region of £600. The industry blames the small size of the UK market for comparatively high costs. Nevertheless, estimates suggest there may be 3 million solar water-heating panels in the UK within 50 years.

Solar energy is also used to supply water, using solar stills. Again the world market is small and capital costs high, but it is hoped that efficient systems will be able to provide emergency supplies in regions that are short of water.

The solar technology which has for some time attracted the greatest interest is photovoltaics - the direct production of electricity from sunlight. These solar cells produce clean, safe and silent energy. Perhaps best known for their application in solar-powered calculators (60 million were sold in 1983, accounting for 10% of world output from solar cells), they are also used to power satellites and spacecraft, and to provide small amounts of electricity for buoys and boats and some remote holiday homes. But costs remain high: in the late 1960s and early 1970s prices of $50,000 per kilowatt of output were being quoted. By the mid-1980s these had fallen to $8-10,000.

Solar energy can also be used to cool buildings. The mechanical equipment is similar to that used in refrigerators, with absorption-desorption principles and evaporating ammonia achieving the cooling effect.

One of the largest growth areas in the field of solar energy is that of "passive solar design", often called solar architecture. This involves designing buildings, both industrial and domestic, to make the most efficient use of solar energy. They are heated by radiation falling on roofs and walls and passing through windows. The heat is then distributed by natural processes of conduction, convection and thermal radiation to retain warmth. The principles can be modified to suit hot climates. During the past ten years solar design has worked at enhancing methods of maximising this "free" energy. At first, designers in France, the USA and Scandinavia led the field, but there have been several notable developments of solar buildings in the UK such as Pennyland Solar estate, Milton Keynes or St Georges School, Wallasey.

Business implications An expansion of the market for solar water-heating panels in temperate countries could lead to a substantial fall in unit price. At present material costs account for only about 20% of the final price, very high labour costs being due to the small market, but the 3 million home units in the UK alone, projected for 2025, could provide a sound base for widespread application to industry. In the other areas of solar energy there is a small but promising market for improved technology. Research into solar energy storage is vital to growth. The market for solar stills in developing countries would be vast were the mechanism affordable. Most development and service industry potential, certainly in the short-term, lies in solar design for houses and factories. New glass-coating materials and more efficient building fabrics are available; new consultancy and fitting industries are being created. There is an established consumer demand for small-scale solar-powered products (such as calculators), boosted by the pollution problems of conventional batteries.

Geothermal Energy

It is estimated that sufficient heat exists about 10 km beneath the earth's surface to supply a large proportion of the world's energy needs for thousands of years. More than 20 countries already produce power from steam tapped from hot water below the earth's surface; processes exist to obtain heat from dry hot rocks.

The world's geothermal output already exceeds 3,500 MW and could reach 8,000 by 1990. The largest geothermal field is in California where over 200 wells have been drilled. Table 4.46 gives the world installed geothermal generating capacity in 1986.

Table 4.46   WORLD INSTALLED GEOTHERMAL ELECTRICITY
GENERATING CAPACITY 1986

Megawatts

USA	2,002
Philippines	894
Mexico	645
Italy	479
Japan	215
New Zealand	167
El Salvador	95
Kenya	45
Iceland	39
Nicaragua	35
Indonesia	32
Turkey	21
China	11
USSR	11
Guadeloupe	4
Azores	3
Others	21
TOTAL	4,719

Source: World Energy Conference Survey of Energy Resources

Natural geysers provide steam and have been used in space- and water-heating projects for many years in New Zealand and Iceland, but man-made aquifer wells are increasingly being used, particularly successfully in France, the USSR and Hungary. Serious drawbacks include the expense of drilling and the corrosive substances encountered. Environmentalists also doubt the desirability of interfering with rock stratas and underground water flows.

A number of successful schemes have been underwritten by governments. In France, for example, a block of flats in Paris is heated with hot water from wells 2 km deep. The French government has supported more than 40 geothermal schemes in the past 15 years and more are under construction in Paris and Bordeaux. It is estimated that government schemes alone will save the equivalent of 1 million tonnes of oil by 1990.

Japan accounts for about two-thirds of the total worldwide consumption of geothermal energy used in spas and hot baths. It also uses it for domestic, horticultural and industrial heating. Excluding spas and baths, the total geothermal heat utilised throughout the world is the equivalent of about 2 million tonnes of oil per year. Iceland is the largest domestic and commercial heating user, closely followed by the USSR, France and Hungary.

The annual growth rate in the output of electricity from geothermal energy has averaged about 14.5% over the past decade and a half.

Business implications Technology in geothermal fields is constantly improving, with an emphasis on new "dry hot rock" techniques. Apart from research programmes aimed at ways of improving efficiency and reducing drilling and maintenance costs, potential exists in groundwater heat pumps, which are widely used in the USA to supply space and water heating in schools, commercial and industrial buildings and in some private homes. There have been similar schemes in Western Europe, notably Sweden where water is drawn from an aquifer 700 metres deep and further heated before being piped to a nearby housing estate. Several areas in the UK are thought to have suitable conditions.

Energy Conservation

Often cited as the most important form of alternative energy, and nicknamed the "fifth fuel", energy conservation offers considerable business opportunities, with a market potential of £52 billion across Europe. In the UK alone, studies have shown that if increased energy consumption targets are to be kept to 3% over the next 12 years, an investment of £8-9 billion in energy-saving technologies and schemes will be needed.

Major industry projects include research into energy saving in power stations throughout Europe. There is also increased political and social interest in incorporating energy conservation into ongoing inner-city regeneration projects. The European Community has a goal of 20% savings on its fuel bill; the UK is aiming at 30%, which could free up to £7 billion for other purposes.

Inner-city energy conservation affects both domestic and business users. The domestic focus is on poor housing stock - poorly insulated, badly heated and ill-maintained. Heating systems are often inefficient and thus expensive to run, and inadequate insulation makes the problem worse. The Association for the Conservation of Energy (ACE) reports that an improvement in energy conservation conditions in this type of housing stock would directly lead to more economically buoyant inner cities: "Firstly residents would have more comfortable homes. Secondly, even though some of the cost savings from energy saving improvements would be taken up through increased comfort levels, there would be money available to spend on other things . . . this extra money would be spent mostly on goods and services in the local areas where such spending is most needed."

Industry and commerce in the inner cities can also benefit from lower fuel costs which energy-saving investments bring. The UK government, in acknowledging the country's poor record in terms of energy cost per unit of output, has pledged to make Britain the most energy-efficient nation in Europe by 1990.

ACE calls for public initiatives to inform businesses of energy conservation techniques: "Reducing waste in inner urban areas would help existing businesses to compete better in their market places, thereby maintaining and even increasing employment opportunities. So businesses stand to gain, first, by reducing company outgoings and, second, by exploiting the new, environment-friendly markets stimulated by increased energy efficiency.

The energy efficiency industry is difficult to define precisely. It comprises many diverse types of activity covering manufacture, distribution, installation and consultancy services. The installation of energy-efficient equipment is well suited to small firms, and many enterprises have been created with limited capital. The manufacture of energy-saving equipment is becoming increasingly capital- rather than labour-intensive, and is dominated by a handful of major companies. ACE forecasts that 52% of jobs will be in installation, with only 15% in manufacture and 5% in supply. This high proportion of installation jobs offers two particular benefits:

1.   Installing energy-saving equipment and materials demands only limited skills and, apart from heating controls, requires only basic training.
2.   Installation jobs can be located anywhere, not necessarily on factorysites.

Energy saving devices include:

1.   Thermal insulation for entire buildings
2.   Mechanical devices to ventilate and to cut heat loss
3.   Thermostats and improved control systems
4.   Larger windows for more sunlight to warm buildings naturally
5.   Energy-efficient household appliances, particularly fridges and freezers
6.   Low-power lamps, usually fluorescent bulbs and tubes
7.   Updated double glazing to minimise heat loss but permit air circulation

8. New materials to coat windows for best heat absorption/insulation purposes
9. Efficient draught-proofing.

The MSC and the Department of Energy have funded a number of "neighbourhood insulation projects", mainly carried out by the voluntary "Neighbourhood Energy Action" movement. UK figures show that 400 projects provided draught-proofing in 200,000 homes during 1986/87. They employed 8,000 people at a total cost of £45 million, of which £9 million was spent directly on insulating materials, mostly draught-proofing.

Growth is also envisaged in the area of energy efficiency consultancy, or energy audits. In 1987 the EC published a draft directive requiring anyone transferring either the ownership or occupation of a home to provide basic information concerning the energy efficiency of the premises. Such a requirement has been operating in Denmark for a number of years, where it has stimulated conservation awareness and thus investment in the market for energy-efficient goods and services. From the outset the scheme generated the equivalent of £4 of private for every £1 of government money. It is now wholly self-financing and has involved over half the Danish housing stock; 1,200 home energy surveyors are now registered.

ACE research shows that its proposed energy-saving improvements in inner cities throughout the UK would generate up to 110,000 new jobs. At present 15,000 people are employed in manufacturing, installing and servicing energy-saving equipment throughout the UK. This could rise by more than five times in inner cities alone to create up to 67,000 new jobs over ten years. Up to 42,000 additional jobs could be created because of increased economic activity. (Figure 4.13)

Figure 4.13   Forecast of Jobs Created in the Energy Conservation Industry 1988

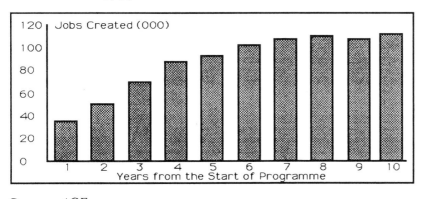

Source: ACE

Business implications A huge market exists for the manufacture and installation of energy-efficient products both for industry and the domestic consumer. If the EC pursues its target of reducing energy consumption by 20% (30% for the UK), investment in energy-saving technology (including grants for householders) must directly affect business.

Natural Cosmetics in the UK

The pursuit of a healthier lifestyle has quickly made inroads into cosmetics, and consumers have accepted that "healthy" and "natural" are two aspects of the same broad concept. Green shoppers, however, are increasingly suspicious at broad claims to "healthy" or "natural" ingredients and, in addition, now expect their environmentally concerned stockists to have considered the question of animal testing. Thus there is a double-check of environmentally sound claims within the cosmetics industry: the proportion of "natural" ingredients, and its animal testing stand.

The natural cosmetics industry attempts to use ingredients as close to their natural state wherever possible. Totally natural products are, in fact, usually impossible to develop as some form of synthetic preservative is required in a majority of cases. Similarly, manufacturers adopting a no animal tests approach cannot claim that absolutely all their ingredients have not been tested on animals at some stage. The most reasonable claim to make would appear to be that companies can claim to use ingredients with a long and proven saftey record, which have long since not needed testing.

The total retail market in 1985 for specialist natural cosmetics in the UK was estimated to be in excess of £20 million. To put this into context, the total retail market for skincare, colour cosmetics, hair care and bathroom products was worth approximately £1,140 million in 1985, with "natural" products accounting for almost 2%. This was more than double their estimated share at the beginning of the decade (see Table 4.47).

Table 4.47   RETAIL MARKET FOR SPECIALIST NATURAL
COSMETICS 1980-1985

£ million rsp	1980	1981	1982	1983	1984	1985
Natural cosmetics	6.1	7.2	8.8	11.0	14.6	20.7
Total cosmetics[1]	735.0	800.0	870.0	955.0	1,050.0	1,140.0
% natural	0.8	0.9	1.0	1.2	1.4	1.8

Source: Euromonitor
Note: [1] *Defined as hair care, skincare, colour make-up, and cosmetics and bathroom products*

Retail Outlets

The Body Shop was founded in 1976. Environmental responsibility and its highly moral selling philosophy are given a high priority. The company now has 88 outlets in the UK and 180 overseas. In 1985 its turnover was over £9 million; in 1986-87 turnover was £17.4 million and profit £7.9 million.

By comparison with Body Shop, the market for natural cosmetics in healthstores has been disappointing. Total retail sales of healthstore cosmetics are estimated to have been worth slightly more than £6 million at rsp in 1985, accounting for less than 4% of total retail sales through healthstores. For Holland & Barrett, the UK's largest healthstore chain, natural cosmetics have been even less successful accounting for only 1% of store turnover.

At the end of 1985 growth in retail sales of cosmetics in healthstores was around 12% per annum, significantly below the 15% rate being achieved by total business in the stores. They seem not to be the ideal places for selling natural cosmetics. This is certainly in part due to their 25-45 age group customer profile, which is a little old for vibrant sales.

Yves Rocher, the French-based natural cosmetic company, operates on a retail franchise basis under the Beauty Centres name. At 1985 Rocher had 33 centres in the UK, 1,000 throughout Europe and more than 2 million regular mail-order customers. Its UK turnover was estimated at about £3 million in 1985, and it is believed this continental giant could mount a significant challenge to Body Shop.

Natural cosmetics sales by manufacturers specialising in health foods for chemists and grocers (excluding own brands) would have been in the region of £1 million in 1985.

Business implications The lid has been lifted from some of the unenvironmental aspects of the cosmetics industry (particularly wasteful packaging, high advertising and marketing costs and cruelty to animals). This leaves a buying public twitchy about the morals of the cosmetics world and suspicious of claims about "natural" ingredients. Companies prepared to take an environmental stand can expect to ride on the current crest of popularity created by Body Shop and Yves Rocher.

4.8 THE ENVIRONMENT AS A PUBLIC RELATIONS TOOL

In an apparent U-turn from the traditional antagonism between industry and the environmental movement, companies worldwide are beginning to take full PR advantage of green links. Environmentalism has moved from its original fringe image to become a more acceptable establishment force, and many more companies are ready, even anxious, to dedicate part of their marketing budgets to perceivably green PR projects. Of course, not *all* companies are prepared to accept the concept of environmentalism, neither are *all* environmental organisations able or willing to adopt an establishment image, but there has undoubtedly been movement on both sides.

Environmental targets in PR terms include:

1.   Opinion formers (such as environmental pressure groups).
2.   The local community.
3.   Regulatory bodies such as planning authorities, service authorities (eg water), technology organisations.
4.   Legislative bodies: national, international and, of increasing influence,the European Community.
5.   Industry organisations. Not simply from within similar industries, but across the board: for instance the CBI, TUC and ILO.
6.   Within the company: board, shareholders and workforce.

Some companies are already well advanced in their environment-linked PR campaigns: to some, such as Body Shop, such PR is a fundamental part of their activity. After ten years of operation, Body Shop, famous for its cruelty-free and no-waste cosmetics and toiletries business, has never bought advertising space (save for some recruitment ads), choosing to rely exclusively on PR methods for its publicity. It is completely convinced by the power of

PR and claims to have enjoyed millions of pounds of free publicity, a fact its high media profile confirms. The Body Shop attitude to PR is that it will always give information freely and honestly, but that entertaining the press or handing out gifts would infringe its ban on unnecessary packaging. This policy is in stark contrast to those of many other cosmetics companies.

Other environment-linked PR campaigns are new additions to regular advertising activities. Cadbury launched its Wildlife chocolate bars, Heinz celebrated its centenary and Nokia reported booming business with its paper products - all with projects benefiting the World Wide Fund for Nature.

Cadbury launched an educational nature project with its animal wrapper chocolate: "Working with WWF has enabled us to consolidate and improve our market share with this new product."

Heinz donated £1 million to WWF projects in its Guardians of the Countryside centenary campaign: "Judging by our mailbag, the timing of our Guardians of the Countryside programme could not have been better. The really enthusiastical response of our customers, a pointer to the fast-growing public interest in conservation, augurs well for this joint venture with the World Wildlife Fund."

Nokia of Finland used the famous WWF Panda logo to launch a product made out of recycled materials: "The company spent only half as much as the competitor on advertising, but outsold the competitor two to one."

Conservation and the environment are favourites when it comes to the "cause-related marketing" tactics of companies worldwide. For example, Harrods in London and I Magnin of the USA increased traffic in their well-known department stores with PR exercises which included specially designed wildlife areas and charity auctions of wildlife art. Kellogg has produced conservation education material in the Nordic countries, Germany and Italy; in Italy American Express donated funds to WWF's Save the Coasts campaign for every card transaction, card usage increasing 20%.

The high incidence of industry partnerships with WWF is a direct result of the organisation seizing the opportunities provided by this surge in the PR value of environment-linked projects. Because of its international structure WWF has become one of the most sophisticated conservationist fund-raisers in the world. As a "clearing house" for millions of pounds donated every year, the organisation has developed a businesslike approach to attracting substantial and regular corporate funds. The tie-up with business partners is based on mutual benefit:

Companies can help save nature and get acknowledgement by funding our projects and publicising important conservation issues. This partnership helps them launch new brands, improve their image, facilitate relations with government regulatory bodies and generate new business contacts.

However, WWF would be the first to admit that these tie-ups with business emanate not from the office of good works but the marketing departments. Its fund-raising literature invites companies to "take advantage of the widespread concern for nature conservation and the proven marketing strength of the WWF Panda".

With the maturing of environmentalism in the public eye, there is less "whitewashing" of issues through PR endeavour. This is due to two main factors: less tolerance of non-environmental products and practice from the consumer, and an increasing acknowledgement from industry that sound environmental practice is linked with corporate success. Both attitudes have been fostered by non-governmental pressure groups such as Friends of the Earth, Greenpeace and the long-established though less flamboyant specialists such as the Royal Society for the Protection of Birds, all of which demonstrate increasing flair in extracting maximum benefit from PR.

These front-line conservationist organisations are therefore not slow to confront unenvironmental activities - even if the alleged perpetrator also happens to be a philanthropist. For instance, Shell UK involves itself in high-profile environmental projects such as the Better Britain campaign, and yet in spite of this Friends of the Earth pulled no punches in its 1987 "Tell Shell to go to Hell . . .!" campaign against the manufacture of certain pesticides.

PR and the World Wide Fund for Nature

Many multinational companies now fully exploit associations with organisations such as WWF. Cadbury, Heinz and Nokia have already been mentioned.

IBM

IBM specifically aims projects at promoting the issue of sustainable development. IBM-Europe made international headlines by presenting a System 38 computer to WWF President, HRH the Prince Philip. The computer, worth many thousands of pounds, is used in the management of WWF's 300 projects.

228

Kodak

Kodak sponsored the WWF Conservation Awards Scheme to assist groups which support their local area. The project also aimed at and, according to the company, succeeded in strengthening visibility of the Kodak product to teenagers.

Office Cleaning Services

OCS is the largest privately owned office cleaning and security group in the UK. It found potential clients reacted much more enthusiastically to nature-oriented presentations prepared in conjunction with WWF than to its traditional sports-related promotions. OCS sponsored a campaign to save the British Barn Owl, which generated positive publicity, and also made a donation to the WWF for each person attending sales meetings. The company reports improved attendance at sales meetings *and* a new company record in attracting new business.

Prudential Assurance

The Pru supports the British Trust for Conservation Volunteers through WWF. This enabled the Pru to enjoy nationwide coverage *and* reach the difficult 18–25 age range. Supported projects included repairing stone walls, digging ditches and restoring the left foot of the chalk giant, Long Man of Wilmington.

Canada Life Assurance

The company used the WWF link to launch a corporate image campaign with the theme "Bringing Protection to Life". Company-funded projects included "Save the White Pelican", and the bird was the first in Canada to be taken off the endangered species list. Canada Life sales increased and staff morale "jumped" because "the employees appreciated the company's nature conservation efforts".

In addition to those mentioned above, a number of European companies have become directly involved with WWF projects, including:

1. *Rentenanstalt*, a major Swiss insurance company, sponsored a WWF teacher's kit on forest conservation. The material supported the company's centenary advertising campaign using the example of a forest protecting an Alpine village from avalanches.

2.   *Produttori Italiani Bierra*, a group of Italian breweries, sponsored *"camminamare"*, a 4,000-km walk around Italy's coast, to draw attention to environmental concerns and WWF's conservation efforts.

3.   *Ente Nazionale* was a well publicised major sponsor in WWF's 25th anniversary activities in Assisi, Italy. The link was continued through its subsidiary, Societa Nazionale Approvigionamento Metano (SNAM) in a WWF-backed campaign successfully launching household methane gas. The company sponsors oasis wildlife protection zones throughout Italy and the Panda gives the natural gas an acceptable image.

Even tobacco companies, which many consider unenvironmental by reason of their very existence, have been successful in improving their image through links with conservation. As a major part of its 25th anniversary celebrations, Scandinavian Tobacco launched an annual conservation prize in conjunction with WWF.

The WWF is not involved with conservation projects at grassroots level: its business is raising money to support specific projects and to distribute to conservation bodies such as the Royal Society for the Protection of Birds and the Royal Society for Nature Conservation, an umbrella group for Britain's naturalist trusts. In this capacity WWF can act as an efficient financial organiser, leaving the actual work to specialist organisations in the field.

The Conservation Foundation

WWF is by no means the only environmental contact being wooed by PR. Another specialist in the area is Britain's Conservation Foundation, formed in 1982 to provide a link between industry and the environment. In practice this results in a variety of sponsored schemes designed to *publicise* and encourage a wide range of constructive conservation activities. The Foundation works at local, national and international levels to meet these ambitions. PR and marketing advantage is high on its lists of benefits for sponsors of schemes.

The concept of industrial sponsorship of the environment led to the creation of the Foundation. Pitney Bowes, the office and mailing equipment company, ran a highly successful "Elms Across Europe" promotion to propagate and plant disease-resistant elms. The promotion continues, the latest launch taking place in Ireland. Every tree sold produces a royalty paid to the Conservation Foundation.

The flagship of the Conservation Foundation's industry/environment projects is the Ford European Conservation Awards. Organised simultaneously throughout 14 European countries, the awards are open to all types of conservation projects in four categories: natural environment; heritage; young people; and conservation engineering. All 14 national winners go through to a European final. The winner of each national category receives £2,000 and each overall national winner £5,000. The European winner receives a further $10,000. Each winner also receives a specially commissioned bronze trophy.

Other Conservation Foundation projects with keen industry participation include:

1. *Trusthouse Forte Community Chest.* This major hotel groups gives well-publicised support for a wide variety of local environmental schemes throughout Britain. Projects have included grants for badger crossings - road crossings with experimental reflectors aimed at warning badgers of oncoming traffic. Since 1984, 54 grants have been made.

2. *Conservation Foundation Special Awards.* Financed by the electricity supply industry since 1984, these make funds available for environmental projects involving the young and the elderly (PR weak spots for electricity companies). The first award enabled a nature reserve especially designed for disabled young people to be built on waste land at the edge of the New Forest.

3. *Aluminium Trees.* A project sponsored by the aluminium industry involving 4,000 schools collecting 1.75 million aluminium cans worth £8,652 for tree planting in the Third World. Meanwhile the Forestry Commission in association with the Nature Conservancy Council and the Nottinghamshire County Council, sponsored by the aluminium industry, created a 60-acre oak tree map of Great Britain in Sherwood Forest in a programme to replace Corsican pine forests.

4. *Puff Fabrics.* A range of fabrics based on a barn owl's tear-drop feather launched by international fabric designers, Osborne & Little, aimed to publicise the plight of the barn owl population and raise funds for conservation. Puff the tame barn owl is one of the Foundation's mascots and inspired the fabric idea.

5. *Country House Awards.* A direct industry link between estate agents Jackson, Stops & Staff and the *Sunday Times* to sponsor a Foundation award for sympathetic country house conversion. Awards are made to the converters of country houses and ancillary buildings for alternative purposes, the judges looking for retention of original qualities.

Other, smaller-scale Foundation projects have included support for the Turkish Delight holiday programme highlighting the plight of turtles along a vulnerable coastline. Royalties have raised £3,000 for the project. *Country*

Living magazine has supported a research and protection scheme for yew trees in British churchyards.

The Benefits of Winning Awards

Companies find that as well as sponsoring environmental excellence awards, they can also enjoy substantial PR from winning awards, thereby giving product or practice "clean" appeal.

The Pollution Abatement Technology Award Scheme promoted by the CBI, with the Royal Society of Arts and the Environment Foundation (a charity formed by the Clarkson Puckle Group of international insurance brokers) as sponsors, is one of the most prestigious. Entries are judged by the extent to which they achieve environmental benefits, are innovative and make economies or improve efficiency. After each award ceremony a booklet is published, describing the successful technologies and giving brief details of all entries. A specially commissioned trophy forms an important part of the award and the winning companies take full PR advantage of immediate publicity and the growing recognition of the award.

The Business and Industry Panel for the Environment Awards are older, launched in 1975 in response to what was perceived as a growing public fear that industry was environment enemy number one. It was also hoped the awards would help persuade industry to pre-empt environmental legislation. Founding organisations included the NCB, CEGB, Reed Paper Group, International Thomson, RTZ and British Rail. A feature of the scheme is that the judges are themselves managers of industry and the awards recognising "good environmental practice" within companies.

Corporate Environmental Policy (CEP)

The publication of a CEP gives the workforce a clear definition of what they are working towards in environmental terms and the public a benchmark against which to measure the performance of both the particular company and its competitors.

The CEP can be used to attack. Legislators can be lobbied to ensure that competitors come up to the same standards. According to leading UK waste-management company Shanks & McEwan, for example: "We are convinced that others are getting away with lower standards. It is important that our example is followed. The regulatory authorities must implement controls over those who operate to the lowest possible standards. In this respect we welcome any legislation . . ."

232

ICI's environmental policy is circulated throughout the company. The fact that its contents are now public knowledge as a result of its publication in various business journals is further indication of the importance attached, not just to having (and implementing) an environmental policy, but also being seen to have a policy.

Perhaps the best known of all CEPs is the 3M 3Ps (Pollution Prevention Pays) programme. Originally developed in the USA, the company now employs the policy worldwide. On receiving its Pollution Abatement Technology award in 1985, the UK company said the 3P programme had saved £4.25 million and had "strengthened 3M's competitive position in world markets".

IBM's CEP (reproduced as Figure 4.10 in Section 4.6) states that all the company's facilities, wherever located, should meet and preferably *exceed* the most stringent government regulations in any of the countries in which it operates. IBM is therefore anxious that legislation should, wherever possible, move to meet its own high standards - a stand which has understandably attracted a great deal of publicity. Where local regulations and set standards do not exist, IBM undertakes to create its own standards. It stresses that environmental protection is tackled just like any other management issue. It starts out with a clearly stated policy, which is issued to all employees and is backed with environmental impact assessment for new projects and the ongoing monitoring of existing works.

The CEPs mentioned above, and many others, foreshadow and reflect much of the Green Code, an environmental policy statement issued by the Chemical Industries Association during the European Year of the Environment in 1987-88. The Code is reproduced later in this section as Figure 4.14.

Formulating and publishing the CEP is only one part of environmental responsibility. The public will increasingly demand to see it carried out. In some activities, environmental impact, and consequently the need for action, is more apparent than others.

Putting the CEP into Practice

In the mid-1960s British Gas was faced with digging up what seemed to be half the countryside to establish a natural gas supply. Doubters warned of a hornet's nest of problems, especially from a public faced with bulldozers and plastic piping.

Today there is a gas transmission system comprising over 11,000 miles of national and regional high-pressure pipeline. British Gas is happy that there was minimum controversy, which it takes as an indication of environmental acceptability. It undertook the huge project on a basis of local consultation and flexibility. PR benefits came from news of a detour to preserve a local beauty spot or protected site. British Gas employed about 50 people specially briefed to minimise local disturbance. About 13,000 acres of land were reinstated.

Britain's largest cement manufacturer, Blue Circle, maintains that environmental protection is now an automatic part of its business agenda. The company constantly finds itself with a high profile in environmental issues, having to answer an increasingly discriminating public. Blue Circle's processes involve quarrying, dust and noise, and its CEP makes its individual works managers responsible for indentifying and dealing with the environmental problems. They are supported by comprehensive environmental guidelines prepared for the company by experts. The performance of individual works is monitored by the CEP group.

In such a front-line occupation, Blue Circle finds environmental PR particularly valuable. It therefore aims for maximum publicity from what it admits is the costly environmental policy of land reinstatement. In the past few years, the company has restored 450 acres to agricultural use and redeveloped over 600 acres in north-west Kent alone.

The Importance of the Consumer to Environmental Activities

In the past many of the environmentally beneficial activities of business and industry have been legislation led, but with the increasing power of "green" consumer spending, shoppers now often produce results through demand.

Recycling

Fundamentally, recycling relies on the consumer's guilt about waste. Thus the recycling of a wide range of materials has a threefold effect - all with PR scope.

1.   It allows the public to participate in environmentalism. By "posting" glass, cans or paper in appropriate recycling containers, the ordinary householder "goes green".

2.   It is often more efficient for industry. Although the UK alone produces 56 million tonnes of waste each year (almost 1 tonne per person) and although it is estimated that burning or dumping costs around £720 million, recycling could be worth £750 million - much of that available to industry.

3.   It has created a recycling industry in its own right. Perhaps best known to the consumer is glass recycling, developed from initial outrage over one-use drink bottles and leading to the 1977 launch of the now well-established bottle banks. Public participation in recycling has been extended to include paper and aluminium cans. It is likely to expand still further with increasing legislation, certainly to include some plastics and, perhaps, household toxics such as batteries.

Sustainable Resource

This is a much-used buzz-phrase in environmental circles and several successful PR campaigns have been based on corporate dedication to sustainability. The Save the Rainforest Campaign currently co-ordinated by Friends of the Earth has majored on persuading both retailers and consumers to use only wood obtained from sustained plantations. Over-harvesting tragedies have led to an increasing awareness of careful husbanding, and extinctions are among the most emotive subjects in the environmental book. PR points are scored by companies pledging to conserve endangered species, especially when substituting one product for a more "acceptable" alternative.

The Environment-Friendly Product

Some household products have long been environmentally conspicuous. Detergents, for example, added "biodegradable" to their list of credits some time ago. Butterfly-friendly garden products, energy-saving light bulbs and non-animal-tested cosmetics are others.

Today, companies are finding substantial PR benefits in stressing the "environment-friendliness" of their products, as these two extracts show.

Thorn EMI: "Since its introduction in 1981, the 2D has established itself as a highly efficient, versatile light source offering considerable energy savings. A more conventional tungsten filament in use during business hours costs roughly £15 a year in energy, with 24-hour use raising the cost to £44. A 2D will cut these energy costs by 75%. The 2D which is rated to last 5,000 hours (five times as long as a normal 60W or 100W bulb) also cuts bulb replacement costs."

"The Body Shop selects its raw, and mostly natural ingredients with great care. It does not test its ingredients or products on animals and most are chosen to be as near to their natural source as possible. Prices are kept at a reasonable level by avoiding costly advertising, fancy packaging, and most importantly, by offering a refill service on some bottle products."

Rolls-Royce's RB211-535E4 turbofan engine created a great deal of publicity by reducing noise pollution - and won the company a Pollution Abatement Technology Award in 1985. The engine is dramatically quieter than other jets, a fact which is demonstrated by its successful application for night flying, even in and out of some of the world's most sensitive airports. The publicity gas helped the company earn a major share of the market, currently reckoned to be worth about £15 billion over the next decade.

Consumer-Led Rejection of Products

Consumer demands can also lead to a rejection of products or services perceived as unenvironmental. Consumers in West Germany, for example, were organised into boycotting products made by Sandoz, the company responsible for polluting the Rhine in 1986. UK shoppers joined with other Europeans to reject fur and whale products: their campaigns led to a substantial reduction (in the case of the whales, a total ban) in these allegedly particularly unenvironmental products. Campaigners hope to achieve similar successes in more recent projects against CFCs, agrochemicals and nuclear power.

Clarks Shoes made a clear stand in the whale product controversy by publicly rejecting the use of whale oil in 1979 (ie well before the EC ban in 1982). Unilever in West Germany took a gamble on converting its brand-leader detergent to a phosphorus-free product while competitors took much more modest steps. And, of course, the threat to the ozone layer caused several retailers (including Boots, Safeway and Tesco) and then aerosol manufacturers to declare publicly against CFCs before either public opinion or legislation forced their hands.

It was in fact on the eve of a much publicised aerosol boycott by Friends of the Earth that the eight largest aerosol manufacturers in the UK (accounting for 65% of the UK toiletries market) announced they were phasing out the use of CFCs "as soon as possible", and "in any event by the end of 1989 at the latest". Meanwhile Osmond Aerosols, which dealt with 800 different products for 200 different companies, introduced "Ozone-Safe" labelling. Johnson Wax (which actually stopped using CFCs in its aerosols in 1976) added to its labels the words: "This product contains no chemicals alleged to damage the ozone layer."

Some companies were quick to exploit the PR potential of "ozone safe", even when the product was not in a risk category. In summer 1988 Mennen ran a national newspaper advertising campaign involving the following text:

Is Your Deodorant Costing the Earth?

If it's an aerosol, chances are it probably is. Most aerosols contain a propellant gas which scientists now believe is destroying the ozone layer. It you are concerned about the harmful effect that these aerosols are having on the ozone layer you may like to consider Speed Stick or Lady Speed Stick as an alternative. Speed Stick and Lady Speed Stick are solid anti-perspirant deodorants. They don't contain aerosol propellants of *any* kind, so you know they can't possibly damage the ozone layer . . .

Some Other Opportunities

Service industries are also acknowledging the PR value of the environment. Many mailings, pamphlets and other public documents are now being printed on recycled paper (usually prominently stated). Local authorities have taken a lead on this; the DoE, on the other hand, introduced recycled paper products only after persuasion from Friends of the Earth. The Electricity Council encourages public use of its nature reserves and leisure areas created on CEGB land, and the nuclear power industry is enthusiastic about PR, holding open days at power stations, complete with family entertainment.

Incidental cataclysms such as the hurricane-force winds in the south of England in the autumn of 1987 lend themselves to non-controversial and opportunist environmental PR. Esso, for example, took full-page advertisements in national newspapers, associating itself with a major tree replanting programme.

The European Year of the Environment (EYE) 1987-88

The EYE stimulated an active response from thousands of large and small companies throughout Europe, many of which discovered the publicity potential of "green". EYE organisers were well aware of the attraction for industry: "A good environmental image is as important as environmental strategy and environmental management when working towards the goal of corporate success."

There were 3,000 organised events and hundreds of additional projects during the year. Among the industries and organisations taking part were:

1. The Chemical Industries Association, which launched its Green Code (see Figure 4.14).
2. National Westminster Bank with its Eyecatcher awards.
3. The CEGB, which spent £1 million on EYE-related projects.

4.   Shell made available £80,000 for grants in its Better Britain Campaign - a £15,000 increase over the previous year.

5.   Pizza Hut and Marvel Comics jointly sponsored a national competition linked with Keep Britain Tidy's Better Beaches Campaign.

6.   Castle Cement (part of RTZ) opened its sponsored College Lake Nature Reserve.

7.   Esso sponsored a teachers' conference aiming to raise awareness of environmental issues and exploring methods of incorporating such issues into the curricula.

8.   Tesco lent trolleys for the Children's Scrap Project in London.

There was an enthusiastic corporate response to the special recycling week held during EYE. Many scrap metal yards opened their doors, including S Sacker, Ipswich; John Moores Ltd, Manchester; and E Barnes and Company, London. Leigh Interests of Walsall opened its toxic plant, Vulcan Materials of Hartlepool its detinning plant, Rockware Glass a number of centres in West Yorkshire, and United Glass Containers centres at Leighton Buzzard and Kellibank, Alloa.

A number of major industry associations were anxious to associate themselves with EYE, including the Institution of Mechanical Engineers, sponsoring the international conference "Vehicle Emissions and their Impact on European Air Quality"; the CBI with its conference, "Excellence"; Institute of Petroleum, with its conference "Ecological Impact of the Oil Industries"; and the Aluminium Federation, which sponsored a Sherwood Forest oak replanting project.

The Chemical Industries Association's Green Code

In 1987 the CIA issued the following statement on their environmental policy:

> The chemical industry recognises that, as with all human activity, its operations will affect the environment. It accepts its duty to manage such operations so that they are socially acceptable as well as complying with all relevant statutory provisions. It is therefore a primary responsibility of the management of the chemical industry in both the short and long term to protect the environment as an integral part of good business practice.

> It is the view of CIA that such good management practices embrace:

> -   Preparation and regular review of company environmental policies, including procedures for their implementation.

- Maintaining an awareness amongst employees at all levels of the importance of environmental issues and providing training appropriate to their responsibilities.

- Using, as far as economically practicable, processes and procedures that minimise the production of wastes.

- Co-operation with the relevant control authorities in developing specific requirements which enable the statutory provisions to be met.

- Participation in the assessment of environmental issues so that a proper balance may be maintained between care for the environment and the benefits to society provided by the industry.

- Taking into account fully any guidance on specific environmental issues provided by government and other appropriate bodies.

- Assessment in advance of the environmental effects of new processes and products and the taking of steps to reduce the environmental effects to a practicable minimum.

- Maintaining an awareness of the environmental effects of operations, supported by monitoring as appropriate.

- Having special regard for the effects of activities on rare or endangered species of flora or fauna.

- Provision of the necessary information to enable products to be stored, transported, used, handled and disposed of without unacceptable effects on the environment.

- Requiring contractors to operate in accordance with legal requirements and acceptable environmental practices.

- Provision of information necessary to enable the public to understand the environmental aspects of an operation, except only where commercial confidentiality is absolutely essential.

On its part, the Association will:

- Draw the attention of its members to environmental legislation and regulations relevant to the continued well-being of their operations.

- Provide advice, when appropriate, to its members on environmental issues.

- Provide written guidance on important environmental issues and encourage its use.

- Make the chemical industry's view known to appropriate audiences.

- Assist government departments and controlling authorities to develop timely and practical environmental controls.

- Maintain a forum for the exchange of views and expertise, and encourage the membership to participate in CIA environmental activities.

Other Environment/Industry Organisations

EYE was a one-off project, but there are permanent organisations dedicated to bridging the gap between environment and industry, and particularly promoting the PR benefits of environmental support for the community. The Conservation Foundation (discussed earlier in this section) is one of the leaders in this field.

CEED

The UK Centre for Economic and Environmental Development (CEED) is also a leading organisation. A non-governmental body, CEED was formed in 1984 to co-ordinate and implement some of the recommendations made in the UK's response to the World Conservation Strategy - "The Conservation and Development Programme for the UK", launched in 1984 by HRH the Prince of Wales. CEED's aim is to reconcile the needs of business and industry with the needs of conservation. It advises, assists and persuades, making use of both its own staff and external experts from universities, trade associations and environmental organisations. It produces a bimonthly newsletter, detailed reports (eg the UK Forestry Policy; Market Mechanisms in the Enforcement of Pollution Control) and organises popular seminars for leading companies (IBM, Shell, etc).

Business in the Community

BiC was formed in the early 1980s with the role of promoting business involvement in local projects aimed at regenerating urban areas. It now has 300 company members, including most major public companies and nationalised industries, all pledged to be "good corporate citizens". Activities include community affairs programmes, featuring the support and servicing of Enterprise Agencies; BiC community affairs forum; Business in the Community Consultants; surveys of companies and their corporate responsibility policies; guidelines for corporate responsibility and a variety of publications. BiC members enjoy considerable publicity for projects involving local communities especially when its President, HRH the Prince of Wales, takes an active interest in proceedings.

Groundwork Trusts

Groundwork Trusts (GT) is a network of environmentally directed trusts with directors drawn from local industry, local authorities and voluntary organisations. Its aim is to improve local environments. The organisation grew out of the Countryside Commission's urban fringe experiments in the early 1980s and GT now has much experience of giving firm direction to local projects by identifying potential clients, identifying what needs to be done and the best means of doing it. Projects attract publicity on both local and national levels and companies involved in both large and small projects include BICC, Ferranti Electronics, ICI, Pilkington Brothers and United Biscuits. Support has also been given by Abbey National Building Society, Halifax Building Society and National Westminster Bank.

Conclusion

Whatever they may call it, companies are spending more on their public relations and therefore on enhancing their environmental image. This follows advice given by the then Minister of State for the Environment, William Waldegrave, in 1986: "An environmentally conscious image is an attractive advertisement in itself for a company which can help promote its products in the market place." But environmental awareness is by no means a matter of course. A 1987 survey of UK organisations showed that of the 70 investigated, only nine had a formal written environmental policy.

Is there, then, a need for specialist help for companies? In the increasingly complex realm of environmental legislation, much of it emanating from the EC in Brussels, the answer is probably yes. Companies will want to know at planning stage what PR benefits are to be gained from either complying with or pre-empting environmental restriction. Three areas of expertise are available to companies:

1.   Existing PR consultants (whether in house or external agencies).
2.   Independent environmental experts. There are a growing number of these consultants (some of whom are willing to go "in house"), mainly spawned by industries traditionally in the front line in the environmental-industrial conflict or from one of the pressure groups.
3.   Direct consultation with the environmental organisations, most of which are increasingly anxious to establish good relations with companies and which, in addition, have a finger very firmly on the pulse of both consumer and legislative leaning.

As the Green Alliance stated in 1986: "A poor environmental performance by industry reinforces and legitimises anti-industrial attitudes. The transformation of public attitudes to industry will be *difficult* to accomplish without a corresponding transformation of industrial attitudes and behaviour, towards the environment."

4.9 LEGISLATION AND POLITICS

There comes a point at which governments act legislatively on environmental matters. Whether the legislation is right or wrong, far-sighted or "too little, too late", business has no choice but to respond. The environmentally aware businessman will not be taken by surprise; the more entrenched may find the write-down of long-term investments forced upon them, profitability destroyed, entire product lines terminated.

The seeds of future legislation lie substantially within the concerns of the environmental movement today. Frequently their predicted time scales have been too short - wildlife extinction through pesticides, the running out of mineral reserves, the total loss of tropical rain forest - but time and again their fears have eventually proved to be well founded. Acid rain, nitrate in the water supply, chlorofluorocarbons (CFCs) and the ozone layer, conservation of fish stocks, desertification, soil salinisation, the spread of waterborne diseases by hydro schemes, are all issues on which governments have been compelled to take action after years of ignoring or refuting the evidence of environmentalists.

Since 1921, 118 international environment agreements have been adopted (see Section 5.2). From 1960 onwards the number adopted has accelerated, not a year passing without an environmental treaty, agreement, protocol, convention or amendment being adopted or coming into force. Moreover, there is a continual increase in the number of signatories to many of them.

This growing body of legislation necessitated an increase in the number of monitoring projects, now standing at 30 (see Section 5.2). In particular, monitoring has become a central part of the EC Fourth Action Programme.

The Brundtland Report

Managers seeking a feel for the way environment legislation *may* develop should examine the report of the World Commission on Environment and Development (WCED), more popularly known as the Brundtland Report, after its chairman Gro Harlem Brundtland, prime minister of Norway.

The Commission examined and pronounced on a whole range of environment/development issues including population growth, food security, energy, urban development, the preservation of ecosystems and the need for industry to "produce more with less". The Commission not only suggested legislation within national boundaries but also tackled an issue little penetrated before by legislation - the "commons".

The Commons

The management of the "commons" was a central theme of the Brundtland Report. The WCED defines commons as "those parts of the planet that fall outside national jurisdictions", specifically the oceans, outer space and Antarctica. Many environmentalists would add "the air"; some would talk of the biosphere itself - the life-supporting part of the plant from just below the surface to just above - as one vast common. Many "new economists" talk also of the global economy as one of the commons.

Hazel Henderson is accepted as one of the leaders of the new economics. In *Resurgence* (No. 125, November/December 1987) she related the new "commons" to their historical equivalent:

> The word "commons" derives from fourteenth-century England where each village had a common greenspace where all could graze their sheep. The now famous "tragedy of the Commons" relates to the behavioural error of villagers who tried to maximise their own gain by grazing more of the sheep on the common - until overgrazing destroyed it for all. In today's globalisation, we now see how we have created the newest "commons": the new, indivisible global economy itself. Each nation and multinational corporation tries to maximise its own position in an all-out

competitive game that can only destroy the global economic commons and bring on a worldwide collapse or depression.

The Oceans

The WCED proposed various measures to improve ocean management, some or all of which may in time form the basis of legislation.

(i) Exclusive Economic Zones

The WCED recommends that, in relation to their EEZs, countries should take steps to reduce "overexploitation of fisheries in coastal and offshore waters", clean up "municipal and industrial pollution" and make inventories of their marine resources. The WCED further believes that where "small island and maritime developing countries" find their EEZs polluted by "powerful countries or companies", international development banks should support "institutional capacity" to protect them. In the Pacific, the report concludes, exploitation or pollution of EEZs by other nations "threatens the political stability of the region".

(ii) Fisheries Management

The WCED believes that extension of EEZs under the Law of the Sea Convention has not achieved the effective conservation and management of living resources that had been required, pointing to declining fish stocks and the destruction of the whaling industry (see Part Three, particularly Sections 3.2 and 3.3).

(iii) Regional Seas Programme

UNEP's Regional Seas Programme involves 130 states bordering 11 different shared seas. The WCED believes that it has been successful but questions the political will for the future, given that "nowhere have the sums been committed" to tackle urban and industrial pollution and agricultural run-off".

(iv) Dumping

The WCED says it "encourages the London Dumping Convention to reaffirm the rights and responsibilities of states to control and regulate dumping within the 200-mile EEZ". In other words, it believes the existing legislative framework is not being properly applied. The Convention, whose full title is the Convention for the Prevention of Marine Pollution by Dumping of Wastes and Other Matter, was concluded in 1972 but did not become operative until 1975. It has 61 contracting parties, among which non-dumping countries are

of other substances provided the national authorities have granted a general permit.

Belgium, the Netherlands, Switzerland and the UK had been dumping low-level radioactive waste in the North-East Atlantic prior to 1983, when the London Dumping Convention meeting called for a moratorium. This was extended indefinitely in 1985, so that nations may not now dump low-level waste unless they can prove it is environmentally safe. This shift in the burden of proof may set a precedent for other areas of environmental legislation, the onus being on companies to demonstrate that something is *not* harmful, rather than on environmentalists to demonstrate that it *is*. Whatever the outcome of investigations into the radioactive waste issue, the WCED urged "all states to continue to refrain from disposing of either low or high-level wastes at sea or in the sea-bed".

(v) The Law of the Sea Convention

The WCED states that ratifying this Convention is "the most significant initial action that nations can take in the interests of the oceans' threatened life-support system". By 1987, 159 nations had signed the Convention but only 32 had ratified it. The WCED supported the Convention because it believed the removal of "35% of the oceans as a source of growing conflict between states" was likely to improve the marine environment. That may or may not be so. But "over 45% of the planet's surface, this sea-bed area and its resources are declared to be the common heritage of mankind, a concept that represents a milestone in the realm of international co-operation". The WCED concludes that "coastal states now have a clear interest in the sound management of the continental shelf and in the prevention of pollution from land and sea-based activities". Many environmentalists are happy with that approach to the "commons".

Space

According to the 1967 Outer Space Treaty, outer space, including the moon and other planets in the solar system, is not subject to national appropriation by claim of sovereignty, by means of use of occupation or by any other means. There is a UN Committee on the Peaceful Uses of Outer Space.

The WCED is concerned that information obtained by remote sensing from space is being retained, rather than pooled, and has called for a strengthening of UNEP's Global Environment Monitoring System to make data obtained from space universally available.

With regard to the pollution of orbital space, the WCED concluded that "the most important measure . . . is to prevent the further testing and deployment of space-based weapons". It was also concerned about radioactive materials, and advocated limiting the size of reactors permitted in orbit, shielding radioactive material for re-entry and the deep-space disposal of spacecraft containing radioactive material, all as a minimum. It concluded that "regulating space debris and nuclear materials in Earth orbit is clearly overdue".

Antarctica

Many environmentalists disagree with the WCED's approach to Antarctica. The WCED accepts that "activities in Antarctica will expand in kind and scale, as will the numbers of participants in such activities . . . Further efforts must be made to ensure effective management of those activities and an orderly expansion of participation in such management."

The WCED "does not propose to adjudicate the status of Antarctica"; it took no position on either the seven states that maintain territorial claims or the opposing view that a common heritage of mankind should not be managed for the benefit of just a few nations. It seems unlikely therefore that any international legislation following on from the WCED's work would prevent the commercial exploitation of Antarctica.

The Report's Conclusions

The Brundtland Report concluded with suggestions for institutional and legal change and with proposals for the principles which should guide legislators. At national level those suggestions included a "foreign policy for the environment"; at the regional level "a new focus on the sustainable use and management of transboundary ecological zones"; and at the global level a new emphasis on sustainable development. At all levels, the WCED called for an increased role for scientific organisations and non-governmental organisations. There was also a call for the UNEP, established in 1972, to be strengthened.

The principles for future environment legislation are summarised below.

1. All human beings have the fundamental right to an environment adequate for their health and well-being.

2. States shall conserve and use the environment and natural resources for the benefit of present and future generations.

3. States shall maintain ecosystems and ecological processes essential for the functioning of the biosphere, shall preserve biological diversity, and shall observe the principle of optimum sustainable yield in the use of living natural resources and ecosystems.

4. States shall establish adequate environmental protection standards and monitor changes in and publish relevant data on environmental quality and resource use.

5. States shall make or require prior environmental assessments of proposed activities which may significantly affect the environment or use of a natural resource.

6. States shall inform in a timely manner all persons likely to be significantly affected by a planned activity and grant them equal access and due process in administrative and judicial proceedings.

7. States shall ensure that conservation is treated as an integral part of the planning and implementation of development activities and provide assistance to other states, especially to developing countries, in support of environmental protection and sustainable development.

8. States shall co-operate in good faith with other states in implementing the preceding rights and obligations.

9. States shall use transboundary natural resources in a reasonable and equitable manner.

10. States shall prevent or abate any transboundary environmental interference which could cause or causes significant harm (subject to certain exceptions in 11 and 12 below).

11. States shall take all reasonable precautionary measures to limit the risk when carrying out of permitting certain dangerous but beneficial activities and shall ensure that compensation is provided should substantial transboundary harm occur even when the activities were not known to be harmful at the time they were undertaken.

12. States shall enter into negotiations with the affected state on the equitable conditions under which the activity could be carried out when planning to carry out or permit activities causing transboundary harm which is substantial but far less than the cost of prevention. (If no agreement can be reached, see 22.)

13. States shall apply as a minimum at least the same standards for environmental conduct and impacts regarding transboundary natural resources and environmental interferences as are applied domestically.

14. States shall co-operate in good faith with other states to achieve optimal use of transboundary natural resources and effective prevention or abatement of transboundary environmental interferences.

15. States of origin shall provide timely and relevant information to the other concerned states regarding transboundary natural resources or environmental interferences.

16. States shall provide prior and timely notification and relevant information to the other concerned states and shall make or require an environmental assessment of planned activities which may have significant transboundary effects.

17. States of origin shall consult at an early stage and in good faith with other concerned states regarding existing or potential transboundary interferences with their use of a natural resource or the environment.

18. States shall co-operate with the concerned states in monitoring, scientific research and standard setting regarding transboundary natural resources and environmental interferences.

19. States shall develop contingency plans regarding emergency situations likely to cause transboundary environmental interferences and shall promptly warn, provide relevant information to and co-operate with concerned states when emergencies occur.

20. States shall grant equal access, due process and equal treatment in administrative and judicial proceedings to all persons who are or may be affected by transboundary interferences with their use of a natural resource or the environment.

21. States shall cease activities which breach an international obligation regarding the environment and provide compensation for the harm caused.

22. States shall settle environmental disputes by peaceful means. If mutual agreement on a solution or on other dispute settlement arrangements is not reached within 18 months, the dispute shall be submitted to conciliation and, if unresolved, thereafter to arbitration or judicial settlement at the request of any of the concerned states.

The European Community

In 1987 the Treaty of Rome was amended by the Single European Act, which in terms of green issues will allow some environmental legislation to be adopted by majority vote in the Council of Ministers rather than the unanimous vote previously required. This is almost certain to result in more and stricter legislation on top of the 100 measures adopted since 1973.

The EC is now engaged in its Fourth Action Programme. The first two can be seen as remedial, legislating to set standards that would - in many cases - reduce the pollution already taking place. With the Third Action Programme 1983 the EC began to think in terms of prevention. In particular it recognised that environmental protection had to be built in to the planning and legislation of other policy creators. The Fourth Action Plan goes further still. Possibly its most significant development is in following through the legislation that has been passed, to ensure that it is implemented. An information sheet produced for the EYE 1987/88 claimed that "once adopted, they *Community decisions* will be implemented smoothly". In reality, the implementation of Community environment policy has been far from smooth. Specifically, businessmen can anticipate economic measures to limit pollution (and perhaps subsidies for pollution control in parts of the Community). The European Commission will undoubtedly aim to increase freedom of information, including environment data, and there will be three-yearly State of the Environment reports.

In *The European Community and Environmental Protection* (1987), the Commission set out the aims and approach of the Fourth Action Programme in general terms.

1.   More effective integration of environmental policy with other Community policies: agriculture, industry, competition, energy, internal market, transport, tourism, social policy, consumer protection, regional policy, development co-operation, etc.

2.   The setting of stricter environmental standards in the context of the completion of the internal market.

3.   The promotion of investment to improve the environment (The Community already plays a significant role in this respect: since 1975 the European Investment Bank has loaned nearly 1,300 million ECU for environmental improvement projects.)

4.   Better information. (The European Commission is looking at ways of improving public access to information held by the authorities responsible for the environment, so that citizens may better know and

defend their rights and interests. In general, the Fourth Programme provides for wider dissemination of information on the environment.)

5.   Effective implementation of Community legislation on the protection of the environment.

6.   Use of a wide range of approaches to prevent and control pollution.

7.   The Community environmental policy is concentrated around two principal themes: the fight against pollution and nuisances; improved management of land, of the environment and of natural resources. Considerable importance is also attached to scientific research and to international action. The fight against pollution and nuisances includes the following topics:
(a) cleaner water;
(b) pure air;
(c) less noise;
(d) better control of chemical products;
(e) safety from the risks involved in biotechnology;
(f) greater nuclear safety.

Conserving nature and natural resources involves:

(a) more rational management of land;
(b) conservation of fauna and flora;
(c) management of waste and promotion of clean technologies.

8.   Scientific research. Some of the research undertaken to date has been concerned with protection of the environment as such: the effects of pollutants on health and ecology, the effect of chemical products, quality of air, water and soil, recycling of waste, clean technologies, etc.

9.   International action.

Politics

In the UK

Green is becoming a well-established political colour throughout the democratic world. There may not be any "Green" prime ministers, but environmental issues are undoubtedly working their way on to political agendas.

Europe's first official Green Party was formed in Britain, in 1973. By 1977, known as the People Party, it gained its first political position with the election of a county councillor in Cornwall. It became the Ecology Party and, in 1985, the Green Party. While not winning any parliamentary seats, Green Party votes have increased over the past few years and the party polled comparatively well in the 1988 North Kensington by-election.

Shortly before the announcement of the 1987 UK general election, all the major parties were more than ready to show their environmental colours. They had good reason. In June, before polling day, MORI found 81% of respondents in a voting survey thought that "the government should be giving a much higher priority to protecting the environment". And 31% said the environment was *very* important or crucial in determining their choice of candidate (see Table 4.48).

Table 4.48   ENVIRONMENTAL VOTING PRIORITIES IN THE 1987 UK
GENERAL ELECTION

%

When you are deciding which political party, if any, you will vote for in the next general election, how important will their policies towards the environment be in making up your mind?

Fairly important	39
Very important	27
Not very important	16
Not at all important	7
Don't know	7
Crucial	4

Source: MORI/FoE

Well before the election, in autumn 1986, the British Labour Party had surprised even its most faithful supporters by issuing a draft environmental policy statement, described as an "impressive" document. "It grasps what is at stake in environmental politics," said Friends of the Earth. "It puts the Liberals on notice that they no longer wear the major parties' green jersey by right." It was felt the Liberals of the day were being influenced by their powerful farming lobby.

Also in autumn 1986 FoE claimed that "the Tories are working hard at their greenery". "Apprehensive though we were at the appointment of Mr Nicholas Ridley as Secretary of State for the Environment, it must be said that the announcement of a unified Pollution Inspectorate, the launching of UK 2000 and the introduction of six Environmentally Sensitive areas are significant steps forward," stated an FoE editorial.

However, the Labour Party was soon backtracking on its earlier pledge to establish a Ministry of Environmental Protection. FoE saw this as pre-election nerves: "Apparently worried about his freedom of action as a future prime minister, and about the danger in setting a precedent by recognising any "minority interests" in such a fashion, he [Neil Kinnock] got the National Executive to delete this commitment from the policy document." Contending that Kinnock was wrong, and well behind the times, FoE pointed out that "the environment is not a special interest to be lobbied by a few, vociferous pressure groups. It concerns *everybody* and every area of government policy."

UK environmentalists saw the 1987 election as the big breakthrough for green politics. In the months before the election politicians of all parties were lobbied for their stand on environmental issues. A computer analysis of candidates' responses to key questions was undertaken, and general optimism prevailed that subjects like nuclear power, changes in planning laws, countryside policies, public transport and greening of the cities would be focused upon. However, the optimism was soon modified as political realities began to intrude upon and water down environmental statements and claims made by the major parties.

After the election the environmentalists admitted disappointment. There was, they decided, no real awareness of the problems facing the UK, Europe and the developing world. No substantial acknowledgement of the type of world needs outlined in the then recently published Brundtland Report. Hope remained, however, that those new MPs who had shown an "unprecedented commitment" to some environmental issues would continue to champion the cause.

In Europe

However, long before the 1987 election, Britain's environmental campaigners were taking their political lobbying further afield - to Brussels and the legislators of the EC. European policy in general and on several issues specific to the environment was taking matters out of the reach of party politics and into higher courts.

252

The UK government had already been "forced" to comply with certain directives, including that on nitrate pollution in drinking water. Yet other EC directives deal with bathing water quality, vehicle emissions, industrial pollution and dumping. The EC's Fourth Action Programme's subtitle, "Enforcement", is causing political watchers to predict fireworks within the Community during the run-up to the 1992 "removal" of intra-Community borders.

Green candidates now stand for election in 16 of the 17 European countries which hold free elections. The West German Green Party, *Die Grünen*, first became known in active politics in 1980 when it won 1.8% of the country's vote. In the 1983 election it took more than 5% of the total vote and became the first new party to enter the West German Parliament, the Bundestag, for 30 years. The 1987 general election saw it take 8% of the vote and win 44 seats.

The background to the rise of the West German greens probably lies in the country's long-running political stability throughout the 1960s and 1970s, which in turn led to localised citizens' action programmes over issues such as the environment. Street-level environmental concern came to a head with the discovery that over half the German forests were badly damaged, probably by acid rain pollution. *Die Grünen's* strength has led to forceful stands on EC issues such as acid rain and vehicle emissions.

In the 1988 French elections the presidential candidate for *Les Verts*, Antoine Waechter, took 3.8% of the first-round vote. As parliamentary candidate for the Haute Rhine in the general election which followed Mitterand's victory, he won 11% of the vote.

Green politicians sit in both houses in the Belgian Parliament, have representatives in the Italian Parliament and form a Europe-wide group in the European Parliament.

In the Far East and Eastern European countries, although green politicians are not yet established, environmentalist pressure groups are making their presence felt.

PART FIVE
REFERENCE SECTION

5.1 INTERNATIONAL ENVIRONMENTAL TREATIES AND PROJECTS

INTERNATIONAL TREATIES AND AGREEMENTS ON THE ENVIRONMENT

Subject	Type*	Adoption Date	Adoption Place	Entry into force	No. of signatory countries
Use of white lead in painting	conv	1921	Geneva	1923	52
Preservation of fauna and flora in their natural state	conv	1933	London	1936	9
Nature protection and wildlife preservation in the western hemisphere	conv	1940	Washington	1942	18
Regulation of whaling	conv	1946	Washington	1948/59	42
Establishment of Inter-American Tropical Tuna Commission	conv	1949	Washington	1950	9
Establishment of a General Fisheries Council for the Mediterranean	agr	1949	Rome	1952/63/76	19
Protection of birds	conv	1950	Paris	1963	10
Establishment of the European and Mediterranean Plant Protection Organisation	conv	1951	Paris	1953/62/64/66/68	31

Continued....

Table cont'd

Subject	Type*	Adoption Date	Adoption Place	Entry into force	No. of signatory countries
Plant protection	conv	1951	Rome	1952	83
Measures for protection of stocks of deep-sea prawns, European lobsters, Norway lobsters and crabs	agr/prot	1952	Oslo	1952/59	3
High seas fisheres of the North Pacific Ocean	conv	1952	Tokyo	1953/60/63	3
(Terminated and replaced by protocol)	prot	1978	Seattle	1979	3
Prevention of pollution of the sea by oil	conv	1954	London	1958/67/68	26
- Tank arrangements and limitation of tank size	amend	1971	London		26
- Protection of Great Barrier Reef	amend	1971	London		27
Plant protection for the Asia and Pacific region	agr	1956	Rome	1956/69/83	24
Conservation of North Pacific fur seals	conv	1957	Washington	1957/64/69/76	4
Fishing in waters of the Danube	conv	1958	Bucharest	1958	6
Continental shelf	conv	1958	Geneva	1964	55
Fishing and conservation of the living resources of the high seas	conv	1958	Geneva	1966	35
High seas	conv	1958	Geneva	1962	57
North-east Atlantic fisheries (Superseded by 1980 convention)	conv	1959	London	1963	19
Fishing in the Black Sea	conv	1959	Varna	1960/65	3
Antarctic	treaty	1959	Washington	1961	30

Continued...

Table cont'd

Subject	Type*	Adoption Date	Adoption Place	Entry into force	No. of signatory countries
Co-operation in the quarantine of plants and their protection against pests and disease	agr	1959	Sofia	1960	10
Protection of workers against ionizing radiation	conv	1960	Geneva	1962	39
Third-party liability in the field of nuclear energy	conv	1960	Paris	1968	14
(Supplementary convention to above)	conv	1963	Brussels	1974	10
Constitution of an international commission for the protection of the Moselle against pollution	prot	1961	Paris	1962	3
African migratory locust	conv	1962	Kano	1963	16
Co-operation in marine fishing	agr	1962	Warsaw	1963	6
International commission to the protection of the Rhine against pollution	agr	1963	Berne	1965/79	5**
Civil liability for nuclear damage	conv	1963	Vienna	1977	10
Compulsory settlement of disputes	op prot	1963	Vienna		1
Banning nuclear weapon tests in the atmosphere, in outer space and under water	treaty	1963	Moscow	1963	112
Establishment of a commission for controlling the desert locust in the eastern region of its distribution area in South-west Asia	agr	1963	Rome	1964	4

Continued....

Table cont'd

Subject	Type*	Adoption Date	Adoption Place	Entry into force	No. of signatory countries
Development of the Chad basin	conv/stat	1964	Fort-Lamy		4
International Council for the Exploration of the sea	conv	1964	Copenhagen	1968	18
Establishment of a commission for controlling the desert locust in the Near East	agr	1965	Rome	1967	14
Conservation of Atlantic tunas	conv	1966	Rio de Janeiro	1969	22
Principles governing the activities of states in the exploration and use of outer space including the moon and other celestial bodies	treaty	1967	London/ Moscow/ Washington	1967	71
Phyto-sanitary convention for Africa (Supersedes an earlier convention London 1954)	conv	1967	Kinshasa		9
African convention on the conservation of nature and natural resources	conv	1968	Algiers	1969	29
European agreement on the restriction of the use of certain detergents in washing and cleaning products	agr	1968	Strasbourg	1971	10
European convention on the protection of animals during international transport	conv	1968	Rome	1971	20

Continued...

Table cont'd

Subject	Type*	Adoption Date	Adoption Place	Entry into force	No. of signatory countries
European convention on the protection of the archaeological heritage	conv	1969	London	1970	17
Co-operation in dealing with pollution of the North Sea by oil	agr	1969	Bonn	1969	8
Conservation of living resources of the South-east Atlantic	conv	1969	Rome	1971	18
Civil liability for oil-pollution damage	conv	1969	Brussels	1975/81	55
Intervention of the high seas in case of oil-pollution casualties	conv	1969	Brussels	1975	47
Intervention on the high seas in cases of marine pollution by substances other than oil	prot	1973	London	1983	17
Benelux convention on the hunting and protection of birds	conv	1970	Brussels	1972/83	3
Establishment of a commission for controlling the desert locust in North-west Africa	agr	1970	Rome	1971/77	4
Wetlands of international importance especially as water-fowl habitat	conv	1971	Ramsar	1975	36
(Amendment to above)	prot	1982	Paris		18

Continued...

Table cont'd

Subject	Type*	Adoption Date	Place	Entry into force	No. of signatory countries
Prohibition of the emplacement of nuclear destruction weapons and other weapons of mass on the sea bed and ocean floor and subsoil	treaty	1971	London/Moscow/Washington	1972	73
Civil liability in marine carriage of nuclear material	conv	1971	Brussels	1975	11
Establishment of an international fund for compensation for oil-pollution damage	conv	1971	Brussels	1978/81	30
Protection against hazards of poisoning arising from benzene	conv	1971	Geneva	1973	26
Prevention of marine pollution by dumping from ships and aircraft	conv	1972	Oslo	1974/82	13
Status of Senegal River and establishment of the Senegal River Development Organisation	conv	1972	Nouakchott		3
Conservation of Antartic seals	conv	1972	London	1978	11
Prohibition of the development, production and stockpiling of bacteriological (biological) and toxin weapons	conv	1972	London/Moscow/Washington	1975	98
Protection of the world cultural and natural heritage	conv	1972	Paris	1975	83

Continued....

Table cont'd

Subject	Type*	Adoption Date	Adoption Place	Entry into force	No. of signatory countries
Prevention of marine pollution by dumping of wastes and other matter	conv	1972	London/ Mexico City/ Moscow/ Washington	1975/79	58
International trade in endangered species of wild fauna and flora	conv	1973	Washington	1975	87
Establishment of a permanent inter-state drought control committee for the Sahel	conv	1973	Ouagadougou		6
Fishing and conservation of the living resources in the Baltic Sea and belts	conv	1973	Gdansk	1974	7
Prevention of pollution from ships	conv	1973	London		15
(Protocol related to above)	prot	1978	London	1983	31
Conservation of polar bears	agr	1973	Oslo	1976	5
Protection of the environment – Scandinavia	conv	1974	Stockholm	1976	4
Protection of the marine environment of the Baltic Sea area	conv	1974	Helsinki	1980	7
Prevention of marine pollution from land- based sources	conv	1974	Paris	1978	12**

Continued...

Table cont'd

Subject	Type[*]	Adoption Date	Adoption Place	Entry into force	No. of signatory countries
Prevention and control of occupational hazards caused by carcinogenic substances and agents	conv	1974	Geneva	1976	22
International energy programme	agr	1974	Paris	1976	19
Protection of the Mediterranean Sea against pollution	conv	1976	Barcelona	1978	17[**]
Prevention of pollution of the Mediterranean sea by dumping from ships and aircraft	prot	1976	Barcelona	1978	17[**]
Co-operation in combating pollution of the Mediterranean Sea by oil and other harmful substances in cases of emergency	prot	1976	Barcelona	1978	17[**]
Protection of the Mediterranean Sea against pollution from land-based sources	prot	1980	Athens	1983	7[**]
Mediterranean specially protected areas	prot	1982	Geneva		11[**]
Protection of animals kept for farming purposes - Europe	conv	1976	Strasbourg	1978	12
Protection of the waters of the Mediterranean shores	agr	1976	Monaco	1981	3
Conservation of nature in the South Pacific	conv	1986	Apia		3
Protection of the archaeological, historical and artistic heritage of the American nations	conv	1976	Santiago	1978	9

Continued...

Table cont'd

Subject	Type*	Adoption Date	Adoption Place	Entry into force	No. of signatory countries
Protection of the Rhine against chemical pollution	conv	1976	Bonn	1979	5**
Protection of the Rhine against pollution by chlorides	conv	1976	Bonn		5
Prohibition of military or any other hostile use of environmental modification techniques	conv	1976	New York	1978	43
Civil liability for oil-pollution damage resulting from exploration for and exploitation of seabed mineral resources	conv	1977	London		6
Protection of workers against occupational hazards in the working environment due to air pollution, noise and vibration	conv	1977	Geneva	1979	14
Kuwait regional convention for co-operation on the protection of the marine environment from pollution	conv	1978	Kuwait	1979	8
Regional co-operation in combating pollution by oil and other harmful substances in cases of emergency	prot	1978	Kuwait	1979	8
Amazonian co-operation	treaty	1978	Brasilia	1980	8

Continued...

Table cont'd

Subject	Type[*]	Adoption Date	Adoption Place	Entry into force	No. of signatory countries
Future multilateral co-operation in the North-west Atlantic fisheries	conv	1978	Ottawa	1979	12[**]
Conservation of migratory species of wild animals	conv	1979	Bonn	1983	13[**]
Protection of animals for slaughter - Europe	conv	1979	Strasbourg	1982	7[**]
Conservation of European wildlife and natural habitats	conv	1979	Berne	1982	13[**]
Long-range transboundary air pollution	conv	1979	Geneva	1983	26
(Protocol to above on long-term financing of the Co-operative Programme by Monitoring and Evaluation of the Long-Range Transmission of Air Pollutants in Europe (EMEP))	prot	1984	Geneva		1
Conservation and management of the vicuña	conv	1979	Lima	1982	4[**]
Conservation of Antarctic marine living resources	conv	1980	Canberra	1982	13
Transfrontier co-operation between territorial communities or authorities - Europe	conv	1980	Madrid	1981	11
Future multilateral co-operation in North-east Atlantic fisheries	conv	1980	London	1982	10[**]
Creation of Niger Basin Authority and protocol relating to the development fund of the Niger Basin	conv/prot	1980	Faranah	1982	8

Continued....

Table cont'd

Subject	Type*	Adoption Date	Adoption Place	Entry into force	No. of signatory countries
Co-operation in the protection and development of the marine and coastal environment of the West and Central Africa region	conv	1981	Abidjan	1984	6
Co-operation in combating pollution in cases of emergency	prot	1981	Abidjan	1984	6
Protection of the marine environment and coastal area of the South-east Pacific	conv	1981	Lima		5
Regional co-operation in combating pollution of the south-east Pacific by oil and other harmful substances in cases of emergency	agr	1981	Lima		5
(Supplementary protocol to above)	prot	1983	Quito		5
Protection of the South-east Pacific against pollution from land-based sources	prot	1983	Quito		5
Conservation of the Red Sea and Gulf of Aden environment	conv	1982	Jiddah		7
Regional co-operation in combating pollution by oil and other harmful substances in cases of emergency	prot	1982	Jiddah		7

Continued....

Table cont'd

Subject	Type*	Adoption Date	Adoption Place	Entry into force	No. of signatory countries
Conservation of salmon in the North Atlantic Ocean	conv	1982	Reykjavik	1983	6**
Benelux convention on nature conservation and landscape protection	conv	1982	Brussels	1983	3
Law of the sea	conv	1982	Montego Bay		131
Protection and development of the marine environment of the wider Caribbean region	conv	1983	Cartagena		15**
Co-operation in combating oil spills in the wider Caribbean region	prot	1983	Cartagena		15
Co-operation in dealing with pollution of the North Sea by oil and other harmful substances	agr	1983	Bonn		8**
Tropical timber	agr	1983	Geneva		19**

Source: UNEP 1985: Register of International Treaties and Other Agreements in the Field of the Environment. United Nations Environment Programme. UNEP/GC/Information/11/Rev.1, Nairobi

Notes: The treaties and agreements listed are all of a multilateral nature and concern mostly the natural environment of man, including flora, fauna, water and air. The objectives and provisions of the agreements are summarised in the source document Also given are the listings of signatory countries. Agreements pending or not yet in force have no entry under "Entry into force". The number of signatory countries is the original number. In some cases, signatory countries have since withdrawn and dependencies have become independent.

* conv:convention; agr:agreement; prot:protocol; op:optional; stat:statute

** + EEC

INTERNATIONAL PROJECTS FOR ENVIRONMENTAL INFORMATION, MONITORING AND CONSERVATION

Project	Headquarters location	Date founded	Participants (countries)
INFORMATION			
INFOTERRA - Interatonal Referral System for Sources of Environmental Information	UNEP, Nairobi	1974	126
IRPTC - International Register for Potentially Toxic Chemicals	UNEP, Geneva	1976	Global
IPCS - International Programme on Chemical Safety	WHO, Geneva		Global
GESAMP- Joint Group of Experts on Scientific Aspects of Marine Pollution	UN, various	1969	Global
MONITORING			
GEMS - Global Environment Monitoring System	UNEP, Nairobi	1975	Global
Climate-related monitoring: BAPOMoN - Background Air Pollution Monitoring NetworkWMO, Geneva		1970	43

Continued...

Table cont'd

Project	Headquarters location	Date founded	Participants (countries)
World Glacier Inventory	ETH, Zurich	1967	21
CSM – Climate System Monitoring Project	WMO, Geneva	1984	
Long-range pollutant transport:			
EMEP – European Monitoring Evaluation Programme	ECE/WMO, Geneva	1977	23
Meteorological Synthesizing Centre-East	IEG/Moscow		
Meteorological Synthesizing Centre-West	NMI/Oslo		
Chemical Co-ordinating Centre	NILU/Lillestrom		
Health-related monitoring:			
GEMS/Air – Urban Air Pollution Monitoring Network	WHO, Geneva	1973	50
GEMS/Water – Global Water Quality Monitoring Network	WHO, Geneva	1976	59
GEMS/Food – Joint FAO/WHO Food Contamination Monitoring Programme	WHO, Geneva	1976	34
Biological monitoring pilot project	WHO, Geneva	1978	10
Personal monitoring pilot project	WHO, Geneva	1979	4
HEAL – Human Exposure Assessment Locations	WHO, Geneva	1982	4
Terrestrial renewable resources monitoring			
Tropical forest resources assessment	FAO, Rome		76
Tropical forest cover monitoring	FAO, Rome		3

Continued...

Table cont'd

Project	Headquarters location	Date founded	Participants (countries)
Pastoral ecosystem monitoring in West Africa	LNERV/ISRA, Dakar		
Desertification monitoring in Latin America	ONERN, Lima		
Soil degradation in North Africa and Middle East	FAO, Rome		
Monitoring status of mammals	CMC, Cambridge	1980*	Global
Monitoring status of birds	ICBP, Cambridge	1980*	Global
Trade in endangered species	CMC, Cambridge	1980*	Global
Parks and protected areas	CMC, Cambridge	1981	Global
Coral reefs	CMC, Cambridge	1980*	Global
Monitoring status of cetaceans	CMC, Cambridge	1982*	Global
GRID - Global Resource Information Database	UNEP, Geneva Nairobi	1985	Global
Ocean monitoring:			
IGOSS - Integrated Global Ocean Station System	IOC, Paris	1975	Global
Regional Seas Programme	UNEP, Nairobi	1974	120
Regional Seas Programme	UNEP, Nairobi	1974	120
Action plans prepared or adopted			
Mediterranean region		1975	
Kuwait region		1976	
Wider Caribbean region		1981	

Continued....

Table cont'd

Project	Headquarters location	Date founded	Participants (countries)
West and Central Agrican region			1981
Eastern Africa region			
Eastern Asian region		1981	
Red Sea and Gulf of Aden region		1982	
South Pacific region		1982	
South-east Pacific region		1981	
South Asian Seas region			
CONSERVATION			
World Conservation Strategy	IUCN, Gland	1980	Global

Source: United Nations Environment Programmes (UNEP)
Notes: * *date beginning UNEP–GEMS association*
ETH   *Swiss Federal Institute of Technology*
IEG   *Institute of Applied Geophysics*
NMI   *Norwegian Meteorological Institute*
NILU *Norwegian Institute for Air Research*
LNERV *Laboratoire National d'Elevage et de la Recherche Vétérinaire*

ONERN *Oficina Nacional Evaluación Recursos Naturales*
ISRA *Institute Sénégalais de Researches Agricoles*
CMC   *Conservation Monitoring Centre (IUCN)*
ICBP *International Council for Bird Preservation*
IOC   *Intergovernmental Oceanographic Commission (UNESCO)*
IUCN *International Union for Conservation of Nature and Natural Resources*

5.2 INFORMATION SOURCES

CONSERVATION AND PRESERVATION SOCIETIES

UK Local

Alvanley Conservation
20 Linden Drive, Helsby, via Warrington, Cheshire
Tel: Helsby 2920

Association for the Protection of Rural Scotland
14a Napier Road, Edinburgh EH10 5AY
Tel: 031-229 1898

Avon Wildlife Trust
209 Redland Road, Bristol, Avon BS6 6YU
Tel: 0272 743396

Black Country Society
49 Victoria Road, Tipton, Staffs DT4 8SW
Tel: 021-557 4662

Broads Authority, The
18 Colegate, Norwich, Norfolk NR3 1BQ
Tel: 0603 610734

Chiltern Society
Silver How, Little Hollis, Great Missenden, Bucks HP16 9HZ

Chippendale Society
c/o Temple Newsam House, Leeds

Cleveland Nature Conservation Trust
The Old Town Hall, Mandale Road, Thornaby, Stockton on Tees, Cleveland
TS17 6AW
Tel: 0642 608405

Conservation Society of the Yorkshire Derwent
The Elms, East Cottingwith, York YO4 4TT
Tel: 07593 296

Cumbria Trust for Nature Conservation
Church Street, Ambleside, Cumbria LA22 OBU
Tel: 0966 32476

Derwent Valley Protection Society
18 Glamis Crescent, Rowlands Gill, Tyne & Wear NE39 1AT
Tel: 02074 2377

Devon Conservation Forum
County Hall, Topsham Road, Exeter EX2 4QQ
Tel: 0392 53327 or 0392 77977 Ext.3327

Devon Trust for Nature Conservation
35 New Bridge Street, Exeter, Devon EX4 3AH
Tel: 0392 79244

Dickens Country Protection Society
Findhorn, Gads Hill, Higham, Rochester, Kent ME3 7PE

Dorset Trust for Nature Conservation
39 Christchurch Road, Bournemouth, Dorset BH1 3NS
Tel: 0202 24241

Droitwich Canals Trust
1 Hampton Road, Droitwich, Worcs WR9 8PN

Durham County Conservation Trust
52 Old Elvet, Durham DN1 3HN
Tel: 0385 69797

Epping Forest & Essex Nature Conservation and Ecology Trust
117 Hatherley Court, Hatherley Grove, London W2 5RG

The Exmoor Society
Hoar Oak House, Alcombe, Minehead, Somerset

Glamorgan Trust for Nature Conservation
The Glamorgan Nature Centre, Fountain Road, Tondu, Bridgend,
Mid-Glamorgan CF32 0EH
Tel: 0656 724100

Gloucestershire Trust for Nature Conservation
Church House, Standish, Stonehouse, Glos GL10 3EU
Tel: 045382 2761

Gwent Trust for Nature Conservation
Shire Hall, Monmouth, Gwent NP5 3DY, Wales
Tel: 0600 5501

Heritage of London Trust Ltd
Second Floor, Chesham House, 30 Warwick Street, London W1R 6AB

Hertfordshire and Middlesex Trust for Nature Conservation
Grebe House, St. Michael's Street, St. Albans, Herts AL3 4SN
Tel: 0727 58901

Hertfordshire Society
29a Mill Lane, Welwyn, Herts AL6 9EU
Tel: 043871 7587

Kent Trust for Nature Conservation
125 High Street, Rainham, Kent ME8 8AN
Tel: 0634 362561

Lancashire Trust for Nature Conservation
Cuerden Valley Park, Cuerden Pavilion, Bamber Bridge, Preston, Lancs
PR5 6AX
Tel: 0772 324129

Leicestershire/Rutland Trust for Nature Conservation
1 West Street, Leicester LE1 6UU
Tel: 0533 553904

Lincolnshire & South Humberside Trust for Nature Conservation
The Manor House, Alford, Lincs LN13 9DL
Tel: 05212 3468

London Green Belt Council
1-4 Crawford Mews, London W1H 1PT
01-262 1477

Manx Nature Conservation Trust
Ballacross, Andreas, Isle of Man
Tel: 062488 434

Marwell Preservation Trust
Marwell Zoological Park, Golden Common, Nr Winchester, Hampshire SO21
1JH
Tel: 096-274 406

Mendip Society
Zennor, The Lynch, Winscombe, Avon, Winscombe BS25 1AR
Tel: 093-484 3103

Montgomery Trust for Nature Conservation
2 Shortbridge Street, Newtown, Powys, Wales
Tel: 0686 24751

North East Civic Trust
3 Old Elvet, Durham DH1 3HL
Tel: 0385 61182/0632 329279

North West Civic Trust
The Environmental Institute, Greaves School, Bolton Road, Swinton,
Manchester M27 2UX
Tel: 061-794 9314

Northamptonshire Trust for Nature Conservation
Lings House, Billing Lings, Northampton NN3 4BE
Tel: 0604 405285

Northern Heritage Trust
3 Old Elvet, Durham DH1 3HL
Tel: 0385 61182

Nottinghamshire Trust for Nature Conservation
2-12 Warser Gate, Nottingham NG1 1PA
Tel: 0602 501034

Orkney Heritage Society
20 Main Street, Kirkwall, Orkneys

Painshill Park Trust
Sandown House, 1 High Street, Esher, Surrey KT10 9RR
Tel: Esher 62111

The Parnham Trust
Parnham House, Beaminster, Dorset

Purbeck Industrial Archaeological Group
71 Thornbury Road, Southbourne, Bournemouth, Dorset
Tel: 0202-318 5219

Scottish Georgian Society
5b Forres Street, Edinburgh EH3 6BJ
Tel: 031-225 9724

Scottish Inland Waterways Association
11 Arden Street, Edinburgh EH9 1BR
Tel: 031-229 7149

Shropshire Trust for Nature Conservation
Barker Street, Shrewsbury, Shropshire SY1 1QP
Tel: 0743 241691

Somerset Trust for Nature Conservation
Fyne Court, Broomfield, Bridgwater, Somerset TA5 2EQ, Kingston St Mary
Tel: 082345 587/8

Southwark Environment Trust
34 Peckham Road, London SE5 8PX
Tel: 01-701 3317

Staffordshire Nature Conservation Trust
Coutts House, Sandon, Staffs ST18 0DN
Tel: 08897 534

Suffolk Preservation Society
Little Hall, Market Place, Lavenham, Sudbury, Suffolk CO10 9QZ
Tel: 0787 247179

Suffolk Trust for Nature Conservation
Park Cottage, Peasenhall, Saxmundham, Suffolk IP17 2NA
Tel: 0728 3765

Surrey Trust for Nature Conservation
Hatchlands, East Clandon, Guildford, Surrey GU4 7RT
Tel: 0483 223526

Sussex Trust for Nature Conservation
Woods Mill, Shoreham Road, Henfield, W. Sussex BN5 9SD
Tel: 0273 492630

Thames Heritage Trust
Gresham House, Twickenham Road, Feltham, Middlesex TW13 6HA

Ulster Architectural Heritage Society
181a Stranmills Road, Belfast, N. Ireland
Tel: 0232 660809

Ulster Countryside Committee
Hut 6, Castle Grounds, Stormont, Belfast BT4 3SS, N. Ireland
Tel: 0232 768716

Ulster Society for the Preservation of the Countryside
West Winds, Carney Hill, Holywood, C. Down BT18 0JR, N. Ireland
Tel: 02317 2300/0232-661222

Ulster Trust for Nature Conservation
Barnett's Cottage, Barnett Demesne, Malone Road, Belfast BT9 5PB, N. Ireland
Tel: 0232 612235

The Vincent Wildlife Centre
Baltic Exchange Buildings, 21 Bury Street, London EC3A 5AV
Tel: 01-283 1266

Warwickshire Conservation Trust
1 Northgate Street, Warwick CV34 4SP
Tel: 0926 496848

Yorkshire Wildlife Trust
20 Castlegate, York Y01 1RP
Tel: 0904 59570

UK National

Animal Welfare Institute
21 Opringe Road, London NW5
Tel: 01-485 6968

Architectural Heritage Fund
17 Carlton House Terrace
London SW1Y 5AW
Tel: 01-930 0914

Association for the Conservation of Energy
9 Sherlock Mews, London W1M 3RH
Tel: 01-935 1495

The Atlantic Salmon Trust
41 Downing Street, Farnham, Surrey GU9 7PH
Tel: 0252 724400

Beautiful Britain
Keep Britain Tidy Group, Bostel House, 37 West Street, Brighton
BN1 2RE
Tel: 0273 23585

British Antarctic Survey
High Cross, Madingley Road, Cambridge CB3 0ET

British Archaeological Trust
15a Bull Plain, Hertford, Herts
Tel: 0992 58170

British Archaeological Society
Stone Raise, 42 Lakeland Park, Keswick, Cumbria CA12 4AT

British Association for Shooting and Conservation
Marford Mill, Rossett, Wrexham, Clwyd LL12 0HL
Tel: 0244-570881

British Association of Nature Conservationists - BANC
Dept of Geography, University of Lancaster, Bailrigg, Lancaster LA1 4YR
Tel: 0524 65201

British Ecological Society
Burlington House, Piccadilly, London W1V 0LQ
Tel: 01-434 2641

British Organic Farmers (BOF)
86 Colston Street, Bristol, Avon BS1 5BB
Tel: 0272 299666

British Organic Standards Group
Elm Farm Research Centre, Hamstead Marshall, Newbury, Berkshire RG15
0HR
Tel: 0488 58298

British Trust for Conservation Volunteers - BTCV
36 St Mary's Street, Wallingford, Oxford OX10 0EU
Tel: 0491 397766

British Wildlife Appeal
164 Vauxhall Bridge Road, London SW1V 2RB
Tel: 01-828 1657

Building Conservation Trust
Apartment 39, Hampton Court Palace, East Molesey, Surrey KT8 9BS
Tel: 01-943 2277

Central Council for Rivers Protection
Fishmongers Hall, London Bridge, London EC4R 9EL
Tel: 01-626 8591

Centre for the Conservation of Historic Parks & Gardens
Institute of Advanced Architectural Studies, King's Manor, York

The Christian Consultative Council for the Welfare of Animals
8a Gaywood Street, London SE1

Christian Ecology Group
58 Quest Hills Road, Malvern, Worcester WR14 1RW
Tel: 06845 2630

Civic Trust
17 Carlton House Terrace, London SW1Y 4AW
Tel: 01-930 0914

Civic Trust for Wales
St Michael's College, Llandaff, Cardiff
Tel: 0222 552388

CoEnCo
Council for Environmental Conservation, Zoological Gardens, Regents Park,
London NW1 4RY
Tel: 01-722 7111

The Commons Society
166 Shaftesbury Avenue, London WC2

Conservation Action Project
Peak National Park Study Centre, Losehill Hall, Castleton, Derbyshire S30
2WB
Tel: 0433 20373

Conservation Bureau
c/o Scottish Development Agency, 102 Telford Road, Edinburgh
EH4 2NP
Tel: 031-343 1911

The Conservation Foundation
11a West Halkin Street, London SW1X 8JL
Tel: 01-235 1743

Conservation Monitoring Centre (CMC)
219c Huntingdon Road, Cambridge CB3 0DL
Tel: 0223 277314

The Conservation Society
12a Guildford Street, Chertsey, Surrey KT16 9BQ
Tel: 09328 60975

The Conservation Trust
c/o George Palmer School, Northumberland Avenue, Reading, Berks RG2 0EN
Tel: 0734 868442

Council for British Archaeology
112 Kennington Road, London SE11 6RE
Tel: 01-582 0494

Council for National Parks
4 Hobart Place, London SW1W 0HY

Council for the Protection of Rural England - CPRE
4 Hobart Place, London SW1W 0HY
Tel: 01-235 9481

Council for the Protection of Rural Wales
Ty Gwyn, 31 High Street, Welshpool, Powys SW21 7JP
Tel: 0038 2525

Country Houses Association
41 Kingsway, London WC2B 6UB
Tel: 01-836 1624

Country Landowners' Association
16 Belgrave Square, London SW1X 8PQ
Tel: 01-235 0511

Countryside Commission
John Dower House, Crescent Place, Cheltenham, Glos GL50 3RA
Tel: 0242 521381

Countryside Commission for Scotland
Battleby, Redgorton, Perth PH1 3EW
Tel: 0738 27921

Countryside Commission for Wales
Broad Street, Newtown, Powys SY16 2LU
Tel: 0686 26799

Crofters Commission
4-6 Castle Wynd, Inverness, Highlands IV2 3EQ, Scotland
Tel: 0463 37231

Elms Across Europe
Pitney Bowes, The Pinnacles, Elizabeth Way, Harlow, Essex
Tel: 0279 37756

English Heritage
(Historic Buildings & Monuments Commission for England)
Fortress House, 23 Savile Row, London W1X 2HE
Tel: 01-734 6010

Fauna and Flora Preservation Society
Zoological Gardens, Regents Park, London NW1 4RY
Tel: 01-586 0872

Forestry Commission
231 Corstorphine Road, Edinburgh EH12 7AT
Tel: 031-334 0303

Friends of the Earth
26-28 Underwood Street, London N1 7JQ
Tel: 01-490 1555

Friends of the Earth (Scotland)
53 George IV Bridge, Edinburgh EH1 1EJ
Tel: 031-225 6906

The Game Conservancy
Fordingbridge, Hants SP6 1EF
Tel: 0425 52381

Groundwork Foundation
Bennetts Court, 6 Bennetts Hill, Birmingham B2 5ST
Tel: 021-236 8565

Groundwork North West
(Country Commission Groundwork Unit), 184 Deansgate, Manchester
M3 3WB
Tel: 061-833 9950

Industrial Buildings Preservation Trust
12/13 Henrietta Street, London WC2E 8LH
Tel: 01-836 1894

Inland Waterways Association
114 Regent's Park Road, London NW1 8UQ
Tel: 01-586 2510/2556

Inland Waterways Protection Society
The Cottage, 69 Ivy Road, Macclesfield, Cheshire SK11 8QN
Tel: 0625 23595(evenings)

Joint Committee for Conservation of British Insects
c/o Institute of Terrestrial Ecology, Furzebrook Research Station, Wareham,
Dorset BH20 5AS
Tel: 09295 51518

Keep Britain Tidy Group
Bostel House, 37 West Street, Brighton, Sussex BN1 2RE
Tel: 0273 23585

Keep Scotland Tidy Campaign
23 Hill Street, Edinburgh EH2 3JP
Tel: 031-225 6336

Land Heritage
(The Trust for the Protection of Britain's Land Heritage), Wellington,
Somerset
Tel: (Greenham) 0832 672610

Leather Conservation Centre
9 St Thomas Street, London SE1 9SA

Linnean Society of London
Burlington House, Piccadilly, London W1V 0LQ

Marine Biological Association of the United Kingdom
The Laboratory, Citadel Hill, Plymouth, Devon PL1 2PB
Tel: 0752 21761

Marine Conservation Society
4 Gloucester Road, Ross-on-Wye, Herefordshire HR9 5BU
Tel: 0989 66017

The Maritime Trust
16 Ebury Street, London SW1N 0LH
Tel: 01-730 0096

National Animal Rescue Association
8 Waterpump Court, Thorpelands, Northampton
Tel: 0604 44797

National Council for the Conservation of Plants and Gardens
c/o RHS, Wisley, Woking, Surrey GU23 6QB

National Heritage Memorial Fund
Church House, Great Smith Street, London SW1P 3BL
Tel: 01-212 5414

National Trust
36 Queen Anne's Gate, London SW1H 9AS
Tel: 01-222 9251

National Trust Junior Division
PO Box 12, Westbury, Wilts BA13 4NA
Tel: 0373 826 302

National Trust for Scotland
5 Charlotte Square, Edinburgh EH2 4DU
Tel: 031-226 5922

Nature Conservancy Council
Northminster House, Peterborough PE1 1UA
Tel: 0733 40345

Nature Reserves Committee
(Northern Ireland), Hut 6, Castle Grounds, Stormont, Belfast BT4 3ST
Tel: 0232 768716

The Otter Trust
Earsham, Bungay, Suffolk NR35 2AF
Tel: 0986 3470

People's Trust for Endangered Species
Hamble House, Meadrow, Godalming, Surrey GU7 3JX
Tel: 04868 24848

Royal Society for Nature Conservation - RSNC
The Green, Nettleham, Lincoln LN2 2NR
Tel: 0522 752326

Royal Society for the Prevention of Cruelty to Animals - RSPCA
The Manor House, The Causeway, Horsham, Sussex RH12 1HG
Tel: 0403 64181

Royal Society for the Protection of Birds - RSPB
The Lodge, Sandy, Bedfordshire SG19 2DL
Tel: 0767 80551

Scottish Civic Trust
24 George Square, Glasgow G2 1EF
Tel: 041-221 1466

Scottish Conservation Projects
70 Main Street, Doune, Perthshire FK16 6BW
Tel: 0786 841479

Seal Sands Conservation Group
Lyndhurst, 111 Roman Road, Linthorpe, Middlesborough, Cleveland
Telephone: 0642 819559

Shell Better Britain Campaign
c/o Nature Conservancy Council, PO Box 6, Godwin House, George Street,
Huntingdon, Cambs PE18 6BU
Tel: 0480 56191

Society for Environmental Improvement
c/o National Centre for Alternative Technology, Llwyngwern Quarry,
Machynlleth, Powys SY20 9AZ, Wales

Society for Protection of Ancient Buildings
37 Spital Square, London E1 6DY
Tel: 01-377 1644

The Soil Association
86 Colston Street, Bristol BS1 5BB
Tel: 0272 290661

Textile Conservation Centre
Apartment 22, Hampton Court Palace, East Molesey, Surrey KT8 9AV

United Kingdom Institute for Conservation
c/o Conservation Dept, Tate Gallery, Millbank, London SW1P 4RG

Wildlife Hospitals Trust
1 Pemberton Close, Aylesbury, Buckinghamshire HP21 7NY
Tel: 0296 29860

The Wildlife Rescue Service
The Old Chequers, Briston, Melton Constable, Norfolk
Tel: 0263 860375

Young People's Trust for Endangered Species - YPTES
19 Quarry Street, Guildford, Surrey GU1 3EH
Tel: 0483 39600

European

European Grassland Federation
c/o Dr JW Minderhaud, Ritzema Bosweg 77, 6706 BD Wageningen,
Netherlands

European and Mediterranean Plant Protection Organisation
1 Rue Le Notre, 75016 Paris, France
Tel: (1) 520-77 94

Foundation for Environmental Conservation
15 Chemin F-Lehmann, 1218 Grand-Saconnex, Geneva, Switzerland
Tel: 022-98-23-83/4

Greek Sea Turtle Protection Society
PO Box 51154, G.R. 14510 Kifissia, Greece

Hellenic Marine Environmental Protection Association (HELMEPA)
1-3 Mavrokoradatou Street, Athens 142, Greece

International

Bureau International de la Recupération
13 place du Samedi, 1000 Brussels, Belgium
Tel: (02) 217-82-51
Telex: 61965

Conservation International
10-15 18th Street, Northwest, Suite 1002, Washington, DC 20036, USA
Tel: +1 (202) 429 5660

Friends of the Earth International
Damrak 26, 1012 LJ, Amsterdam, Netherlands

Inter-American Tropical Tuna Commission - IATTC
c/o Scripps Institution of Oceanography, La Jolla, Calif 92093, USA
Tel: (619) 453-2820
Telex: 697115

International Association for Ecology
Harvest House, 62 London Road, Reading, Berks RG1 5AS

International Association of Meteorology and Atmospheric Physics - IAMAP
NCAR, POB 3000, Boulder, Colo 80307, USA

International Association against Noise
Hirschenplatz 7, 6004 Lucerne, Switzerland
Tel: (041) 513013

International Commission for the Conservation of Atlantic Tunas
Calle Principe de Vergara 17, 28001 Madrid, Spain
Tel: 431 03 29
Telex: 46330

International Commission for the Protection of the Rhine against Pollution
5400 Koblenz, Kaiserin-Augusta-Anlagen 15, POB 309, Federal Republic of Germany
Tel: (0261) 33623
Telex: 862499

International Commission for the Southeast Atlantic Fisheries
Paseo de la Habana 65, Madrid 16, Spain

International Council for Bird Preservation
219c Huntingdon Road, Cambridge CB3 0DL
Tel: 0223 277318

International Environment Bureau
61 Route de Chene, CH-1208, Geneva, Switzerland
Tel: + 41 22 865111

International Institute for Biological Husbandry
9 Station Approach, Needham Market, Ipswich, Suffolk IP6 8AT
Tel: 0449 720838

International Institute for Conservation
The Tate Gallery, Millbank, London SW1P 4RG

International Institute for Conservation of Historic and Artistic Works
6 Buckingham Street, London WC2N 6BA
Tel: 01-839 5957

International Institute of Environment and Development
3 Endsleigh Street, London WC1H 0DD
Tel: 01-388 2117

International League for the Protection of Cetaceans
2 Meryon Court, Rye, East Sussex EN13 7AH
Tel: 0797 2234649

International League for the Protection of Horses
PO Box No 166, 67a Camden High Street, London NW1 7JL

International Planned Parenthood Federation
18-20 Lower Regent Street, London SW1Y 4PW
Tel: 01-839 2911

International Primate Protection League
19-25 Argyll Street, London W1V 2DU
Tel: 01-837 7227

International Regional Organisation of Plant Protection and Animal Health
(Organismo Internacional Regional de Sanidad Agropecuaria - OIRSA
Edif. Carbonell 2, Carretera a Sta Tecla, San Salvador, El Salvador
Tel: 232391
Telex: (0373) 20746

International Society for the Prevention of Water Pollution
Little Orchard, Bentworth, Alton, Hants GU34 5RB
Tel: 0420-62225

International Society for the Protection of Animals
106 Jermyn Street, London SW1 6EE
Tel: 01-839 3026/3066

International Society for Tropical Ecology
c/o Botany Dept, Banaras Hindu University, Varanasi, 221005 India

**International Union for Conservation of Nature and Natural Resources -
IUCN**
219c Huntingdon Road, Cambridge CB3 0DL
Tel: 0223 277314 and 277420 (Species Conservation Monitoring Unit) and
277427 (Wildlife Trade Monitoring Unit)

Head Office
Avenue du Mont-Blanc, CH-1196 Gland, Switzerland
Tel: 022-64-71-81

International Whaling Commission
The Red House, Station Road, Histon, Cambridge CB4 4NP, England
Tel: 022 023 3971
Telex: 817960

North Pacific Fur Seal Commission
c/o National Oceanic and Atmospheric Administration, National Marine
Fisheries Service, Washington, DC 20235, USA

Northwest Atlantic Fisheries Organisation
POB 638, Dartmouth, Nova Scotia, B2Y 3Y9, Canada
Tel: 469 9105
Telex: 019-31475

Permanent Inter-State Committee on Drought Control in the Sahel - CILSS
POB 7049, Ouagadougou, Burkina Faso

World Coalition for the Abolition of Vivisection
84100 Uchaux, France
Tel: (90) 34-17-60

World Wide Fund for Nature (WWF)
Panda House, 11-13 Ockford Road, Godalming, Surrey, England
GU7 1QU
Tel: 04868 20551

Head Office
World Conservation Centre, 1196 Gland, Switzerland
Tel: (022) 647181
Telex: 28183

Canada

Friends of the Earth/Les Amis de la Terre
53 Queen Street, Room 16, Ottawa K1P 5CS, Ontario

Japan

Chikyu no Tomo (Friends of the Earth)
501 Shinwa Building, 9-17 Sakuragaoka, Shibuya-ku, Tokyo 150

USA

Ecosphere Associates
2521 East 6th Street, Tucson, Arizona 85716
Tel: +1 (602) 327 5558

The Conservation Foundation of America
1717 Massachusetts Avenue NW, Washington, DC 20036

Partners for Livable Places
1429 21st Street NW, Washington, DC 20036

EDUCATIONAL AND ADVISORY BODIES

UK national

Advisory Board for Redundant Churches
Fielden House, Little College Street, London SW1P 3SH
Tel: 01-222 9603

Advisory Committee on Animal Experiments
c/o Home Office, 50 Queen Anne's Gate, London SW1H 9AT
Tel: 01-213 3000

Advisory Committee on Pollution of Sea
1 Cambridge Terrace, London NW1
Tel: 01-486 4930

Advisory Council on Energy Conservation
c/o Deptartment of Energy, Thames House South, Millbank,
London SW1P 4QJ
Tel: 01-211 3000

Agricultural Training Board
Bourne House, 32-34 Beckenham Road, Beckenham, Kent BR3 4PB
Tel: 01-650 4890

Centre for Alternative Technology
Llywntwern Quarry, Machynlleth, Powys SY20 9AZ
Tel: 0654 2400

Centre for Environmental Education (CEE)
School of Education, University of Reading, Reading RG1 5AQ
Tel: 0734 85234

Centre for Environmental Interpretation (CET)
Manchester Polytechnic, John Dalton Building, Chester Street, Manchester M1
5GD
Tel: 061-228 6171

Centre for Human Ecology
115 Buccleuch Place, Edinburgh EH8 9LN
Tel: 031-667 1011 ext 6696/6799

City Farm Advisory Service
c/o Inter-Action, 15 Wilkin Street, Kentish Town, London NW5 3NG
Tel: 01-485 0881

Common Ground
45 Shelton Street, London WC2H 9HJ
Tel: 01-379 3109

Council for Environmental Education School of Education
University of Reading, London Road, Reading, Berkshire RG1 5AQ
Tel: 0734 875234 ext 218

Environmental Education Advisers' Association
Pendower Hall Teachers' Centre, West Road, Newcastle-upon-Tyne NE15 6PP

Environmental Information Centre
15 Goosegate, Nottingham NG1 1FE
Tel: 0602 582561

Glasgow Environmental Education Urban Projects
Education Offices, 129 Bath Street, Glasgow G2 2SY
Tel: 041-204 2900 ext 2639

Heritage Education Group
Civic Trust, 17 Carlton House Terrace, London SW1Y 5AW
Tel: 01-930 0914

Inland Waterways Amenity
Advisory Council, 122 Cleveland Street, London W1P 5DN
Tel: 01-387 7973

The Land Decade Education Council
The London Science Centre, 18 Adam Street, London WC2N 6AH

National Association for Environmental Education
c/o West Midlands College of Higher Education, Gorway, Walsall,
West Midlands WS1 3BD

Nuclear Electricity Information Group
22 Buckingham Gate, London SW1
Tel: 01-828 8248

Recycling Advisory Unit, Warren Spring Laboratory
Gunnels Wood Road, Stevenage, Hertfordshire SG1 2BX
Tel: 0438 313388

Royal Forestry School
102 High Street, Tring, Hertfordshire HP23 4AH
Tel: 044282 2028

Society for the Interpretation of British Heritage
Centre for Environmental Interpretation, 4 Holmewood Close, Kenilworth,
Warwicks CV8 2JE
Tel: 021-300 6456

Working Weekends on Organic Farms (WWOOF)
19 Bradford Rd, Lewes, E Sussex BN7 1RB
Tel: 07916 6286

International

International Centre for Agricultural Education - CIEA
Federal Office of Agriculture, Mattenhofstrasse 5, 3003 Berne, Switzerland
Tel: 31 612619

International Centre for Conservation Education (ICCE)
Greenfield House, Guiting Power, Cheltenham, Glos GL54 5TZ

ENERGY BODIES AND GROUPS

UK National

The Charter for Energy Efficiency
99 Midland Road, London NW1 2AH

Department of Energy
Thames House South, Millbank, London SW1P 4QJ
Tel: 01-211 3000

Energy Conservation Group
Building 156, AERE Harwell, Didcot, Oxon OX11 0RA
Tel: 0235 834621 ext 218

Energy Efficiency Office
Department of Energy, Thames House South, Millbank, London
SW1P 4QJ

Energy Equipment Testing Service
Department of Mechanical Engineering and Energy Studies, University
College, Newport Road, Cardiff CF2 1TA
Tel: 0222 44211 ext 7116

Energy Support Unit
20 Foyle Street, Sunderland, Tyne & Wear SR1 1LE
Tel: 0783 42860

Wind Energy Group
345 Ruislip Road, Southall, Middlesex UB1 2QX
Tel: 01-578 2366

Information Sources

European

European Atomic Energy Society
c/o Institute for Energy Technology, PB 40, 2007 Kjeller, Norway

International

International Solar Energy Society
19 Albermarle Street, London W1X 3HA
Tel: 01-493 6601

Head Office
PO Box 52, National Science Centre, 191 Royal Parade, Parkville, Melbourne,
Victoria 3052, Australia

World Energy Conference
34 St James's Street, London SW1A 1HD
Tel: 01-930 3966

Canada

Atomic Energy of Canada Ltd
275 Slater St, Ottawa K1A 0S4
Tel: (613) 237-3270
Telex: 053-3126

Israel

Israel Atomic Energy Commission
26 Rehov Hauniversita, Ramat Aviv, POB 7061, Tel-Aviv
Tel: 03-415111
Telex: 33450

South Africa

Atomic Energy Corporation of South Africa Ltd (AEC)
POB 582, Pretoria 0001
Tel: 284775
Telex: 321047

USA

Department of Energy
1000 Independence Ave, SW, Washington, DC 20585
Tel: (202) 252-5000

Nuclear Energy Program
Washington, DC 20585

Nuclear Regulatory Commission (NRC)
1717 H St, NW, Washington, DC 20555
Tel: (202) 492-7715

ENVIRONMENTAL PRESSURE GROUPS

Band Aid
PO Box 4TX
Tel: 01-408 1999

Beauty Without Cruelty International
11 Lime Hill Road, Tunbridge Wells, Kent TN1 1LJ
Tel: 0892 25587

Campaign Against Lead in Petrol
171 Barnett Wood Lane, Ashtead, Surrey KT21 2LP

Campaign for Lead Free Air (CLEAR)
3 Endsleigh Street, London WC1H 0DD
Tel: 01-278 9686

Campaign for the Countryside
11 Cowley Street, London SW1P 3NA
Tel: 01-222 9134

Campaign for Real Ales - CAMRA
34 Alma Road, St Albans, Hertfordshire AL1 3BW
Tel: 0727 67201

CLEAR
2 Northdown Street, London N1 9BG
Tel: 01-278 9686

Coastal Anti-Pollution League
94 Greenway Lane, Bath, Avon BA2 4LN
Tel: 0225 317094

Compassion in World Farming
20 Lavant Street, Petersfield, Hampshire GU32 3EW
Tel: 0730 64208

Cumbrians Opposed to a Radioactive Environment (CORE)
98 Church Street, Barrow-in-Furness, Cumbria LA14 2HJ
Tel: 0229 33851

Environmental Forum
12a Ennis Road, Finsbury Park, London N4 3HD
Tel: 01-263 8505

The Georgian Group
37 Spital Square, London E1 6DY
Tel: 01-377 1722

Greenpeace
29-31 Islington Green, London N1 8XE
Tel: 01-354 5100

International

Temple House
25-26 High Street, Lewes, E Sussex
Tel: 0273 478787

League Against Cruel Sports
83-87 Union Street, London SE1 1SC
Tel: 01-407 0979/01-403 6155

National Campaign for the Protection of Badgers
The Paddock, Westonbirt, Nr Tetbury, Gloucestershire GL8 8QJ

National Society for Clean Air
136 North Street, Brighton BN1 1RG
Tel: 0273 26313

Neighbourhood Energy Action
2nd Floor, 2/4 Bigg Market, Newcastle-upon-Tyne NE1 1UW

Noise Abatement Society
PO Box 8, Bromley, Kent BR2 0UH
Tel: 01-460 3146

Scottish Campaign to Resist the Atomic Menace
11 Forth Street, Edinburgh EH1 3LE

Suffolk Countryside Campaign
Greenacre, Beyton, Bury St. Edmunds, Suffolk IP30 9AB
Tel: 0359 70491

The Other Economic Summit (TOES)
4 Streche Road, Swanage, Dorset BH19 1NF
Tel: 0929 425 627

MANUFACTURERS AND RETAILERS OF ENVIRONMENTAL PRODUCTS

Body Shop International plc
Dominion Way, Rustington, West Sussex BN16 3LR
Tel: 0903 717107

Boots Co plc
Nottingham NG2 3AA
Tel: 0602 56111

British Aerospace plc
Aircraft Group HQ, Richmond Road, Kingston-upon-Thames, Surrey KT2
5QS
Tel: 01-546 7741

British Gas plc
Rivermill House, 152 Grosvenor Road, London SW1V 3JL
Tel: 01-821 1444

British Nuclear Fuels plc
Risley, Warrington WA3 6AS
Tel: 0925 832000

British Petroleum Company plc (BP)
Britannic House, Moor Lane, London EC2Y 9BU
Tel: 01-920 2703

Cranks Health Foods
8 Marshall Street, London W1V 1LP
Tel: 01-437 9431

Ecology Building Society
43 Main Street, Cross Hills, Keighley, West Yorkshire BD20 8TT
Tel: 0535 35933

Esso UK plc
Esso House, Victoria Street, London SW1E 5JW
Tel: 01-834 6677

Gaia Books
Umbrella Studios, 12 Trundle Street, London SE1 1QT
Tel: 01-403 5124

Green Books
Ford House, Hartland, Bideford, Devon EX39 6EE
Tel: 02374 293621

IBM UK Ltd
IBM Southbank, 76 Upper Ground, London SE1 9PZ
Tel: 01-928 1777

Imperial Chemical Industries plc
Imperial Chemical House, Millbank, London SW1P 3JF
Tel: 01-834 4444

Johnson Matthey plc
New Garden House, 78 Hatton Garden, London EC1N 8JP
Tel: 01-430 0011

McCann Erickson International
McCann Erickson House, 36 Howland Street, London W1P 6BD
Tel: 01-580 6690

Safeway Food Stores Ltd
Beddow Way, Aylsford, Nr Maidstone, Kent ME20 7AT
Tel: 0622 77822

Sainsbury plc
Stamford House, Stamford Street, London SE1 9LL
Tel: 01-921 6000

Shell International Petroleum Company
Shell Briefing Service PAC/221, Shell Centre, London SE1
Tel: 01-934 1234

Thorn EMI Lighting Ltd
Tricity House, 284 Southbury Road, Enfield, Middlesex EN1 1TJ
Tel: 01-363 5353

Unilever plc
Unilever House, Blackfriars, London EC4P 4BQ
Tel: 01-822 5252

NATURALISTS' ASSOCIATIONS AND SOCIETIES

UK Local

Bedfordshire & Huntingdonshire Naturalists' Trust Ltd
38 Mill Street, Bedford, Beds MK40 3HD
Tel: 0234 64213

Berks Bucks & Oxon Naturalists' Trust
3 Church Cowley Road, Rose Hill, Oxford OX4 3JR
Tel: 0865 775476

Berwickshire Naturalists' Club
The Hill, Coldingham, Eyemouth, Borders TD14 5QB
Scotland
Tel: 03903 209

Bracken Hall Countryside Centre
Glen Road, Baildon, Shipley, West Yorkshire BD17 5EA

Brecknock Naturalists' Trust
Chapel House, Llechfaen, Brecon, Powys, Wales
Tel: 087486 688

Brent Lodge Bird & Wildlife Trust
Eartham, Chichester, West Sussex PO18 0LP
Tel: 024 365 314

Cambridgeshire & Isle of Ely Naturalists' Trust Ltd
1 Brookside, Cambridge CB2 1JF
Tel: 0223 358144

Cornwall Naturalists' Trust
Trendrine, Zennor, St Ives, Cornwall TR26 2BW
Tel: 0736-796926

Derbyshire Naturalists' Trust
Elvaston Castle Country Park
Derby DE7 3EP
Tel: 0332 756610

Essex Naturalists' Trust Ltd
Fingringhoe Wick Nature Reserve, South Green Road, Fingringhoe,
Colchester, Essex CO5 7DN
Tel: 020628 678

Hampshire Gardens Trust
c/o The Planning Dept., The Castle, Winchester

Hampshire and Isle of Wight Naturalists' Trust
8 Market Place, Romsey, Hants SO5 8NB
Tel: 0794 513786

Herefordshire and Radnorshire Nature Trust Ltd
25 Castle Street, Hereford HR1 2NW
Tel: 0432 56872

Jersey Wildlife Preservation Trust
Les Augres Manor, Trinity, Jersey, Channel Islands
Tel: 0534 61949

London Wildlife Trust
1 Thorpe Close, London W10 5XL
Tel: 01-968 5368/9

Norfolk Naturalists' Trust
72 Cathedral Close, Norwich, Norfolk NR1 4DF
Tel: 0603 25540

Norfolk Ornithologists' Association
Aslack Way, Holme next Sea, Hunstanton, Norfolk PE36 6LP
Tel: Holme 266

Norfolk Wildlife Park Trust
Norfolk Wildlife Park, Great Witchingham, Norwich, Norfolk NR9 5QS
Tel: 060544 274

North Wales Naturalists' Trust
154 High Street, Bangor, Gwynedd LL57 1NU
Tel: 0248 351541

North Western Naturalists' Union
59 Moss Lane, Bramhall, Stockport, Cheshire SK7 1EQ
Tel: 061-439 2899

Northumberland Wildlife Trust
Hancock Museum, Barras Bridge, Newcastle-upon-Tyne NE2 4PT
Tel: 0632 320038

Peak & Northern Footpaths Society
15 Parkfield Drive, Tyldesley, Manchester M29 8NR
Tel: 061-790 4383

Peak National Park Study Centre
Losehill Hall, Castleton, Derbyshire S30 2WB
Tel: 0433 20373

West Wales Naturalists' Trust
7 Market Street, Haverfordwest, Dyfed SA61 1NF
Tel: 0437 5462

Wick & Wickhams (Dorset) Association
71 Thornbury Road, Southbourne, Bournemouth, Dorset
Tel: 0202 318 5219

Yorkshire Mammal Group
c/o Miss Beryl Cronin, 23 Adelaide Street, York

UK national

Amateur Entomologists Society
355 Hounslow Road, Hanworth, Feltham TW13 5JL

Anglers' Cooperative Association
Midland Bank Chambers, Westgate, Grantham, Lincs NG31 6LE
Tel: 0476 6108

The Angling Foundation
The Limes, Alvechurch, Worcs

Arboricultural Association
Ampfield House, Ampfield, Romsey, Hants SO5 9PA
Tel: 0794 68717

Association of British Herb Growers and Producers
c/o Yorkshire Herbs, Middleton Tyas, Richmond, North
Yorkshire

Association of British Wild Animal Keepers
21 Northcote Road, Clifton, Bristol BS8 3HB

Botanical Society of the British Isles
c/o British Museum (Natural History), Cromwell Road, London
SW7 5BD
Tel: 01-589 6323 ext 701

British Bird & Wildlife Hospitals Association
Eartham, Chichester, West Sussex PO18 0LP

British Bryological Society
AR Perry, c/o Department of Botany, National Museum of Wales, Cardiff
CF1 3NP

The British Butterfly Conservation Society
Tudor House, Quorn, Loughborough, Leicestershire LE12 8AD
Tel: 0509 412870

The British Deer Society
Green Lane, Ufton Nervet, Reading, Berkshire RG7 4HA
Tel: 073-592 4133

British Entomological and Natural History Society
c/o the Alpine Club, 74 South Audley Street, London W1Y 5FF

British Herpetological Society
c/o Zoological Society of London, Regents Park, London NW1 4RY

British Lichen Society
c/o Department of Botany, British Museum (Natural History), Cromwell Road,
London SW7 5BD

British Mountaineering Council
Crawford House, Precinct Centre, Booth Street East, Manchester
M13 9RZ
Tel: 061-273 5835

British Museum Society
c/o British Museum, Great Russell Street, London WC1
Tel: 01-636 1555 ext 605

British Mycological Society
c/o Department of Plant Sciences, Wye College, Nr Ashford, Kent
TH25 5AH

British Naturalists' Association
6 Chancery Place, The Green, Writtle, Essex CM1 3DY
Tel: 0245 420756

British Ornithologists' Club
c/o British Ornithologists' Union, Zoological Society of London, Regents Park,
London NW1 4RY
Tel: 01-586 4443

British Ornithologists' Union
c/o Zoological Society of London, Regents Park, London NW1 4RY
Tel: 01-586 4443

British Pteridological Society
42 Lewisham Road, Smethwick, Warley, West Midlands B66 2BS

British Trust for Ornithology
Beech Grove, Station Road, Tring, Hertfordshire
Tel: 044-282 3461

British Waterfowl Association
25 Dale Street, Haltwhistle, Northumberland NE49 9QB
Tel: 0498 21176

British Wildlife Hospital Field Centre
Little Sturdington, Cheltenham, Nr Gloucester
Tel: 0242 862166

Captive Animals's Protection Society
17 Raphael Road, Hove BN3 5QP
Tel: 0273 732363

Cat Survival Trust
Marlind Centre, Codicote Road, Welwyn, Hertfordshire AL6 9TU

Conchological Society of Great Britain and Ireland
c/o Hon Secretary, 51 Wychwood Avenue, Luton, Beds LU2 7HY

Domestic Fowl Trust
Honeybourne Pastures, Honeybourne, Evesham, Worcestershire
Tel: 0386 833083

Ecological Parks Trust
c/o The Linnean Society, Burlington House, Piccadilly, London W1V 0LQ
Tel: 01-734 5170

Freshwater Biological Association
The Ferry House, Far Sawrey, Ambleside, Cumbria LA22 0LP
Tel: 09662 2468

Garden History Society
66 Granville Park, London SE13 7DX

The Geological Society
Burlington House, Piccadilly, London W1V 0JU
Tel: 01-734 2356/2510

The Geologists' Association
Dept of Geology, University College London, Gower Street, London WC1E 6BT

Hardy Plant Society
10 St Barnabas Road, Emmer Green, Reading, Berkshire

The Hawks Trust
c/o Birds of Prey Section, Zoological Gardens, Regents Park, London NW1 4RY

High Society
34 Boscobel Place, London SW1W 9PE
Tel: 01-235 1530

The Irish Wildlife Federation
112 Grafton Street, Dublin 2
Tel: 0001-608346

The Mammal Society
c/o the Linnean Society, Burlington House, Piccadilly, London W1V 0LQ

Organic Farmers and Growers Ltd
Abacus House, Station Approach, Needham Market, Ipswich, Suffolk
IP6 8AT
Tel: 0449 720838

Pheasant Trust
Great Witchingham, Norwich, Norfolk NR9 5QS
Tel: 060544 274

Ramblers' Association
1-5 Wandsworth Road, London SW8 2LJ
Tel: 01-582 6878

Rare Breeds Survival Trust
4th Street, National Agricultural Centre, Stoneleigh Park, Kenilworth,
Warwicks CV8 2LG
Tel: 0203 51141

Red Deer Commission
Knowsley, 82 Fairfield Road, Inverness, Highland IV3 5LH, Scotland
Tel: 0463 231751

Royal Agricultural Society of England
National Agricultural Centre, Stoneleigh, Kenilworth, Warwicks CV8 2LZ
Tel: 0203 555100

Royal Botanic Gardens
Kew, Richmond, Surrey TW9 3AB
Tel: 01-940 1171

Royal Botanical & Horticultural Society
55 Brown Street, Manchester M2 5DS
Tel: 061-834 8317

Royal Entomological Society
41 Queens Gate, London SW7 5HU
Tel: 01-584 8361

Royal Geographical Society
1 Kensington Gore, London SW7 2AR

Royal Horticultural Society
Horticultural Hall, Vincent Square, London SW1P 2PE
Tel: 01-834 4333

Royal Horticultural Society of Ireland
Thomas Prior House, Merrion Road, Dublin 4, Eire
Tel: 0001 68 4358 (mornings)

Royal Scottish Forestry Society
1 Rothesay Terrace, Edinburgh EH3 7UP
Tel: 031-225 1300

Scottish Countryside Rangers Association
Lochore Meadows Country Park, Crosshill, Lochgelly, Fife KY5 8BA
Tel: 0592 860086

Scottish Marine Biological Association
Dunstaffnage Marine Research Laboratory, PO Box 3, Oban, Argyll,
Strathclyde PA34 4AD
Tel: 0631 62244

Scottish Ornithologists' Club
21 Regent Terrace, Edinburgh EH7 5BT
Tel: 031-556 6042

Scottish Wildlife Trust
25 Johnstone Terrace, Edinburgh EH1 2NH
Tel: 031-226 4602

Seabird Group
c/o British Trust for Ornithology, Beech Grove, Tring, Herts HP23 5NR
Tel: 044282 3461

Wild Flower Society
69 Outwoods Road, Loughborough, Leics

The Wildfowl Trust
Slimbridge, Glos GL2 7BT
Tel: 045-389 333

Wildfowlers' Association of Great Britain & Ireland
Marford Mill, Rossett, Clwyd
Tel: 0244 570881

Wildlife Link
Unit 22, Finsbury Business Centre, 40 Bowling Green Lane, London EC1R
0BJ
Tel: 01-837 4405

Woodland Trust
Autumn Park, Dysart Road, Grantham, Lincs NG31 6LL
Tel: 0476 74297

Young Ornithologists' Club
The Lodge, Sandy, Bedfordshire SG19 2DL

The XYZ Club
(Young Zoologists Club), London Zoo, Regent's Park, London NW1

The Zoological Society of London
Regent's Park, London NW1 4RY

International

International Dendrology Society
Whistley Green Farmhouse, Hurst, Reading, Berkshire

International Dolphin Watch
1 Woodgates Mount, North Ferriby, Humberside HU14 2JQ
Tel: 0482 634346

International Federations of Organic Agricultural Movements
La Maioun, F-84410, Bedoin, France

International Fund for Animal Welfare (IFAW)
Little Mead, Marsh Green, Hartfield, East Sussex TN7 4ET

POLITICAL GROUPS

Conservative Ecology Group
11 Church Road, Portsmouth, Hants PQ1 1QA

Green Party
36-38 Clapham Road, London SW9 0JQ
Tel: 01-735 2485

Green Party of Ireland
Washington Lodge, Grange Road, Rathfarnham, Dublin 14, Eire

Parliamentary Alternative Energy Group
House of Commons, London SW1A 0AA

Social Democratic Green Group
69 Cambridge Road, Oakington, Cambs CB4 5BG
Tel: 022023 3200

**Socialist Environment & Resource Association (ERA) and
Socialist Countryside Group**
9 Poland Street, London W1V 3DG
Tel: 01-439 3749

PROFESSIONAL, INDUSTRIAL AND TRADE BODIES WITH ENVIRONMENTAL RELEVANCE

UK National

Association of Professional Foresters
Brokerswood Park, Brokerswood, Westbury, Wilts BA13 4EH
Tel: 0373 822238

British Reclamation Industries Confederation
16 High Street, Brampton, Huntingdon, Cambridgeshire PE18 6TU
Tel: 0480 55249

British Waste Paper Association
Highgate House, 214 High Street, Guildford, Surrey GU1 3JB
Tel: 0483 37980/37989

Business and Industry Panel for the Environment
Saxley Hill Barn, Meath Green Lane, Horley, Surrey
Tel: 02934 4903

Business in the Community
227A City Road, London EC1V 1LX
Tel: 01-253 3716

Business Network
18 Well Walk, London NW3
Tel: 01-435 5000

Can Makers Recycling Information Service
25 North Row, London W1R 2BY
Tel: 01-629 9621

Centre of Economic and Environmental Development (CEED)
12 Upper Belgrave Street, London SW1X 8BA
Tel: 01-245 6440

Chemical Industries Association (CIA)
Kings Buildings, Smith Square, London SW1P 3JJ
Tel: 01-834 3399

Combined Heat and Power Association
Bedford House, Stafford Road, Caterham, Surrey CR3 6JA

Confederation of British Industry (CBI)
Centre Point, New Oxford Street, London WC1
Tel: 01-379 7400

Consumers' Association
2 Marylebone Road, London NW1 4DX
Tel: 01-486 5544

Federation of British Craft Societies
8 High Street, Ditchling, East Sussex

Federation of Environmental Trade Associations
Unit 3, Phoenix House, Phoenix Way, Heston, Greater London TW5 9ND
Tel: 01-897 2848

The Industry Committee for Packaging and the Environment (INCPEN)
161-6 Fleet Street, London EC4A 2DP
Tel: 01-353 4353

Institute of Complementary Medicine
21 Portland Place, London W1N 3AF
Tel: 01-636 9543

Institute of Environmental Health Officers
Chadwick House, 48 Rushworth Street, London SE1 0QT
Tel: 01-928 6006

Institute for European Environmental Policy
3 Endsleigh Street, London WC1H 0DD
Tel: 01-388 2117

Institute for Marine Environment Research
Prospect Place, The Hoe, Plymouth, Devon PL1 3EH
Tel: 0752 21371

Institute for Terrestrial Ecology
Monks Wood Experimental Station, Abbots Ripton, Huntingdon
Tel: Abbots Ripton 381

Institute of Estuarine and Coastal Studies
University of Hull, Cottingham Road, Hull, Humberside HU6 7RX
Tel: 0482 46311 ext 7511

Institute of Foresters of Great Britain
22 Walker Street, Edinburgh EH3 7HR
Tel: 031-225 2705

Institute of Marine Biochemistry
St Fittick's Road, Aberdeen AB1 3RA, Scotland
Tel: 0224 875695

Institute of Paper Conservation
PO Box 17, London WC1N 2PE

Institute of Rural Life at Home and Overseas
27 Northumberland Road, New Barnet, Herts EN5 1EA
Tel: 01-440 4165

Institute of Waste Management
28 Portland Place, London W1N 4DE
Tel: 01-580 5324

Institute of Water Pollution Control
Ledson House, 53 London Road, Maidstone, Kent ME16 8JH
Tel: 0622 62034

Institution of Environmental Sciences
Centre for Extension Studies, University of Technology, Loughborough,
Leics LE11 3TU
Tel: 0509 263171

Landscape Institute
Nash House, Carlton House Terrace, London SW1
Tel: 01-839 4044

Lawyers' Ecology Group
c/o Denton Hall & Burgin, 3 Gray's Innn Place, London WC1
Tel: 01-242 1212

National Association of Field Studies Officers
Everdon Field Centre, Everdon, Daventry, Northants NN11 6BL

National Association of Loft Insulation Contractors
PO Box 12, Haslemere, Surrey GU27 3AN
Tel: 0428 54011

Organic Growers Association
86 Colston Street, Bristol BS1 5BB
Tel: 0272 299800

Plant Breeding Institute
Maris Lane, Trumpington, Cambridge CB2 2LQ
Tel: 0223 840411

Professional Institutions Council for Conservation
12 Great George Street, Parliament Square, London SW1P 3AD
Tel: 01-222 7000

Scottish Landowners' Federation
18 Abercromby Place, Edinburgh EH3 6TY
Tel: 031-556 4466

The UK Centre for Economic & Environment Development - CEED
10 Belgrave Square, London SW1X 8PH
Tel: 01-245 6440

UK Waste Materials Exchange
PO Box 51, Stevenage, Herts SG1 2DT
Tel: 0438 3388

Wildlife Trade Monitoring Unit
219c Huntingdon Road, Cambridge CB3 0DL
Tel: 0223 277314

International

International Group of National Associations of Agrochemical Manufacturers
12 ave Hamoir, 1180 Brussels, Belgium
Tel: (02) 374-59-81
Telex: 62120

International Organisation of Consumers' Unions - IOCU
Emmastraat 9, 2595 EG The Hague, Netherlands

PUBLIC AND OFFICIAL BODIES

UK national

Ancient Monuments and Historic Buildings Directorate
c/o Dept of the Environment, 2 Marsham Street, London SW1P 3EB
Tel: 01-212 3434

Ancient Monuments Board for England
Fortress House, 23 Savile Row, London W1X 2HE
Tel: 01-734 6010

Ancient Monuments Board for Scotland Scottish Development Dept
(Ancient Monuments), 17 Atholl Crescent, Edinburgh
Tel: 031-229 9321

Ancient Monuments Board for Wales
Welsh Office, Cathays Park, Cardiff CF1 2NQ
Tel: 0222 825111

Bodleian Library
University of Oxford, Oxford OX1 3BO
Tel: 0865 44675

British Waterways Board
Melbury House, Melbury Terrace, London NW1 6JX
Tel: 01-262 6711

Department of the Environment
2 Marsham Street, London SW1P 3EB
Tel: 01-212 3434

Department of the Environment
(Northern Ireland), Conservation Branch, Hut 6, Castle Grounds, Stormont,
Belfast BT4 3ST, N. Ireland
Tel: 0232 768716

Department of the Environment
(Republic of Ireland), Custom House, Dublin 1
Tel: 0001-74 2961

Department of the Environment
(Wildlife Division), Tollgate House, Houlton Street, Bristol, Avon
BS2 9DJ
Tel: 0272 218811

Highlands & Islands Development Board
Bridge House, Bank Street, Inverness, Highland IV1 1QR, Scotland
Tel: 0463 34171

Historic Buildings Bureau for England
25 Savile Row, London W1X 2BT
Tel: 01-734 6010

Historic Buildings Bureau (Scotland)
Scottish Development Dept, New St Andrew House, Edinburgh EH1 3SZ
Tel: 031-556 8400 ext 4618

Historic Buildings Bureau (Wales)
New Crown Buildings, Cathays Park, Cardiff CF1 2NQ
Tel: 0222 823864

Historic Buildings Council for Scotland
25 Drumsheugh Gardens, Edinburgh EH3 7RN
Tel: 031-226 3611

Historic Buildings Council for Wales
Crown Building, Cathays Park, Cardiff CF1 2NQ
Tel: 0222-825111

Historic Churches Preservation Trust
Fulham Palace, London SW6 6EA

Ministry of Agriculture, Fisheries and Food
Whitehall Place, London SW1
Tel: 01-233 3000

Ministry of Defence Conservation Department (MOD)
Defence Lands 3, Room 22, Spur 3, B Block, Government Buildings,
Leatherhead Road, Chessington, Surrey
Tel: 01-397 5266

Public Records Office, Conservation Department
Portugal Street, London WC2A 3PH
Tel: 01-405 3488

Royal Commission on Environmental Pollution
Church House, Great Smith Street, London SW1P 3BL
Tel: 01-212 3434

Royal Environmental Health Institute of Scotland
62 Virginia Street, Glasgow G1 1TX
Tel: 041-552 1533

Town & Country Planning Association
17 Carlton House Terrace, London SW1Y 5AS
Tel: 01-930 8903/4/5

Tree Council
Room 101, Agriculture House, Knightsbridge, London SW1X 7NJ
Tel: 01-235 8854

South Africa

Council for Nuclear Safety
POB 284, Pretoria 0001

RESEARCH/STUDY GROUPS AND BODIES

UK National

Agricultural and Food Research Council
160 Great Portland Street, London W1N 6DT
Tel: 01-580 6655

A Rocha
(Christian Field Study Centre & Bird Observatory in South West Portugal)
c/o Dr R A Pullan, 13 West Drive, Upton, Wirral, Merseyside L49 6JX

Association for Studies in the Conservation of Historic Buildings
Institute of Archaeology, 31-34 Gordon Square, London WC1H 0PY
Tel: 01-387 6052

Brathay Centre for Exploration and Field Studies
Old Brathay, Ambleside, Cumbria LA22 0HN
Tel: 09663 3042

Centre for the Study of Rural Society
Bishop Grosseteste College of Education, Lincoln LN1 3DY
Tel: 0522 27347 ext 23 or 35

Centre for Village Studies
Yoxford, Saxmundham, Suffolk LP17
Tel: 072877 327

Earth Resources Research
258 Pentonville Road, London N1 9JY
Tel: 01-278 3833

Ecological Physics Research Group
Cranfield Institute of Technology, Cranfield, Bedford MK43 0AL
Tel: 0234 750993

Economic and Social Research Council (ESRC)
1 Temple Avenue, London EC4Y 0BD
Tel: 01-353 5252

Field Studies Council
Preston Montford, Montford Bridge, Shrewsbury, Salop SY4 1HW
Tel: 0743 850880

Forestry Commission
Forestry Commission Research Station, Alice Holt Lodge, Wrecclesham,
Farnham, Surrey GU10 4LH
Tel: 0420 22255

The Future Studies Centre
The Birmingham Settlement, 318 Summer Lane, Birmingham B19 3RL
Tel: 021-359 3662/2113

Henry Doubleday Research Association
National Centre for Organic Gardening, Ryton on Dunsmore, Coventry CV8
3LG
Tel: 0203 303517

The Humane Research Trust
Broom House, 29 Bramhall Lane South, Bramhall, Cheshire SK7 2DN
Tel: 061-439 8041

Natural Environment Research Council
Polaris House, North Star Avenue, Swindon, Wiltshire SN2 1EU
Tel: 0793 40101

Political Ecology Research Group
PO Box 14, 34 Cowley Road, Oxford OX4 1HZ
Tel: 0865 725354

Scottish Field Studies Association
Nairn Estate Office, Priory Lodge, Victoria Road Kirkcaldy, Fife
KY1 2QU
Tel: 0592 264702

European

European Association for Research on Plant Breeding
c/o POB 128, 6700 AC Wageningen, Netherlands

European-Mediterranean Seismological Centre
5 rue Rene Descartes, 67084 Strasbourg Cedex, France
Tel: (88) 61 48 20
Telex: 890826

European Organisation for Nuclear Research
European Laboratory for Particle Physics, 1211 Geneva 23, Switzerland
Tel: (022) 836111
Telex: 41900

International

African Timber Organisation
BP 67, Libreville, Gabon

Asian Vegetable Research and Development Center
POB 42, Shanhua, Tainan 741, Taiwan
Tel: (06) 5837801
Telex: 73560

Association for the Advancement of Agricultural Science in Africa - AAASA
POB 30087, Addis Ababa, Ethiopia

Caribbean Food and Nutrition Institute
Jamaica Centre, UWI Campus, POB 140, Kingston 7, Jamaica
Tel: 92 78338
Trinidad Centre, UWI Campus, St Augustine, Trinidad
Tel: 66 31544

Charles Darwin Foundation for the Galapagos Isles
c/o Juan Black, Casilla 38-91, Quito, Ecuador

Collaborative International Pesticides Analytical Council Ltd - CIPAC
c/o Plantenziektenkundige Dienst, Postbus 9102, 6700 HC Wageningen,
Netherlands

Desert Locust Control Organisation for Eastern Africa
POB 4255, Addis Ababa, Ethiopia
Tel: 18 14 75

Intergovernmental Oceanographic Commission
UNESCO,
7 place de Fontenoy, 75700 Paris, France
Tel: (1) 568-39-83
Telex: 204461

International Association for Earthquake Engineering
Kenchiku Kaikan, 3rd Floor, 5-26-20, Shiba, Minato-ku, Tokyo
108 Japan
International Association of Photobiology
c/o L O Björn, Department of Plant Physiology, Box 7007, 221 01 Lund,
Sweden

International Bee Research Association
Hill House, Gerrards Cross, Bucks SL9 0NR, England
Tel: 0753 885011
Telex: 23152

International Centre for Advanced Mediterranean Agronomic Studies
11 rue Newton, 75116 Paris, France

International Centre of Insect Physiology and Ecology
POB 30772, Nairobi, Kenya

International Centre for Tropical Agriculture
(Centro Internacional de Agricultura Tropical)
Apdo Aéreo 6713, Cali, Colombia
Tel: 57-3-680111
Telex: 05769

International Commission for Agricultural and Food Industries
35 rue du Général Foy, 75008 Paris, France
Tel: (1) 293-19-24

International Council for the Exploration of the Sea - ICES
Palaegade 2-4, 1261, Copenhagen K, Denmark
Tel: (01) 15-42-25
Telex: 22498

International Crops Research Institute for the Semi-Arid Tropics - ICRISAT
Patancheru Post Office, Andhra Pradesh 502 324, India
Tel: 224016
Telex: 0152 203

International Institute for Sugar Beet Research
47 rue Montoyer, 1040 Brussels, Belgium
Tel: (02) 515-65-06
Telex: 21287

International Institute of Tropical Agriculture - IITA
Oyo Rd, PMB 5320, Ibadan, Nigeria
Tel: 413244
Telex: 31417

International Laboratory for Research on Animal Diseases
POB 30709, Nairobi, Kenya
Tel: 592311
Telex: 22040

International Livestock Centre for Africa - ILCA
POB 5689, Addis Ababa, Ethiopia
Tel: 183215
Telex: 21207

International Peace Research Association
Mershon Center, Ohio State University, 199 West 10th Ave, Columbus,
OH 43201, USA
Tel: (614) 422 1681

International Rice Research Institute - IRRI
POB 933, Manila, Philippines
Tel: 88-48-69
Telex: 45365

International Service for National Agricultural Research - ISNAR
POB 93375, 2509 AJ The Hague, Netherlands
Tel: (070) 472991
Telex: 33746

International Society for Soilless Culture - ISOSC
POB 52, 6700 AB Wageningen, Netherlands
Tel: (08370) 19012

International Waterfowl Research Bureau
Slimbridge, Glos GL2 7BX, England

Joint Institute for Nuclear Research
POB 79, 101000 Moscow, USSR

Israel

Weizmann Institute of Science
POB 26, Rehovot
Tel: 08 482111
Telex: 361900

South Africa

The National Nuclear Research Centre
Pelindaba, Private Bag X256, Pretoria 0001
Tel: 213311
Telex: 322948

EUROPEAN BODIES

Commission of the European Communities (Belgium)
Rue de la Loi 200, B1049 Brussels, Belgium
Tel: +32 2 235 11 11

Commission of the European Communities (UK)
8 Storey's Gate, London SW1P 3AT
Tel: 01-222 8122

Council of Europe
BP 431R6-, F67006 Strasbourg, Cedex, France
Tel: +1 (88) 614961

European Centre for Environmental Communication (ECEC),
55 rue de Varenne, F-75341 Paris, Cedex 07, France
Tel: +33 1 42 22 12 34

European Environmental Bureau
29 rue Vautier, 1040 Brussels, Belgium
Tel: +32 2 647 0199

European Network for Environmental Technology Transfer (NETT)
-see Commission of the European Communities

Plant Genetic Systems
Josef Plateaustraat 22, 9000 Gent, Belgium
Tel: +32 91 242525

Scientific Committee on Problems of the Environment (SCOPE)
Secretariat, 51 Boulevard de Montmorency, 75016 Paris, France
Tel: +33 1 4 525 0498

UN AND SIMILAR INTERNATIONAL BODIES

International Energy Agency
2 rue André Pascal, 75775 Paris Cedex 16, France

Organisation for Economic Co-operation and Development (OECD)
Chateau de la Muette, 2 rue André Pascal, 75775 Paris Cedex 16, France

OECD Nuclear Energy Agency - NEA
38 boulevard Suchet, 75016 Paris, France
Tel: (1) 524-82-00

United Nations Environment Programme - UNEP
POB 30552, Nairobi, Kenya
Tel: 333930
Telex: 22068

Europe: Palais des Nations, 1211 Geneva 10, Switzerland
Asia and the Pacific: UN Bldg, 10th Floor, Rajadamnern Ave, Bangkok, Thailand
Latin America: Presidente Mazaryk 29, Ap. Postal 6-718, México 5, DF, Mexico
West Asia: POB 4656, Ouiedat Bldg, Bir Hassan, Beirut, Lebanon

Food and Agriculture Organisation - FAO
Via delle Terme di Caracalla, 00100 Rome, Italy
Tel: Rome 57971
Telex: 610181

Regional offices
Afric .. UN Agency Building, North Maxwell Rd, POB 1628, Accra, Ghana
Tel: 66851
Telex: 2139
Centre for Integrated Rural Development in Africa: Arusha, Tanzania
Asia and the Pacific: Maliwan Mansion, Phra Atit Rd, Bangkok 2, Thailand
Tel: 2817844
Telex: 82815
Latin America: Avenida Providencia 871, Casilla 10095, Santiago, Chile
Tel: 462061
Telex: 340279

Liaison offices
North America: 1001 22nd St, NW, Suite 300, Washington, DC 20437, USA
Telex: 64255
United Nations: Suite DC-1125, United Nations, New York, NY 10017, USA
Telex: 236350

FAO Councils and Commissions
(Based at Rome unless otherwise indicated: G = Ghana, T = Thailand)

African Commission on Agricultural Statistics:(G)
African Forestry Commission
Asia and Pacific Commission on Agricultural Statistics:(T)
Asia and Pacific Plant Protection Commission:(T)
Caribbean Plant Protection Commission
Commission for Controlling the Desert Locust in the Eastern Region of its
 distribution area in South West Asia
Commission for Controlling the Desert Locust in the Near East
Commission for Controlling the Desert Locust in North-West Africa
Commission for Inland Fisheries of Latin America
European Commission for the Control of Foot-and-Mouth Disease
European Commission on Agriculture
European Forestry Commission
European Inland Fisheries Advisory Commission
FAO Regional Commission on Farm Management for Asia and the Far
 East:(T)
FAO/WHO Codex Alimentarius Commission
General Fisheries Council for the Mediterranean - GFCM
Indian Ocean Fishery Commission:(T)
Indo-Pacific Fishery Commission:(T)
International Poplar Commission
International Rice Commission
Joint FAO/WHO/OAU Regional Food and Nutrition Commission for
 Africa:(G)

Latin American Forestry Commission
Near East Forestry Commission
Near East Regional Commission on Agriculture
Near East Regional Economic and Social Policy Commission
North American Forestry Commission
Regional Animal Production and Health Commission for Asia, the Far
 East and the South-West Pacific:(T)
Regional Commission on Food Security for Asia and the Pacific:(T)
Regional Commission on Land and Water Use in the Near East
Regional Fisheries Advisory Commission for the South-West Atlantic
Western Central Atlantic Fishery Commission

UN Industrial Development Organisations (UNIDO)
PO Box 300, 1400 Vienna, Austria
Tel: Vienna 2631-3674

UN Publications
Vereinte Nationen, Veroffent Lichungen, Palais des Nations, CH-1211 Geneva
10, Switzerland

World Bank
1818 H Street, NW Washington DC 20433, USA
Tel: +1 (202) 477 1234

World Health Organisation - WHO
Avenue Appia, 1211 Geneva 27, Switzerland
Tel: (022) 346061
Telex: 27821

Regional offices
Africa: POB 6, Brazzaville, Congo
Americas: Pan-American Sanitary Bureau, 525 23rd St. NW, Washington, DC
20037, USA
Eastern Mediterranean: POB 1517, Alexandria, Egypt
Europe: 8 Scherfigsvej, 2100 Copenhagen 0, Denmark
South-East Asia: Indraprastha Estate, Ring Rd, New Delhi 1, India
Western Pacific: POB 2932, Manila, Philippines

World Resources Institute
1735 New York Avenue, NW Washington DC 20006, USA
Tel: +1 (202) 638 6300

5.3 BIBLIOGRAPHY

Environmental reports

Bontius, GH, Kema, NV and Doelman, (1986) *CHP in the Netherlands*, Paper presented to the 13th Congress of World Energy Conference

Central Board of Finance of the Church of England (1987) GS Misc 259.

EIRIS (1987) *Ethical Investment Dilemmas: The Church of England as a Case Study.*

El Hinnawi, E (1985) *Environmental Refugees*, UNEP.

Friends of the Earth (1988) *Good Wood Guide.*

European Commission (1987) *The European Community and Environmental Protection.*

Hurst, P *The Trade Union Perspective on Pesticides*, TGWU.

IIED (1987) *A Low Energy Strategy for the UK.*

Management Information Services (1986) *Cost and Impact of Environmental Control Investments.*

NEDO (1989) *Directions for Change: Land Use in the 1990s.*

TUC (1987) *Health and Safety at Work: The Way Forward.*

UNEP (1985) *Register of International Treaties and Other Agreements in the Field of the Environment.*

WCED (1987) *Our Common Future* (Brundtland Report).

Books on environment issues

OECD (1984) "Impact of Environmental Measures on Growth, Productivity, Inflation and Trade", in *Environment and Economics*, Vol 1, pp 117-94.

Smith, RA (1872) *Air and Rain: The Beginnings of a Chemical Climatology.*

Ward, S (1986) *Socially Responsible Investment,* Directory of Social Change/ EIRIS.

Journals with environmental relevance

Hahn, RW and Noll, RG (1983) "Barriers to Implementing Tradable Air Pollution Permits", *Yale Journal of Regulation*, Vol 1.

Henderson, H (1987) "Mutually Assured Development", *Resurgence*, No 125, November/December.

Seskin, EP, Anderson, RJ Jr and Reid, RO (1983) "An Empirical Analysis of Economic Strategies for Controlling Air Pollution", *Journal of Environmental Economics and Management*, June.

INDEX

INDEX